The Dog Lover's Companion to Philadelphia

1ST EDITION

Christine Matturro McLaughlin

AVALON TRAVEL

THE DOG LOVER'S COMPANION TO PHILADELPHIA
THE INSIDE SCOOP ON WHERE TO TAKE YOUR DOG

Published by
Avalon Travel Publishing
1400 65th Street, Suite 250
Emeryville, CA 94608, USA

Avalon Travel Publishing
An Imprint of
Avalon Publishing Group, Inc.

Printing History
1st edition—April 2005
5 4 3 2 1

ISBN: 1-56691-774-3
ISSN: 1554-320X

Editor and Series Manager: Kathryn Ettinger
Acquisitions Editor: Rebecca K. Browning
Copy Editor: Elizabeth Wolf
Designer: Jacob Goolkasian
Graphics Coordinators: Susan Snyder, Tabitha Lahr
Production Coordinator: Jacob Goolkasian
Map Editors: Kevin Anglin, Olivia Solís
Cartographer: Kat Kalamaras
Indexer: Judy Hunt

Cover and interior illustrations by Phil Frank

Printed in USA by Malloy Inc.

ABOUT THE AUTHOR

© Francie Scott

Although Christine Matturro McLaughlin had been writing for magazines and websites for more than a decade, it was her silly yet inquisitive golden retriever, Linus, who made her an author. His goofy personality and love for nature gave her many ideas for her articles, and eventually this book.

She and Linus took their weekend fun seriously, checking out the dog-friendly park sites, events, and restaurants of Philadelphia together. In the process, McLaughlin got bitten by not just a tick or two but also the travel bug. So she decided there'd be no better opportunity to write a book in which she could include her slobbery yet sweet poochie and their travels together. And *The Dog Lover's Companion to Philadelphia* emerged . . .

Sadly, though, during the course of writing this book, her beloved Linus passed away at the young age of seven. It was a difficult time for McLaughlin and her family. "Who knew you could be so dependent on the peace and comfort you get from a being who says no words . . . until it's gone?" she wondered.

In the meantime, McLaughlin enlisted the help of her equally sweet golden neighbor, Nellie. Similar to Linus, although a bit more refined (no drooling), Nellie is extremely friendly, loves people and other dogs, and enjoys everything that Linus would, so the transition went smoothly.

All in all, this book turned out to be a poignant yet therapeutic way for McLaughlin to honor her favorite dog of all time, Linus, and their favorite places of all time—in and around Philadelphia.

To Linus (Liney-Lou, Dolly, Louie, McDoodles, Noodley McDoodley, Lolly Dolly, Dolly Lamma, Drooly Looly)

CONTENTS

Resources 225

Indexes 235

PHILADELPHIA

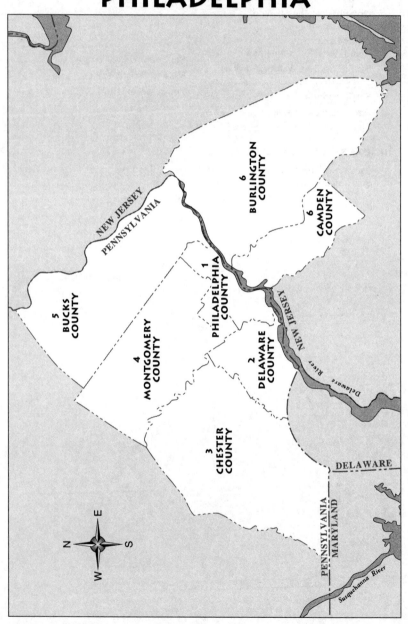

MAPS

Introduction

When it comes to cities, Philadelphia is a paws-down favorite. Residents of the City of Brotherly Love tend to be as loyal as their dogs—people who grow up here usually stay here. Philadelphia is also known as a city of neighborhoods, each of which has a distinct personality. Philadelphians are fiercely critical of their city (not to mention their sports teams) but in the same breath will defend it to the end; this is a city that's full of life and beaming with pride.

Being the birthplace of our country also gives Philadelphia a certain dignity. It's the fifth-largest city in the nation and has the third-largest downtown population, after New York and Chicago. But despite its greatness, the city tends to get lost between New York and Washington, D.C. Just look at a weather map of the nation and you'll see. It's a city of underdogs (no pun intended), but maybe that's why it's so beloved.

Philadelphia is one of the best-kept secrets around, and those who live here like it that way. It's a livable city—not exorbitantly expensive, yet stylish and modern, offering all the culture of the world-class city that it is. Plus, it offers breathtaking architecture and history on virtually every block, and more outdoor sculpture and public art than in any other city in the country. What's more, Philadelphia is home to the world's largest urban landscaped park, Fairmount Park. At this 8,900-acre citywide park system, leashed dogs are permitted everywhere.

Best of all, dogs are an integral part of the lives of Philadelphians. Nearly every existing off-leash dog park in the city was a major grassroots effort undertaken by dog-loving city dwellers, not city officials. When you see the results of their hard work, fundraising, and organizing, you'll be amazed by these dogged volunteers.

Philadelphia's off-leash areas have grown in number in recent years. They include everything from small, fenced neighborhood parks with makeshift dog pools to larger, more sophisticated fenced areas with working doggy water fountains.

In the suburbs you'll find fewer off-leash areas but just as much variety, from off-leash wooded trails to wide-open fields and fenced parks. Policies in suburbs vary greatly: Some parks in some counties don't allow dogs at all, other parks in other counties have their own dog parks as part of the park system, and others simply allow leashed dogs everywhere.

Some harsh realities exist though. State parks are losing funding and are closing parks or certain areas of parks due to less staff. City park budgets have been cut, too, so some parks have been threatened with closing.

Sad to say, there have even been three separate incidents of dog deaths at area dog parks. All were small dogs killed by larger, aggressive dogs. Important reminder: Immediately leave a park if your dog is threatened in any way.

Despite these misfortunes, the Philadelphia area is embracing dogs like never before. In fact, it was rated the fourth-healthiest city in the U.S. for pets by the Purina Pet Institute's Healthy Pets 21 Consortium, a think tank of leaders in the pet health and welfare community. The University of Pennsylvania's Ryan Veterinary Hospital is the busiest veterinary teaching hospital in the country, with more than 28,000 small-animal patient visits a year and canine-care specialists ranging from oncology to opthalmology. The hospital is open 24 hours for emergency care.

The media have picked up the scent of dog devotion, too. Most area television stations include regular pet segments in their news programs, especially publicizing dog-adoption programs. One radio station hosts a wildly popular dog walk in the city. There's even a radio show, "Doggy Talk," that discusses dog fun and behavioral issues. It airs Tuesdays at 6 P.M. (89.3 Warminster/ Hatboro, 107.3 Philadelphia, 97.1 Bensalem).

And we can't forget that this city is renowned for its prestigious Kennel Club of Philadelphia Dog Show, which takes place at the Fort Washington Convention Center and is aired nationally on Thanksgiving Day.

Nowhere else can you eat and party with your pooch at so many of the leading restaurants and bars, stay at the finest hotels and comfy B&Bs together, conquer endless activities on weekends, and experience four seasons a year, while being one to two hours from the mountains and the shore—all without spending an arm and a dog leg. And nowhere else can you do these things in and around a city that's so unique, so colorful and interesting, and so drastically underrated as Philadelphia.

To tackle an incredible city like Philadelphia and its surrounding area, I had an incredible dog join me. His name: Linus, my extra-large (90 pounds, skinny), silly, sweet, and slobbery golden retriever. He was the inspiration for this book.

It was his good nature, unbounded happiness, and friendly disposition that dared me to take him to places I'd never taken a dog before. He opened a world of fun I'd only dreamt about before he entered my life: dog parks, street festivals, inner cities, rural areas, restaurants, parades, stores, B&Bs, hotels, cabins, the mountains, the lake, the beach, the list went on. Philadelphia and the surrounding area, especially, brim with things to do and places to stay, and Linus happily lapped it all up…with a few googlers hanging from his mouth. (I wasn't kidding about the slobber.)

It still pains me to use the past tense when referring to him. Very sadly and abruptly, while working on this book together, Linus became urgently ill, hospitalized, heavily medicated, and died shortly thereafter of complications due to megaesophagus—a serious medical condition in which the esophagus no longer effectively moves food to the stomach. He was only seven years old.

In the midst of my grieving, I saw my sweet golden retriever neighbor, Nellie, one day and I thought how happy she had made Linus. She is his female counterpart in every way: very much the same friendly personality (loves people and dogs), only gentler, girlier, and no slobber. There was no doubt she would be best to finish the book with me.

In fact, she actually helped me grieve (we had some tearful outings) and eventually come to grips with losing my hairy best friend.

The Paws Scale

At some point, we've got to face the facts: Humans and dogs have different tastes. We like eating oranges and smelling lilacs and covering our bodies with soft clothes. They like eating roadkill and smelling each other's unmentionables and covering their bodies with horse manure.

The parks, beaches, and recreation areas in this book are rated with a dog in mind. Maybe your favorite park has lush gardens, a duck pond, a few acres of perfectly manicured lawns, and sweeping views of a nearby skyline. But unless your dog can run leash-free, swim in the pond, and roll in the grass, that park doesn't deserve a very high rating.

The lowest rating you'll come across in this book is the fire hydrant 🔥 . When you see this symbol, it means the park is merely "worth a squat." Visit one of these parks only if your dog just can't hold it any longer. These parks have virtually no other redeeming qualities for canines.

Beyond that, the paws scale starts at one paw 🐾 and goes up to four paws 🐾 🐾 🐾 🐾 . A one-paw park isn't a dog's idea of a great time. Maybe it's a tiny park with only a few trees and too many kids running around. Or perhaps it's a magnificent-for-people national park that bans dogs from every inch of land except paved roads and a few campsites. Four-paw parks, on the other hand, are places your dog will drag you to visit. Some of these areas come as close to dog heaven as you can imagine. Many have lakes for swimming or hundreds of acres for hiking. Some are small, fenced-in areas where leash-free dogs can tear around without danger of running into the road. Just about all four-paw parks give you the option of letting your dog off leash (although most have restrictions, which I detail in the park description).

In addition to finding paws and hydrants, you'll also notice an occasional foot symbol 👣 in this book. The foot means the park offers something special for the humans in the crowd. You deserve a reward for being such a good chauffeur.

The Dog Lover's Companion is not meant to be a comprehensive guide to all of the parks in the Philadelphia region. If I included every single park, this book would be larger than a multi-volume set of the *Encyclopædia Britannica.* Instead, I tried to find the best, dog-friendliest, and/or most convenient parks. Some counties have so many wonderful parks that I had to make tough choices about which to include and which to leave out. Other counties have such a limited supply of parks that, for the sake of dogs living and visiting there, I ended up listing parks that wouldn't otherwise be worth mentioning.

To help you along in your quest for the perfect pooch playground, whether local or far-flung, I've provided specific directions to all the parks listed in this book from the nearest major highway, city, or town. Although I tried to make this as easy as possible for you, signposts can be confusing. I highly recommend picking up a detailed street map before you and your dog set out on your travels.

He, She, It

In this book, whether neutered, spayed, or au naturel, dogs are never referred to as "it." They are either "he" or "she." I alternate pronouns so no dog reading this book will feel left out.

To Leash or Not to Leash...

This is not a question that plagues dogs' minds. Ask just about any normal, red-blooded American dog whether she'd prefer to visit a park and be on leash or off, and she'll say, "Arf!" (Translation: "Duh!") No question about it, most dogs would give their canine teeth to frolic about without that cumbersome leash.

Whenever you see the running dog  in this book, you'll know that under certain circumstances, your dog can run around in leash-free bliss. Fortunately, Philadelphia and its suburbs are home to dozens of such parks. The rest of the parks require leashes. I wish I could write about the parks where dogs get away with being scofflaws. Unfortunately, those would be the first parks the animal control patrols would hit. I don't advocate breaking the law, but if you're going to, please follow your conscience and use common sense.

Also, just because dogs are permitted off leash in certain areas doesn't necessarily mean you should let your dog run free. In national forests and large tracts of wild land, unless you're sure your dog will come back when you call or will never stray more than a few yards from your side, you should probably keep her leashed. An otherwise docile homebody can turn into a savage hunter if the right prey is near. Or your curious dog could perturb a rattlesnake or dig up a rodent whose fleas carry bubonic plague. In pursuit of a strange scent, your dog could easily get lost in an unfamiliar area. (Some forest rangers recommend having your dog wear a bright orange collar, vest, or backpack when out in the wilderness.) And there are many places where certain animals would love to have your dog for dinner—and not in a way Miss Manners would condone.

Be careful out there. If your dog really needs leash-free exercise but can't be trusted off leash in remote areas, she'll be happy to know that some beaches permit well-behaved, leashless pooches, as do a growing number of beautiful, fenced-in dog exercise areas.

There's No Business Like Dog Business

There's nothing appealing about bending down with a plastic bag or a piece of newspaper on a chilly morning and grabbing the steaming remnants of what your dog ate for dinner the night before. It's disgusting. Worse yet, you have to hang onto it until you can find a trash can. And how about when the newspaper doesn't endure before you can dispose of it? Yuck! It's enough to make you wish your dog could wear diapers. But as gross as it can be to scoop the poop, it's worse to step in it. It's really bad if a child falls in it, or—gasp!—starts eating it. And have you ever walked into a park where few people clean up after their dogs? The stench could make a hog want to hibernate.

Unscooped poop is one of a dog's worst enemies. Public policies banning dogs from parks are enacted because of it. At present, a few good Philadelphia area parks that permit dogs are in danger of closing their gates to all canines because of the negligent behavior of a few owners. A worst-case scenario is already in place in several communities—dogs are banned from all parks. Their only exercise is a leashed sidewalk stroll. That's no way to live.

Just be responsible and clean up after your dog everywhere you go. (And, if there's even a remote chance he'll relieve himself inside, don't even bring him into hotels or stores that permit dogs!) Anytime you take your dog out, stuff plastic bags in your jacket, purse, car, pants pockets—anywhere you might be able to pull one out when needed. Or, if plastic isn't your bag, newspapers will do the trick. If it makes it more palatable, bring along a paper bag, too,

and put the used newspaper or plastic bag in it. That way you don't have to walk around with dripping paper or a plastic bag whose contents are visible to the world. If you don't enjoy the squishy sensation, try one of those cardboard or plastic bag pooper-scoopers sold at pet stores. If you don't like bending down, buy a long-handled scooper. There's a scooper for every preference.

A final note: Don't pretend not to see your dog while he's doing his bit. Don't pretend to look for it without success. And don't fake scooping it up when you're really just covering it with leaves. I know these tricks because I've been guilty of them myself—but no more.

Etiquette Rex: The Well-Mannered Mutt

While cleaning up after your dog is your responsibility, a dog in a public place has his own responsibilities. Of course, it really boils down to your responsibility again, but the burden of action is on your dog. Etiquette for restaurants and hotels is covered in other sections of this chapter. What follows are some fundamental rules of dog etiquette. I'll go through it quickly, but if your dog's a slow reader, he can read it again: no vicious dogs; no jumping on people; no incessant barking; no leg lifts on tents, backpacks, human legs, or any other personal objects you'll find hanging around beaches and parks; dogs should come when they're called; dogs should stay on command.

Linus managed to infringe on many of these rules in his time. Do your best to remedy any problems. It takes patience and it's not always easy. If Linus knew I had to leave the house, he would only come in from outside when he felt like it. I'd have to chase him all over with cookies as a ploy just to get him inside. He was also a fan of legs and large stuffed animals in his youth. Once he violated a giant, talking Winnie the Pooh who decided to tell Linus his thoughts on the behavior while in the act: "Goodness!"

Safety First

A few essentials will keep your traveling dog happy and healthy.

Beat the Heat: If you must leave your dog alone in the car for a few minutes, do so only if it's cool out and you can park in the shade. Never, ever, ever leave a dog in a car with the windows rolled up all the way. Even if it seems cool, the sun's heat passing through the window can kill a dog in a matter of minutes. Roll down the window enough so your dog gets air, but also so there's no danger of your dog getting out or someone breaking in. Make sure your dog has plenty of water.

You also have to watch out for heat exposure when your car is in motion. Certain cars, like hatchbacks, can make a dog in the backseat extra hot, even while you feel okay in the driver's seat.

Try to time your vacation so you don't visit a place when it's extremely warm. Dogs and heat don't get along, especially if the dog isn't used to heat. The opposite is also true. If your dog lives in a hot climate and you take him to a freezing place, it may not be a healthy shift. Check with your vet if you have any doubts. Spring and fall are usually the best times to travel.

Water: Water your dog frequently. Dogs on the road may drink even more than they do at home. Take regular water breaks, or bring a heavy bowl (the thick clay ones do nicely) and set it on the floor so your dog always has access to water. I use a non-spill bowl, which comes in really handy on curvy roads, and a foldable vinyl one I stick in my bag (I found it in a dollar store). When hiking, be sure to carry enough for you and a thirsty dog.

Rest Stops: Stop and unwater your dog. There's nothing more miserable than being stuck in a car when you can't find a rest stop. No matter how tightly you cross your legs and try to think of the desert, you're certain you'll burst within the next minute…so imagine how a dog feels when the urge strikes, and he can't tell you the problem. There are plenty of rest stops along the major freeways. I've also included many parks close to freeways for dogs who need a good stretch with their bathroom break.

How frequently you stop depends on your dog's bladder. If your dog is constantly running out the doggy door at home to relieve himself, you may want to stop every hour. Others can go significantly longer without being uncomfortable. Watch for any signs of restlessness and gauge it for yourself.

Car Safety: Even the experts differ on how a dog should travel in a car. Some suggest doggy safety belts, available at pet-supply stores. Others firmly believe in keeping a dog kenneled. They say it's safer for the dog if there's an accident, and it's safer for the driver because there's no dog underfoot. Still others say you should just let your dog hang out without straps and boxes. They believe that if there's an accident, at least the dog isn't trapped in a cage. They say that dogs enjoy this more, anyway.

I'm a follower of the last school of thought. Linus loved sticking his snout out the window to smell the world go by. The danger was that if the car had kicked up a pebble or bothered a bee, Linus's nose and eyes could have been injured. He was okay, as was Nellie, but I've seen dogs who needed to be treated for bee stings to the nose because of this practice. If in doubt, try opening the window just enough so your dog can't stick out much snout.

Whatever travel style you choose, your pet will be more comfortable if he has his own blanket or bed with him. A veterinarian I know brings a faux-sheepskin blanket for his dogs. At night in the hotel, the sheepskin doubles as the dog's bed.

Planes: Air travel is even more controversial. Personally, unless my dog could fly with me in the passenger section (which tiny dogs are sometimes allowed to do), I'd rather find a way to drive the distance or leave them at home with a friend. I've heard too many horror stories of dogs suffocating in what was supposed to be a pressurized cargo section, dying of heat exposure, or ending up in Miami while their people go to Seattle. There's just something unappealing about the idea of a dog flying in the cargo hold, like he's nothing more than a piece of luggage. Of course, many dogs survive just fine, but I'm not willing to take the chance.

But if you need to transport your dog by plane, try to fly nonstop, and make sure you schedule takeoff and arrival times when the temperature is below 80°F (but not bitterly cold in winter). You'll want to consult the airline about regulations, required certificates, and fees. Be sure to check with your vet to make sure your pooch is healthy enough to fly.

The question of tranquilizing a dog for a plane journey causes the most contention of all. Some vets think it's insane to give a dog a sedative before flying. They say a dog will be calmer and less fearful without a disorienting drug. Others think it's crazy not to afford your dog the little relaxation she might not otherwise get without a tranquilizer. Discuss the issue with your vet, who will take into account the trip length and your dog's personality.

Many websites deal with air-bound pooches. Check them out for further info on air travel with your dog: http://airconsumer.ost.dot.gov/publications/animals.htm (Department of Transportation info about transporting animals); www.aa.com (American Airlines); www.nwa.com (Northwest Airlines); www.delta.com (Delta Air Lines); www.continental.com (Continental Airlines);

www.usairways.com (US Airways Airlines); www.united.com (United Airlines); www.southwest.com (Southwest Airlines).

The Ultimate Doggy Bag

Your dog can't pack her own bags, and even if she could, she'd probably fill them with dog biscuits and chew toys. It's important to stash some of those in your dog's vacation kit, but here are other handy items to bring along: bowls, bedding, a brush, towels (for those muddy days), a first-aid kit, pooper-scoopers, water, food, prescription drugs, tags, treats, toys, and—of course—this book.

Make sure your dog is wearing her license, identification tag, and rabies tag. On a long trip, you may even want to bring along your dog's rabies certificate. Some parks and campgrounds require rabies and licensing information. You never know how picky they'll be.

It's a good idea to snap a disposable ID on your dog's collar, too, showing a cell phone number or the name, address, and phone number either of where you'll be vacationing or of a friend who'll be home to field calls. That way, if your dog should get lost, at least the finder won't be calling your empty house.

Some people think dogs should drink only water brought from home, so their bodies don't have to get used to too many new things. I never had a problem giving my dog tap water from other parts of the state, nor has anyone else I know. Most vets think your dog will be fine drinking tap water in most U.S. cities.

Bone Appétit

In some European countries, dogs enter restaurants and dine alongside their folks as if they were people, too. (Or at least they sit and watch and drool while their people dine.) Not so in the United States. Rightly or wrongly, dogs are considered a health threat here. But many health inspectors say they see no reason why clean, well-behaved dogs shouldn't be permitted inside a restaurant.

Fortunately, you don't have to take your dog to a foreign country in order to eat together. The Philadelphia area is full of restaurants with outdoor tables, and many of them welcome dogs to join their people for an alfresco experience. The law on outdoor dining is somewhat vague, and you'll encounter many different interpretations of it. In general, as long as your dog doesn't go inside a restaurant (even to get to outdoor tables in the back) and isn't near the food preparation areas, it's probably legal. The decision is then up to the restaurant proprietor.

The restaurants listed in this book have given us permission to tout them as dog-friendly eateries. But keep in mind that rules can change and restaurants

can close, so I highly recommend phoning before you set your stomach on a particular kind of cuisine. Since some restaurants close during colder months, phoning ahead is a doubly wise thing to do. (Although you can safely assume that when its snowing or just cold, the outdoor tables will move indoors for a while each year. Hence, poochie can't come.) If you can't call first, be sure to ask the manager of the restaurant for permission before you sit down with your sidekick. Remember, it's the restaurant proprietor, not you, who will be in trouble if someone complains to the health department.

Some fundamental rules of restaurant etiquette: Dogs shouldn't beg from other diners, no matter how delicious the steak looks. They should not attempt to get their snouts (or their entire bodies) up on the table. They should be clean, quiet, and as unobtrusive as possible. If your dog leaves a good impression with the management and other customers, it will help pave the way for all the other dogs who want to dine alongside their best friends in the future.

A Room at the Inn

Good dogs make great hotel guests. They don't steal towels, and they don't get drunk and keep the neighbors up all night. The Philadelphia region is full of lodgings whose owners welcome dogs. This book lists dog-friendly accommodations of all types, from motels to bed-and-breakfast inns to elegant hotels—but the basic dog etiquette rules are the same everywhere.

Dogs should never be left alone in your room. Leaving a dog alone in a strange place invites serious trouble. Scared, nervous dogs may tear apart drapes, carpeting, and furniture. They may even injure themselves. They might also bark nonstop and scare the daylights out of the housekeeper. If at all possible, just don't do it.

Only bring a house-trained dog to a lodging. How would you like it if a house guest relieved himself in the middle of your bedroom?

Make sure your pooch is flea-free. Otherwise, future guests will be itching to leave.

It helps to bring your dog's bed or blanket along for the night. Your dog will feel more at home and will be less tempted to jump on the hotel bed. If your dog sleeps on the bed with you at home, bring a sheet or towel and put it on top of the bed so the hotel's bedspread won't get furry or dirty.

After a few days in a hotel, some dogs come to think of it as home. They get territorial. When another hotel guest walks by, it's "Bark! Bark!" When the housekeeper knocks, it's "Bark! Snarl! Bark! Gnash!" Keep your dog quiet, or you'll both find yourselves looking for a new home away from home.

For some strange reason, many lodgings prefer small dogs as guests. All I can say is, "Yip! Yap!" It's really ridiculous. Large dogs are often much calmer and quieter than their tiny, high-energy cousins.

If you're in a location where you can't find a hotel that will accept you and your big brute, it's time to try a sell job. Let the manager know how good and quiet your dog is (if he is). Promise he won't eat the bathtub or run around and shake all over the hotel. Offer a deposit or sign a waiver, even if they're not required for small dogs. It helps if your sweet, soppy-eyed pooch is at your side to convince the decision-maker.

You could sneak dogs into hotels, but I don't recommend trying it. The lodging might have a good reason for its rules. Besides, you always feel as if you're going to be caught and thrown out on your hindquarters. You race in and out of your room with your dog as if ducking the dogcatcher. It's better to avoid feeling like a criminal and move on to a more dog-friendly location. In these situations, it's helpful to know that just about every Motel 6 permits one small pooch per room. Some have more lenient rules than others. I also found that a healthy percentage of two other chains, Red Roof Inn and Best Western, permit pooches. Space precludes me from listing all the locations, but if you find yourself in a town anywhere in the United States, and you don't know where to look for a dog-friendly lodging, those are good starting points.

The lodgings described in this book are for dogs who obey all the rules. I provide a range of rates for each lodging, from the least expensive room during low season to the priciest room during high season. Most of the rooms are doubles, so there's not usually a huge variation. But when a room price gets into the thousands of dollars, you know we're looking at royal suites here.

Some lodgings charge extra for your dog. If you see "Dogs are $10 (or whatever amount) extra," that means $10 extra per night. Some charge a fee for the length of a dog's stay, and others ask for a deposit—these details are noted in the lodging description. A few places still ask for nothing more than your dog's promise that she'll be on her best behavior. So, if no extra charge is mentioned in a listing, it means your dog can stay with you for free.

Also included in this book are websites for those lodgings whose site names aren't too long and convoluted. (When the URL takes up more space than this sentence, I generally don't include it.) Not all lodgings have a website, but when they do, it can be very helpful in deciding where to stay. Sites often provide lots of details, photos, and a way to reserve online. But generally, when staying with a pooch, it's a good idea to reserve by phone so you can let the staff know you'll be bringing your sweet beast.

Natural Troubles

Chances are your adventuring will go without a hitch, but you should always be prepared to deal with trouble. Make sure you know the basics of animal first aid before you embark on a long journey with your dog.

The more common woes—ticks, foxtails, poison ivy and oak, and skunks—can make traveling with a dog a somewhat trying experience. Ticks are hard to avoid in many parts of the Philadelphia area. They can carry Lyme disease, so you should always check yourself and your dog all over after a day in tick country. Don't forget to check ears and between the toes. If you see a tick, just pull it straight out with tweezers, not with your bare hands.

The tiny deer ticks that carry Lyme disease are more difficult to find since they're usually the size of a pin head. Consult your veterinarian if your dog is lethargic for a few days, has a fever, loses her appetite, or becomes lame. These symptoms could indicate Lyme disease. Some vets recommend a new vaccine that is supposed to prevent the onset of the disease.

Foxtails—those arrow-shaped pieces of dry grass that attach to your socks, your sweater, and your dog—are an everyday annoyance. In certain cases, they can also be lethal. They may stick in your dog's eyes, nose, ears, or mouth and work their way in. Check every nook and cranny of your dog after a walk in the country. Despite my constant effort to find these things in Linus's fur,

I've missed a few and they've beaten a path through his foot and into his leg. Be vigilant.

Poison ivy is also a common menace. Get familiar with it through a friend who knows nature or through a guided nature walk. Dogs don't generally have reactions to poison ivy, but they can easily pass its oils on to people. If you think your dog has made contact with some poison ivy, avoid petting her until you can get home and bathe her (preferably with rubber gloves). If you do pet her before you can wash her, don't touch your eyes and be sure to wash your hands immediately.

If your dog loses a contest with a skunk (and she always will), rinse her eyes first with plain warm water, then bathe her with dog shampoo. Towel her off, then apply tomato juice. I once went through four gallons of the stuff before Linus started smelling less offensive. (Walking into the store to buy it was a real hoot. I had obviously absorbed some of the stench myself. Everyone kept turning around and saying, "Whew! Do you smell a skunk?" as I wafted by.) If you can't get tomato juice, try using a solution of one pint of vinegar per gallon of water to decrease the stink instead.

Ruffing It Together

Whenever we went camping, Linus insisted on sleeping in the tent. He sprawled out and wouldn't budge. At the first hint of dawn, he'd tiptoe outside (sometimes right through the bug screen) as if he'd been standing vigil all night. He tried not to look shamefaced, but under all that hair lurked an embarrassed grin.

Actually, Linus might have had the right idea. Some outdoor experts say it's dangerous to leave even a tethered dog outside your tent at night. The dog can escape or become bait for some creature hungry for a late dinner.

The few Philadelphia area state parks that allow dogs to camp require that they be kept in a tent or vehicle at night. Some county parks follow suit. Other policies are more lenient. Use good judgment.

If you're camping with your dog, chances are you're also hiking with him. Even if you're not hiking for long, you have to watch out for your dog's paws, especially the paws of those who are fair of foot. Rough terrain can cause a dog's pads to become raw and painful, making it almost impossible for him to walk. Several types of dog boots are available for such paws. It's easier to carry the booties than to carry your dog home.

Be sure to bring plenty of water for you and your pooch. Stop frequently to wet your whistles. Some veterinarians recommend against letting your dog drink from a stream because he could ingest giardia or other internal parasites, but it's not always easy to stop a thirsty dog.

A Dog in Need

If you don't currently have a dog but could provide a good home for one, I'd like to make a plea on behalf of all the unwanted dogs who will be euthanized tomorrow—and the day after that and the day after that. Animal shelters, humane organizations, and rescue groups are overflowing with dogs who would devote their lives to being your best buddy, your faithful traveling companion, and a dedicated listener to all your tales. The people who work in these organizations are dedicated to matching the right dog to the right person, so you can be assured you'll find the best friend for you. For a first step, try petfinder.org, where you can see hundreds of dogs available in your area or close by.

Need a nudge? Remember the oft-quoted words of Samuel Butler: "The great pleasure of a dog is that you may make a fool of yourself with him and not only will he not scold you, but he will make a fool of himself, too."

Keep in Touch

Readers of *The Dog Lover's Companion to Philadelphia* mean everything to us. Linus, Nellie, and I explored the region so you and your dogs can spend true quality time together. Your input is very important. Since I first started working on this book, I've heard from many wonderful dogs and their people about new dog-friendly places or old dog-friendly places I didn't know about. If you have any suggestions or insights to offer, please contact us using the information listed in the front of this book.

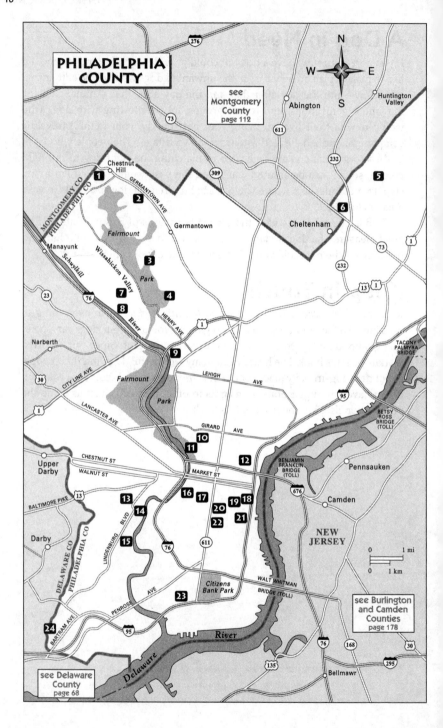

PHILADELPHIA COUNTY

see Montgomery County page 112

Abington

Huntington Valley

Chestnut Hill

1

GERMANTOWN AVE

2

Germantown

Cheltenham

5

6

Fairmount

Wissahickon Valley

Manayunk

Schuylkill

Park

3

7

4

8

River

HENRY AVE

Narberth

9

LEHIGH AVE

TACONY PALMYRA BRIDGE

City Line Ave

Fairmount

Park

Lancaster Ave

GIRARD AVE

BETSY ROSS BRIDGE (TOLL)

Upper Darby

CHESTNUT ST

WALNUT ST

10

11

12

BENJAMIN FRANKLIN BRIDGE (TOLL)

Pennsauken

MARKET ST

BALTIMORE PIKE

13

LINDENBURG BLVD

14

15

16 **17**

20

22

19 **18**

21

676

Camden

Darby

NEW JERSEY

Citizens Bank Park

AVE

23

WALT WHITMAN BRIDGE (TOLL)

0   1 mi
0   1 km

PENROSE

see Burlington and Camden Counties page 178

BARTRAM AVE

24

River

Delaware

Bellmawr

see Delaware County page 68

CHAPTER 1

Philadelphia County

> There are three faithful friends—an old wife, an old dog, and ready money.
>
> Benjamin Franklin

Philadelphia—the city of neighborhoods. Sure, every city can say it has neighborhoods, but there's no doubt it's different here. Philadelphia is a large city with the personality and soul of a small town. Each neighborhood has its own character and within those neighborhoods definitely live some characters…who love their dogs. According to recent estimates, nearly 200,000 dogs live in the city limits. That's a lot of playful pups.

These pups live with a zealous bunch of dog lovers. Everyone in Philadelphia has something they're wildly passionate about. And their dogs tend to reflect their passions and lifestyles. Whether it's watching sports, viewing art, making art, enjoying the outdoors, shopping, or eating cheesesteaks, it's a city where you can do it all with your dog—and Philadelphians do.

PICK OF THE LITTER—PHILADELPHIA COUNTY

BEST ALL-AROUND DOG PARK
Schuylkill River Dog Run, The Business District (page 45)

BEST ARTSY DOG PARK
Orianna Hill Dog Run, Northern Liberties (page 39)

BEST LESSER-KNOWN DOG PARK
Eastern State Dog Pen, Fairmount/Art Museum Area
(page 35)

BEST LEASHED WALK IN THE PARK
Wissahickon Valley Park: Forbidden Drive, Chestnut Hill
(page 21)

BEST LEASHED WALK IN THE CITY
Independence National Historical Park, Historic and
Waterfront Districts (page 54)

BEST PLACE TO HAVE A BEER
Standard Tap Bar & Restaurant, Northern Liberties
(page 41)

BEST PLACES TO EAT
Bliss, The Business District (page 46)
Rouge, Rittenhouse Square (page 51)
City Tavern, Historic and Waterfront Districts (page 57)

BEST PLACES TO STAY
Loews Philadelphia Hotel, The Business District
(page 48)
The Rittenhouse Hotel, Rittenhouse Square (page 52)

BEST EVENT
DeBella Dog Walk, Fairmount/Art Museum Area (page 34)

These neighborhoods are exactly why Philly could be dubbed the City of Brotherly Dog Lovers because of the tight-knit community of dog owners that has developed in nearly every one. These dog lovers form their own make-shift town watch as walking dogs tends to be a great way to report and deter crime. And since the law is to clean up after your dog, community groups tend to be an enforcer by default, since there are not enough law enforcers due to budget constraints.

Sadly, Philadelphia parks are also losing funding, which means some city parks have been threatened with closing or losing services. But that doesn't stop Philadelphians. They raise money for parks, as well as build and organize their own dog parks. Take Orianna Hill in Northern Liberties, Seger Dog Park in Washington Square, and Eastern State Dog Pen in Fairmount, for example. These off-leash parks were not started by the city, but by dog lovers who care about the health and happiness of their furry friends.

Your pup will be pleased to know that off-leash dog runs are becoming more common all over the city due to the community groups who've started them. But while visiting do not be deterred by the close ties in community groups: They welcome anyone and everyone to visit their parks and donate to their causes to better the lives of everyone's canine companions.

In addition to all the off-leash frolicking pups can do in the city, Philadelphians love to take their leashed pups to Fairmount Park, the largest inner-city park in the world. Because of its size, covering nearly 9,000 acres, Fairmount Park travels through many neighborhoods in the Northwest and West sections of the city. Every dog lover has his or her own favorite part, and ours is Wissahickon Valley's Forbidden Drive. Your leashed pup is welcome all over the park including its nearly 100 miles of hiking paths.

Then there's the peaceful and gorgeous 1,600-acre Pennypack Park in the Northeast section of the city, where your dog and you can walk and hike in the wooded and quiet oasis, and stop for a picnic lunch by the creek.

While its neighborhoods are its pride, Philadelphia is best known for its heart being the region of Center City. Why not simply call it downtown Philadelphia? Because this is Philadelphia and not much is typical here. It is dubbed Center City because it's the center or hub of everything that's exciting in the region, especially when it comes to dog fun. The borders that define Center City are Vine to South Street and Front to 25th Street. Center City encompasses many of the neighborhoods that Philadelphia is known for, like Rittenhouse Square and Old City.

Here you can attend a doggy breakfast, take in some serious American history, go for a romp at a nearby dog run, stay at some of the finest hotels, and dine at some of the city's best restaurants. In fact, outdoor eateries where dogs are welcome abound downtown and have doubled in number in recent years due to the restaurant boom.

DIVERSIONS

Philadelphia Murals: While you and your doggy are cruising the streets of the city together, you'll likely see more than one public art mural. That's because there are more than 2,000 indoor and outdoor murals in the city. As an anti-graffiti initiative started in 1984, the Mural Arts Program has completed more murals than any other public art program in the nation; it is used as a model program around the world. While they vary in size, an average mural is about the size of a Philadelphia row house—three stories high (35 feet) by 30 feet across. Subject matter includes heroes, landscapes, and inspiring scenes. No matter what your taste in art, you will likely be captivated when you approach one. They're amazing. For a detailed description of the murals and their locations, visit the program's website, www.muralarts.org.

Walking Tour of the City: Philadelphia was named the fourth-best walking city in the nation by a group that appreciates the foot like no other, the American Podiatric Medical Association. That nomination may have stemmed from the walker-friendly direction/signage program called Walk!Philadelphia. The largest and most visually dynamic pedestrian wayfinding system in North America, Walk!Philadelphia encompasses more than 2,200 colorful, bold signs across Center City. You can't miss them. The system consists of directional signs and heads-up diskmaps (with the direction the user is facing at the top of the map). Neighborhoods are color coded to make it easy to use. With this practical system you and your pup can explore on your own and never worry about getting lost.

Plus, all of Center City is walkable with your pup on a leash and is easily navigated from its color-coded maps on nearly every corner (see Diversions). In recent years more hotels have opened their doors to dogs or added new dog-friendly programs.

If you're interested in seeing Philadelphia via public transit and have a smaller pooch, SEPTA (the Southeastern Pennsylvania Transit Authority) allows caged pets on all its buses and trains. If not, driving into the city is not tough, although parking can be hard to come by and expensive. If you're headed to Center City, be sure to have at least $20 available for parking in case you can't find a street spot. And don't forget your roll of quarters in case you do!

All in all, Philadelphia is a ball and no doubt you both will have one and maybe even fetch one when you visit.

Chestnut Hill, Mount Airy, and Blue Bell Hill

Some of the most magnificent homes and gardens in the entire Philadelphia region dating back to the early 1700s stand in these sections of the city. Not only is this area a sight to see in and of itself, the residents here adore their dogs as evidenced by all the different breeds you'll see shopping or eating with humans along the busy downtown street of Germantown Avenue, which runs through both Chestnut Hill and Mount Airy. Whenever we drove down Germantown Avenue, the windows would go up as Linus had a hard time not jumping out of the car to say hi to one of his cousins.

PARKS, BEACHES, AND RECREATION AREAS

1 Wissahickon Valley Park: Forbidden Drive

🐾 🐾 🐾 (See Philadelphia County map on page 16)

The single best thing about having a dog in your life is going to a place together like Wissahickon Valley Park, specifically Forbidden Drive. The Wissahickon Valley is actually a seven-mile long alpine gorge cut by the Wissahickon Creek before it empties into the Schuylkill River. The wooded trail of Forbidden Drive gets its name from a 1920s ordinance that banned cars on it. Yes, it is clever.

Spanning about 1,800 acres with 45 miles of trails, Wissahickon Valley Park (a.k.a. "The Wissahickon" to locals) is one of the largest and most commonly used sections of Fairmount Park. Because it's one of the few remaining urban wilderness areas that is so scenic and distinctive, the federal government designated it a National Natural Landmark in 1972.

Although the park requires you to keep your pup on a leash, Forbidden Drive is one of the most enjoyable walks you'll likely have in the city together. In fact, it was Linus's favorite Sunday activity, aside from sleeping on the couch while watching football.

While walking you truly feel as though you're embedded in nature, not in the fifth-largest city in the nation. Here you'll traverse the drive's gravel path along scenic Wissahickon Creek and run into lots of other canine and non-canine walkers, joggers, and runners, as well as a few equestrian types, anglers, and picnickers, especially on the weekends. One of the highlights is a picturesque, antique covered bridge you'll see in the first half of the walk. Forbidden Drive has mile markers so you can even track how far you've traveled. At about the halfway point, you can both stop for a bite at the Valley Green Inn or for a refreshing drink from the water fountain.

Maps of the entire Wissahickon Valley can be purchased online for $6 from the Friends of the Wissahickon website.

DOG-EAR YOUR CALENDAR

Annual Manayunk Arts Festival: You and your pup will enjoy the sights and sounds of the largest outdoor arts and crafts show in the Philadelphia region. The juried show features more than 250 artists from across the country. A feast for the senses, the always-crowded arts festival has live entertainment setting the summer party mood with food and drink vendors up and down Main Street. Drinking water is available for your dog at many booths. It's fun for the whole family with special children's activities including a Children's Clothesline Art Exhibition. Shuttle buses are available throughout the festival. Parking at pick-up areas is free and the shuttle fare just $1 per person. A portion of the proceeds benefits North Light Community Center. 215/482-9565.

Philadelphia Live Arts Festival & Philly Fringe: Let's just say it's like nothing you've ever seen. This renowned Philadelphia event, which usually begins early September and runs for two weeks, hosts a variety of live shows intended to truly stretch your conception of what is art. Many of the performances are funny; others are a bit sad. The best part is they love dogs at all the outdoor performances. Pups are even welcome to the box office. 211 Vine St.; 215/413-9006; www.livearts-fringe.org. Box office: 620 Chestnut St.; 215/413-1318.

Fall for the Arts Festival: A great event to attend in Chestnut Hill on a brisk autumn day is the Fall Festival, held on Germantown Avenue, on Sunday of Columbus Day weekend. Here you and your pup can view the works of over 130 fine artists and craftspeople in a festive atmosphere that includes live entertainment, amusement rides, food, wine, and beer. Free admission. 215/247-6696.

First Fridays: The first Friday of every month the arts community in Old City holds its "open house" event where galleries stay open late (5–9 P.M.) and the streets are filled with people strolling about and dining at many of the great eateries. It's something every art and dog lover should do. Although dogs are not allowed in all the galleries for various reasons (such as breakable items at dog level), they are welcome at some of the more than 40 that participate. Ask first before bringing your pup inside. Regardless, the two of you are welcome to tool through the streets and enjoy the ambiance at this famous community event. 215/625-9200; www.oldcityarts.org.

There are many ways to get to Forbidden Drive, but one of the easiest is at the far end of the drive. Take Germantown Avenue to Northwestern Avenue. Take a left on Northwestern until it dead-ends and park in the parking spots or on the street. Hours are sunrise–1 A.M. 215/247-0417; office@fow.org; www.fow.org.

🐾 Pastorius Park

🐾 🐾 (See Philadelphia County map on page 16)

Our first introduction to dog parks nearly a decade ago, Pastorius Park was actually the park of choice for Linus and me when he was a wee rascally puppy. We heard rumors about dogs running off leash here and couldn't imagine more fun to be had. So we discovered it and made it a habit.

Established in 1915, Pastorius Park is a 16-acre unfenced park named in honor of Francis Pastorius, a leader of early German immigrants to the area. The park is removed from any busy streets and loaded with benches and trees and even a pond for doggy paddling. Weekly summer concerts are also held at its amphitheater.

But this is an unofficial dog park—"unofficial" being the operative word. On any given day, you can let Fido run free with lots of other doggies, especially in the mornings and late afternoons, but be mindful of the authorities who tend to lurk nearby (the two of us were nearly ticketed on more than one occasion). The people who come here know the drill and will happily give you fair warning if they see a ranger on the way. If uncertain, keep your dog leashed and out of the pond.

Take Germantown Pike North to Hartwell Lane and take it until it dead-ends at Roanoke. The park is at Roanoke and Abington Streets. Street parking is available. Hours are sunrise–sunset. 215/247-6696.

🐾 Carpenter Woods Dog Park

🐾 🐾 🐾 🐾 (See Philadelphia County map on page 16)

One of the treasures of Mount Airy to dog-loving locals is Carpenter Woods. This segment of Fairmount Park is not just a wooded and peaceful escape but also a ton of fun for Fido and you. You'll love that you can traverse the dirt pathways under the shade of hundred-year-old trees, and your dog will love it because it's full of great smells, foliage, and friends.

But it must be stressed this is an unofficial dog park, with many pups going unlawfully leash-less. If you're caught by authorities with your dog off leash, you could face a fine of between $25–300, so please use caution. Still, once you get into the thick of the woods and see the regulars, you'll feel ready to let loose. Here you both will be greeted by breeds from Corgis to Rottweilers to poodles, and everything in between. Many of these friendly dogs here know each other, of course. Plus, it's a hot spot for area pet sitters who have the low down on all things dog.

FETCHING NECESSITIES

The next time you're in Chestnut Hill and need to run a few errands you can check out a couple dog-friendly spots. At the bottom of the hill, you and your doggy are welcome to check out *Air-Bud: Golden Receiver* (one of Linus's favorites) or any variety of films at **TLA Video** (7630 Germantown Ave., 215/248-4448); at the top of the hill you both are welcome to shop at the **Hill Company** (8615 Germantown Ave.; 215/247-7600), which specializes in gardening supplies, outdoor furniture and accessories.

Plus, close by to the Hill Company is **Bone Appetite K-9 Bakery** (8505 Germantown Ave.; 215/247-4292), a super-friendly place that sells everything from homemade gourmet dog biscuits to doggone fancy collars and leashes, carriers, car seats, pet furniture, custom dog beds and gift items for pet lovers. They love all dogs and encourage everyone who visits to bring their pooch in with them.

Carpenter Woods is a pawticularly excellent destination all year round, but especially in the summer as it's completely shaded and there's a creek for dogs to stop and refresh. Benches are also scattered throughout the woods, but Linus and I found the toppled-over trees made more naturalistic rest spots.

Although the area comprises only about two city blocks, it feels like miles when you're in the midst of the woods. Remember to bring your own poop bags as there are none available.

From Chestnut Hill take Allens Lane, which turns into Wissahikon Avenue. Take a left on Mount Pleasant Street. The entrance is on South Mount Pleasant Street at Ellet Street. Street parking is ample. Hours are 6 A.M.–1 A.M. 215/683-0200.

🯁 Clifford Park

 (See Philadelphia County map on page 16)

Arriving here, it doesn't appear like much of a park, or even a dog park, for that matter. It's a ballfield with a large outfield and some woods and a meadow near the Thomas Mansion. But this is a very special place for dog-loving residents of Blue Bell Hill, this section of Philadelphia. It is not what's on the outside of the park, but more of what's on the "inside." It's here that friendships are made and flourish through the common thread: dogs.

Every morning and evening, Blue Bell Hillers congregate here with their dogs walking them in the woods together and along the trails behind the Mansion, as well as in the outfield of Clifford Park. The regulars are a close-knit community and often socialize outside of the dog park and help each other out with dog sitting or house sitting when needed. In fact, one mem-

DOG-EAR YOUR CALENDAR

Pennypack Park Music Festival: You and your outdoors-loving, music-appreciating poochie are welcome to bring your lawn chairs and blankets and check out the live concerts featuring music like big band, pop, classic rock, and Irish folk held at Pennypack Park twice a month in the summer starting in May, usually on Wednesday evenings 7–9:30 P.M. info@pennypackpark.com; www .pennypackpark.com.

Summer Outdoor Concerts: For 10 Wednesday nights in the summer, the Chestnut Hill Community Association produces free outdoor concerts in Pastorius Park, located just off Germantown Avenue. Bring your own dinner or grab one at a Chestnut Hill restaurant and head to the park with your pooch by 7:30 P.M. to enjoy the sweet sounds of summer. 215/248-8810.

Lawnchair Drive-In: Get out your lawn chair, grab your leash, and head down to Liberty Lands Park (3rd Street north of Poplar) in Northern Liberties for a fun midweek break. This free outdoor movie feature occurs in the summer on Wednesday evenings at dusk. The program has shown everything from *The Exorcist* to *The Wizard of Oz*. In past years, early black and white Popeye cartoons were aired to start the show. The season usually begins the last week in July and runs through the month of August. Northern Liberties Neighborhood Association; 215/627-6562.

ber says that his dog neighbors are the closest neighbors he has. Blue Bell residents include artists, broadcasters, academics, and nonprofit employees whose dogs represent a diverse range of breeds, each with a distinctive personality.

The dogs here look to play with other dogs and are visibly disappointed when one of their favorite friends doesn't show up that day, according to one regular.

Dogs go off leash as long as they're familiar with the other dogs. Park rangers rarely give out citations here, but they will warn people to put their dogs on leashes.

You and your pup are always welcome here, but come early (between 6:30 and 7 A.M. or late in the afternoon (4–6 P.M.), as that's when the greatest number of furry friends will be around. As long as your dog has good recall, it shouldn't be a problem letting him off leash. However, there are some busy streets surrounding the area, so be absolutely positive your dog will come when called.

From Chestnut Hill take Allens Lane, which turns into Wissahickon Avenue. Follow Wissahickon to Walnut Lane. The park will be on your left. Street parking is the only option here. Hours are sunrise–sunset. 215/683-0200.

PLACES TO EAT

Bruno's: What a shame, we thought, as the owner of this excellent greasy spoon sadly explained that dogs are not allowed here anymore due to recent complaints. This was one of our favorite places to go after a vigorous walk on Forbidden Drive. Linus and I would sit on the porch and have a cool drink, and share a Father Casey egg sandwich or one of the most scrumptious milkshakes you'd ever consume in your life. But since it's so close to our hearts and a favorite of the locals, we're hoping by the time you read this, they'll change their policy back to welcoming pups. Call first and see. 9800 Germantown Ave.; 215/242-1880.

Cafette: Creative home-style dishes are the trademark of this comfy and casual BYOB restaurant. Both the vegetarian and non-vegetarian soups, salads, and sandwiches are consistently delicious and moderately priced. Cafette is open for dinner, too. You can sit with your doggy in the front patio or the intimate sculpture garden in the back and enjoy your home-cooked meal together. 8136 Ardleigh St.; 215/242-4220; www.cafette.com.

Cresheim Cottage: This absolutely adorable cottage doubles as a very cozy restaurant located in Mount Airy. Because the interior is so cute, it's too bad your doggy won't be able to see it, but they'll happily serve you and your pup on the lovely garden patio around the back. The service is friendly and professional, and the food is just as impressive. If you love seafood, try the crab and rock shrimp cakes. Yum! 7402 Germantown Ave.; 215/248-4365.

Labrador Coffee: The store owners here love dogs so much, they named their coffee shop after them. But it's not just Labs they adore, they appreciate all varieties of canines at the restaurant. (Ironically, they're former golden retriever owners.) While smaller, well-behaved pups are allowed inside, the outside eating area, a small outdoor garden, welcomes your any-size-doggy to accompany you as you enjoy bagels, sandwiches, and pastries. Treats and water are available for your four-legged friend. 8139 Germantown Ave.; 215/247-8487.

Roller's: At the top of the hill in Chestnut Hill, you will find this beloved high-end diner filled with Hillers (the native people and dogs). You and your doggy are welcome to sit outside on the patio and enjoy fresh fruit, seafood, salads, and homemade desserts. 8705 Germantown Ave.; 215/242-1771.

Solaris Grille: If you can swing grabbing a table outside the fence of this creative and upbeat restaurant, do so. The food is well worth it, and dogs are allowed at the few tables in this outdoor area. A perfect spot to come for brunch, lunch, or dinner, Solaris Grille offers some of the tastiest food—everything from omelets to potstickers to fresh fruit—at reasonable prices. It never disappoints. 8201 Germantown Ave.; 215/242-3400; www.solarisgrille.com.

Valley Green Inn: A leisurely stroll or quick jog with your furry friend along the Wissahickon Creek on Forbidden Drive will likely bring you right by the Valley Green Inn, a beautiful old roadhouse. It's the only restaurant located in the confines of the park. And because it's park-central, of course they love dogs and will happily provide water and treats for your pup on their outside patio directly in front of the porch. Plus, there's a snack bar open in warm-weather months. Although there was no place to sit down and eat with your dog at the time of printing of this book, plans are in the works for allowing dogs on the terrace with their people. Valley Green Road at Wissahickon; 215/247-1730; www.valleygreeninn.com.

Northeast Philly

If you're a Philadelphia native and you're talking about the Northeast, you're definitely not discussing New England (why would you?), but instead this distinctive region of the city. The Northeast is as ethnic as neighborhoods come. Generations of Italian, Jewish, Polish, Irish, and African American people have called it home. Residents rarely leave for extended periods, let alone move away. Why should they when they have the gorgeous Pennypack Park in their back yard and all their bi-legged and four-legged friends and family are here?

PARKS, BEACHES, AND RECREATION AREAS

🖥 Pennypack Park

🐾 🐾 🐾 ◀● (See Philadelphia County map on page 16)

Like taking a step inside another, more remote world, Pennypack Park is famous for having this effect on its visitors, many of whom choose to live near it, so they can have a taste of the country in the city limits. Encompassing 1,600 acres of woodlands, meadows, wetlands, fields, the Pennypack Creek, bike paths, playgrounds, picnic areas, and hiking trails, this park has it all.

DIVERSION

Yappy Hour: You and your pup need a little socialization and fun indoors? Look no further than the PetSmart on Route 1 in Northeast Philadelphia. Every week for a half hour (days and times may vary), poodles canoodle and Labs gab at the store's Yappy Hour, and you get the pleasure of seeing your dog having a great time playing with friends. 4640-60 E. Roosevelt Blvd.; 215/743-9602.

This park has a rich history as it was once the home of the Lenni-Lenape Indians who named it Pennypack, which translates to "dead, deep water" or "water without much current." It still behaves that way.

Your pup will have a tail-wagging time walking with you through this green oasis along the trails. In many parts, you can get right down to the water to cool off. Most of the park is shaded with huge, old trees that serve as a border to the noise and cityscape.

Along the way, depending on your route you can pass by some historic structures like the Pennypack Bridge, which dates to 1697 and is still used on Frankford Avenue (previously Kings Highway), or the Verree House on Verree Road, the site of a raid by British troops during the Revolutionary War. You and your pup might also see abandoned railroad grades, as well as evidence of early mills and mill races.

You might even catch a few deer here as there are large numbers residing in Philadelphia (uh…Pennypack), as well as rabbits and turtles.

Linus was a huge fan of Pennypack; the minute I parked the car, his nose was in the corner of the window ready for the door to open and him to come flying out and down the bike path with me.

There are several entrances to Pennypack Park since it's so huge, but our favorite is to take Bustleton Avenue to Winchester Avenue, which borders the park. Park along Winchester and walk down the bike path toward the wooded area of the park. Hours are sunrise–1 A.M. 215/934-PARK; FriendsPennypack@comcast.net; www.philaparks.org/pp.htm.

DOG-EAR YOUR CALENDAR

Dog Lovers Holiday Bazaar: Just when there's a chill in the air and it's hard to find fun things to do with your pup, here's an annual indoor event that you two should make a tradition. This all-day affair aims to educate and entertain you and your doggy (who is welcome on a leash) with the latest from more than 50 dog-related vendors and information from rescue groups. Canine good citizen tests are performed as well as lots of other dog skill activities. Best of all, your pup can get into the holiday spirit and have his photo taken with (or without) Santa. The free bazaar is typically held the first weekend in November at the National Guard Armory on Roosevelt Boulevard in Northeast Philadelphia, but call first to be sure the location hasn't changed. (At press time, the location was uncertain.) 215/338-6870; gpdfa@aol.com.

6 Burlholme Park

🐾 🐾 (See Philadelphia County map on page 16)

Comprising about 70 acres with a beautiful pinkish Italianate-style mansion on its grounds, Burlholme Park dates back to the early 19th century. Named after an estate in England, it means "house in a woodland setting." The Ryerss family, the home's original owners, were animal lovers. The headstones marking the graves of their beloved pets, buried under a tree on the west side of the mansion, are still visible.

Today the park is used for various activities, especially dog walking. It even hosts the Paws for the Cause walk that benefits Fox Chase Cancer Center next door. It has ball fields, a picnic pavilion, shaded picnic areas, portable toilets, a playground, and trash cans for the poop you scoop. The open areas really beg your pup to run off leash, but it's not advisable here since it's really in the middle of the park and would turn a head or two.

From Center City, take Route 1 North (Roosevelt Boulevard) then turn left on Rising Sun Avenue. Take a left on Cottman Avenue (Route 73) then a right on Central Avenue; park along Central. Hours are sunrise–sunset. 215/685-0544 or 215/685-0599.

PLACES TO EAT

Blue Ox Brauhus Restaurant: Excellent service and a good, authentic German meal are the hallmarks of this enjoyable spot located in the Fox Chase section of Northeast Philly. Like Octoberfest anytime of the year, this eatery has an outstanding selection of beer on tap and tasty eats. You and poochie will have a true German experience dining in the beer garden together. And the staff will happily provide your pup with some water and a treat, too. 7980 Oxford Ave.; 215/728-9440.

PLACES TO STAY

Although there are no dog-friendly hotels specifically in Northeast Philly, you'll have good luck in surrounding towns such as Bensalem and Trevose, covered in the Bucks County chapter.

Manayunk

A historic textile milling district just a few minutes' drive from Center City, Manayunk is a happening place to shop and eat, and quite accommodating to dogs on its bustling Main Street. This neighborhood has reinvented itself to stand the test of time. One of the trendiest spots in the city, it is located along the shoulders of the Schuylkill River and borders the historic Manayunk Canal. Main Street is lined with distinctive boutiques, galleries, and dog-friendly restaurants. The neighborhood also hosts many festivals and

DOG-EAR YOUR CALENDAR

Dad Vail Regatta: For Philadelphians it seems like every other day in the springtime, there's a regatta that shuts down Kelly Drive to traffic. As annoying as this may be to drivers, it's also a source of pride for Philadelphians. In fact, the father of all regattas, the annual Dad Vail Regatta is the largest collegiate regatta in the United States. Thousands of student athletes representing hundreds of colleges converge on the city the second week of May to watch the exciting rowing competition, held on the Schuylkill River. You and your pup are welcome to join the party for free along Kelly Drive. www.dadvail.org.

Wachovia Bike Race: Established more than two decades ago, Wachovia Bike Race (formerly the First Union USPRO Cycling Championship) is the longest-running, richest single-day cycling race in the U.S., with a $130,000 purse. Held the first Sunday in June, 140 of the world's best professional cyclists travel on a 14.4-mile circuit through the Benjamin Franklin Parkway and Kelly Drive. Once they enter Manayunk, the cyclists lap the grueling and infamous Manayunk Wall, with a 17 percent grade, an unbelievable 10 times. With cheers and beers flowing in the streets, the experience of seeing the cyclists conquer The Wall is definitely one of the year's highlights in Philadelphia. 215/482-9565.

outdoor activities, including the ever-so-fun, longest-running single-day cycling race in the U.S., the Wachovia Bike Race (formerly the First Union USPRO Cycling Championship); www.manayunk.com.

PARKS, BEACHES, AND RECREATION AREAS

🖪 Pretzel Park Dog Run

🐾 🐾 🐕 (See Philadelphia County map on page 16)

Maybe you've met your friends in Manayunk and your dog wants to meet some of her own. Try taking a walk a couple of blocks north of Main Street and stopping at Pretzel Park. Also known as Manayunk Park, this dog run is a relative newcomer to the Philadelphia dog park scene. While visiting with poochie you'll be happy to know it is completely fenced in with a wood chip surface; bags and water are available, too. The last time Linus and I visited the park, tree trunks served as a makeshift obstacle course for him and his two rowdy mixed-breed buddies. Although the park isn't big, it's well taken care of, and appreciated by residents and visitors alike. Most people are very responsible about picking up after their pets and help out to keep the park looking great. Afternoons are busiest, but also the most fun.

It's located at Cresson, Silverwood, and Rector Streets. From Main Street take a right on Cotton and then a right at Cresson. Follow Cresson to Silverwood and take a left. You'll see the park on your left at Rector Street. Park anywhere along the street. Hours are sunrise–sunset. 215/683-0200.

🐾 Manayunk Canal Towpath

🐾 🐾 (See Philadelphia County map on page 16)

While visiting Manayunk you and puppers might enjoy seeing the neighborhood through its "back door" via the Manayunk Canal Towpath. This path, located behind the shops on Main Street, parallels the canal and the Schuylkill River. It's also a portion of the Philadelphia-Valley Forge Bikeway that stretches 22 miles along the river. No matter how far you and your dog want to walk along the path (the surface varies between gravel, hard ground, and boardwalk), you'll see other nature lovers and signs describing the industrial history of Manayunk and its famed canal. Also, you'll see former textile mills, old rail lines, canal locks, and ruins of the lock lender's house, as well as wildlife and even a fisherman here and there. Because dogs and their people frequent this part of Manayunk, poop-bag dispensers and trash cans are now available along the tow path.

The Manayunk Development Corporation is in the process of organizing a full restoration of the Manayunk Canal to allow canoes and small boats to sail through on their way down the Schuylkill River.

The towpath is accessible directly behind Main Street. Take Exit 338 from the Schuylkill Expressway. At the bottom of the ramp make a left turn, cross the Green Lane Bridge to the traffic light at Main Street, and make a right turn. Park anywhere along the street or in the first parking lot on your right. Hours are sunrise–sunset. 215/482-9565.

PLACES TO EAT

Adobe Cafe and Sante Fe Steakhouse: Not too far from the action on Main Street, but far enough to provide a little more peace in a laid-back atmosphere with better parking, is the friendly Adobe Cafe. It's known for its interesting and always good Tex-Mex fare; you will likely enjoy the tacos, burritos, and enchiladas as well as more offbeat dishes like chicken stuffed with goat cheese and spinach. Vegetarians will also find many mouth-watering choices. Best of all, you and your pup are welcome to gobble it all up together outside on the patio. 4550 Mitchell St.; 215/483-3947.

Bucks County Coffee Company: There's nothing like a piping hot cup of joe on a brisk fall day, especially here. Known as one of the first specialty coffee micro roasters, the java from this ambitious shop is among the best in the area. The even better part is that staffers let your doggy come inside with you while ordering, and welcome the two of you to sit street-side together while sipping your brew. 4311 Main St.; 215/487-3927; www.buckscountycoffee.com.

Le Bus: This popular eatery's humble beginnings stemmed from a make-shift bread shop out of a school bus on the University of Pennsylvania campus. It's come a long way. Now it's one of the most admired, least expensive restaurants in Manayunk. While Linus felt its bread was reason alone to dine here—restaurants around town even give it a mention in their menus—leave room to sample the healthy and hearty soups, salads, and sandwiches. Definite must-tries include the turkey burger, the Thai turkey salad, and Mom's meatloaf. You and your canine companion are welcome to sit outside. 4266 Main St.; 215/487-2663.

Sonoma: Most people who've spent some time on Main Street have eaten a meal or two at the casually hip Sonoma, a Manayunk favorite. Serving what's best described as "Italifornia cuisine," Sonoma offers fresh produce, meats, and seafood on its mostly organic menu. Its pizzas are equally fresh-tasting and delicious. No matter what you order at this moderately priced eatery, you'll probably love it. You and your pup are welcome to sit on the sidewalk overlooking Main Street. 4411 Main St.; 215/483-9400.

Zesty's (formerly Café Zesty): If you're looking for an unpretentious eatery with great service, try Zesty's, a long-time local favorite. The food is a mix of Greek and Italian, but there's no mix in how distinctively good each dish is. For a fun appetizer try the saganaki, a Greek cheese pan-fried with ouzo and lemon. For an entrée, the marinated tuna is a solid bet. You and your pup are welcome at the restaurant's street-side seating area. 4382 Main St; 215/483-6226.

Fairmount/Art Museum Area

Just northwest of Center City, you'll be in the neighborhood known as Fairmount, also referred to as the "Art Museum Area." Linus always found it curious that we'd call the Philadelphia Museum of Art "the art museum," as if there were only one. He knew better: There are a slew of museums all over Philadelphia. But for clarification purposes, the big one where Rocky ran up the steps is the one locals call "the art museum." Hence, the surrounding area of the city is the Art Museum Area. Interesting tidbit: To commemorate its appreciation of canine companions, this world-famous museum recently held a "dog show" art exhibit displaying paintings of pups from the 17th to 20th centuries, an event appreciated by dog lovers and art lovers alike.

DIVERSION

Laurel Hill Cemetery: Overlooking Kelly Drive and the Schuylkill River, this 100-acre Gothic cemetery welcomes you and your leashed four-footed friend on its grounds. The first architecturally designed cemetery and the first burial ground to be named a National Historical Landmark, Laurel Hill was the "afterlife address of choice" for the city's elite during the 18th and 19th centuries. Thomas McKean, a signer of the Declaration of Independence, is buried here. In the 19th century, Laurel Hill was a popular retreat not for mourning but for picnickers and strollers because of its beautiful landscape. Its monuments include everything from marble headstones to granite obelisks and massive mausoleums that entomb the families of Philadelphia's industrial leaders. Interesting tidbit: The William Warner tomb, designed by Alexander Milne Calder, the sculptor of the William Penn statue atop City Hall, shows the soul arising from the tomb in a cloud of smoke. The grounds are open Monday–Friday 8 A.M.–4 P.M., Saturday 9:30 A.M.–1:30 P.M. 3822 Ridge Ave., 215/228-8200.

PARKS, BEACHES, AND RECREATION AREAS

⑨ East and West Parks of Fairmount Park (Kelly Drive and West River Drive Areas)

🐾 🐾 🐾 🐾 (See Philadelphia County map on page 16)

While some of Philadelphia's parks make you feel as if you're anywhere but in a city, the East and West Parks do the opposite. They give you a taste of nature while at the same time provide an incredible view of some of Philadelphia's finest offerings: its skyline, the Philadelphia Museum of Art (one of the oldest and most respected museums), Boathouse Row (19th-century Tudor boathouses, home to private rowing clubs and illuminated at night), and the Water Works (stunning neoclassical buildings that supplied water to the city for more than a century). This eight-mile stretch of pathway surrounds both sides of the Schuylkill River on Kelly Drive over the Falls Bridge to West River Drive and back down to the art museum.

It's an excellent hike if your pup is in good shape and likes to run, jog, or walk with you on a leash for extended lengths along the scenic Schuylkill River. Plus, on weekend days from April through October, West River Drive is closed to traffic providing even more room for your favorite form of exercise with your favorite friend.

But you don't have to do the entire loop; you can do as much or as little as you'd like. Case in point: The last time we were walking the loop, Linus was

DOG-EAR YOUR CALENDAR

DeBella Dog Walk: A great way to say thank you to your pup for being such a good friend is to take him to the DeBella Dog Walk celebrating all things canine at Fairmount Park's Memorial Hall. One Sunday in April from 10 A.M.–2 P.M., you both can learn about rescue groups, adoption programs, animal shelters, health issues, microchip identification, and training demonstrations. You can also participate in fun events like agility demos and even a dog/person look-alike contest. The field behind Memorial Hall transforms into a canine paradise complete with doggy watering stations, training seminars, and green pastures for as far as the eye can see. The event is free and open to the dog-loving public. Every dog must be on a nonretractable leash. 610/617-4866.

Walk for the Park: Sponsored by the Fairmount Park Commission, you and your pooch are invited to walk a 2.5-mile stretch along Benjamin Franklin Parkway from the Philadelphia Museum of Art to JFK Plaza and back again to raise awareness and money for Philadelphia's Park System. Usually held in September, walkers should meet at 8:30 A.M. at the art museum. The event starts at 9 A.M. A picnic is held for all participants after the walk. Cost is $10 for adults; free for children under 12. 215/685-0045.

Alzheimer's Association Memory Walk: Your pup is encouraged to join you in raising awareness and funds for people with Alzheimer's Disease and their families at the annual Memory Walk that takes place at Fairmount Park's Memorial Hall. Usually held a Sunday in October, starting at 8 A.M., there are no fees to enter, but collected donations are encouraged. Alzheimer's Association; 215/561-2919, ext. 310.

Fundraising Dog Walk: Help prevent cancer by walking with your doggy in the annual "Paws for the Cause" walk that benefits Fox Chase Cancer Center. The event held one Sunday in October at Burlholme Park includes pet demonstrations, vendors, and contests for amazing pet tricks and best tail wagger, and a dog-owner look-alike contest. Registration is $10 and begins at 8 A.M. Participants can walk anywhere from one to three miles. Pledges will be collected and prizes given for the highest amount. Donations can be sent to Department of Diagnostic Imaging, Fox Chase Cancer Center, 333 Cottman Ave., Philadelphia, PA 19111; 215/728-3024.

intent on making it until the last mile when he politely pooped out. He gently slowed down to a complete stop and had that "that's all for now" look in his eye. So we took a break for an hour before heading back to the car, where he happily snoozed all the way home.

On this invigorating walk you'll be right alongside walkers, joggers, inline skaters, bikers, skateboarders, and lots of four-legged companions. On the East Side along Kelly Drive, you'll see countless sculptures that are so moving they may actually make you both stop in your tracks. You'll see the Ellen Phillips Samuel Memorial Sculpture Garden (you can't miss it), featuring three terraces and 17 striking sculptures referencing American history. One other section that always brings a smile is farther north on Kelly Drive, the happy sculpture of the three "Playing Angels," so powerful you can practically hear them playing music and dancing above you.

On West River Drive, near Montgomery Drive, you'll see the Boelson Cottage, a charming little house that looks like it was coaxed off the pages of *Hansel and Gretel.* More than 300 years old, the cottage is one of the oldest buildings in Fairmount Park. Also, the West Park provides some of the best views of Boathouse Row and the Waterworks.

From Center City take the Benjamin Franklin Parkway to either Kelly Drive or West River Drive and park in one of the many parking sections along the roads. Hours are sunrise–1 A.M. 215/683-0200.

10 Eastern State Dog Pen

🐾 🐾 🐾 🐾 🐕 (See Philadelphia County map on page 16)

The people of Philadelphia continue to surprise and delight, especially with the addition of this dog park. It keeps a low profile, but it deserves some praise. The fact that it's alongside the historic Eastern State Penitentiary is interesting enough, but that it's basically immaculate with friendly people and pups in the cozy neighborhood of Fairmount, makes it even more noteworthy. The best time to visit the park is weekdays 4–7 P.M., when you'll find at least a half-dozen or so dogs.

It has all the amenities you could ask for in a dog park: double-gated entrance, biodegradable poop bags and dispenser, trash cans, park benches, water bowls, and shade. In addition, there are two sections, one for bigger dogs and one for smaller pups. There's even a makeshift dog pool (a baby pool) for extra-hot days. Light-colored stone covers the ground, making it easy to spot and clean up poop. Plus, the park has plans to install a doggy water fountain in the future.

Like nearly all of the dog parks in Philly, this park was started and is maintained by a group of determined dog lovers, rather than by the city. It is actually an offshoot of the Friends of Eastern State Penitentiary, called Fairmount D.O.G. (dog owners group). Regular fundraisers are held to help pay back

DOG-EAR YOUR CALENDAR

Fourth of July Welcome America! Festival: If you're going to celebrate Independence Day, what better place to do it than the city where it all began? It's bigger and better here. That's why Philadelphia's Independence Day lasts 12 days, usually starting the week before the Fourth. This famous festival features more than 80 events and activities. Standouts include the 4th of July parade, the fireworks display, outdoor movies, and concerts at various locations. Just make sure your four-legged patriot can handle the noise and crowds. 800/537-7676; www.americasbirthday.com.

Thanksgiving Day Parade: Sure, everybody knows about the one in New York, but did you know that pups and their people have been coming to see the Philadelphia parade since 1920, and that it was the first Thanksgiving Day parade ever? Well, it may not receive the buzz that the one up north gets, but Philadelphia's parade is just as much fun, with festive floats, big balloons, and tons of bands and dancers, but with a Philly bent. Plus, at its conclusion Santa and his helpers happily arrive to ring in the holiday season. A great community event. 215/581-4529.

Christmas in the Air: The month of December in Center City is jam-packed with activities for you and poochie. Some of the best include tree-lighting ceremonies at City Hall and the Avenue of the Arts, the Market Street East Holiday Parade, and Santa presiding in a festive gazebo in Rittenhouse Square every weekend of the month. Plus, you'll both enjoy the many displays of lights at the Philadelphia Museum of Art and City Hall, as well as in Rittenhouse Square, Franklin Square, and Logan Circle. www.gophila.com.

Mummer's Parade: Although January is a darned cold time of year to be outside with your pooch, this New Year's Day parade is one major Philadelphia tradition you don't want to miss. It's string bands and struts, costumes and floats, bizarre yet fascinating. How can you explain a parade that officially begins at 9 A.M., but is unofficially still going on 14 hours later? Picture a plumber in a kilt pretending that he's a "Scot on Viagra," or 15 men in green sequin tuxedos doing a karaoke version of Frank Sinatra's "My Way," or a 60-man string band dressed as angels playing "Joy to the World." And that is just some of what you might see. All we can say it's a sight to see up close, and nothing like this happens anywhere else. It's usually held on Broad Street. www.mummers.com.

the start-up loan that built the dog park, and Yappy Hours and park clean-up days are held monthly. It's truly a community at this special park.

To become a member or make a donation, write a check to FESPP and note "for the dog park." Send to Fairmount D.O.G., c/o H. Faunce, 877 N. 24th St., Philadelphia, PA 19130; fairmountdog@yahoo.com; www.fairmountdog.org.

Another perk of the park is that just around the corner are dog-friendly Fairmount Avenue eateries.

The park is located at the eastern side of Eastern State Penitentiary at the intersection of Brown and Corinthian Streets, and Fairmount Avenue. Park anywhere along Corinthian or Brown.

11 Fairmount Area Dog Walk

 (See Philadelphia County map on page 16)

If your pup has excellent recall and you're in the art museum area and want to take him off leash, this is definitely a good option. The "dog walk," as it's called, is actually an open, hilly, tree-lined field located along Kelly Drive, behind the Philadelphia Museum of Art on the opposite side of the road. Although it's not an official dog park and isn't fenced, if you visit in the warm-weather months, your pup is sure to find lots of other dogs to run with on this quarter-mile stretch of land. There are always balls and toys flying in abundance and many friendly people, especially in the late afternoon. But realize that it is close to a very busy street, so please be extra-careful with your pooch. Hours are sunrise–sunset.

From Center City, take Kelly Drive past the art museum and look for the fields on your right. Pass them and park on the right along Sedgely Drive.

PLACES TO EAT

London Grill: Have you ever wanted to simply order great bar food at a restaurant or great restaurant food at a bar? If so, this is the place to come for both served to you and your dog in a laid-back setting. Its moderately priced creative cuisine is a favorite with the locals. The fish-and-chips are among the best in the city. You and your furry friend are welcome in the eatery's sidewalk seating. 2301 Fairmount Ave.; 215/978-4545.

Mace's Crossing: Even if you don't imbibe, the fun atmosphere of Mace's Crossing, a happy hour favorite among the nine-to-fivers, beckons your name if you pass it on a warm day. The patio located along the Ben Franklin Parkway gets so packed with revelers that you can't help but feel compelled to join the party. The pub serves not only an expansive selection of microbrews but also soups, salads, and sandwiches. The best part is that the staffers love dogs and will welcome them with a bowl of water to go along with your choice of beverage. 1714 Cherry St.; 215/564-5203.

Mugshots: Located directly across from the Eastern State Penitentiary, this little coffee shop boasts a creative vegan and nonvegan menu, and the service couldn't be friendlier. You and your pup can enjoy your tasty dish or coffee concoction streetside together. 2100 Fairmount Ave.; 267/514-7145.

Peacock on the Parkway: This friendly, family-run restaurant specializes in moderately priced Mediterranean food with a huge menu that will appeal to anyone's tastes. Some of the menu items are Turkish while others are Italian and even Greek and Spanish. But no matter what choice you make, it's sure to be a good one, as the food here is top notch. You and your doggy can sit on the patio along the Ben Franklin Parkway. 1700 Benjamin Franklin Parkway; 215/569-8888.

Rembrandt's Restaurant & Bar: An old standby of artsy types and Fairmount residents, Rembrandt's is located in a renovated historic tavern filled with beautiful stained-glass windows and interesting antique lighting fixtures. Although your pup isn't allowed inside to see the decorative accents, the friendly staff is happy to serve you salads, sandwiches, and a variety of new American entrées in its sidewalk seating. Doggy cookies and water are also available for your pooch. 741 N. 23rd St.; 215/763-2228 or 215/763-2229; www.rembrandts.com.

PLACES TO STAY

Best Western Center City Hotel: A bargain of a hotel and close to lots of open space to take your pup, the Best Western Center City is a good bet, but don't expect beauty or luxury. It's pretty drab on the inside. Also because it's located near the art museum and a lot of open space, it's pretty far from other attractions. While there are no weight restrictions for your pooch here, the hotel does charge a $10 pet fee per night. Rates are $95–125. 501 N. 22nd St.; 215/568-8300.

The Wyndham Franklin Plaza: Move along the northern border of Center City, and you'll find the Wyndham. No, it's not in the center of all the action, but that may be a good thing depending on your preference. If your dog is under 50 pounds and you can swing the $50 nonrefundable fee, you and Fido can stay here together. Rates are $69–179 and $759 for suites. 17th and Race Streets; 215/448-2000; www.wyndham.com/hotels/PHLFP/main.wnt.

Northern Liberties

East of Fairmount and north of Old City is Northern Liberties, the burgeoning artsy, hip Philadelphia neighborhood of the decade. This place is so cool and so inclusive to dogs, you'll find pups hanging out with their people at the park, and frequently in restaurants and bars, too. Because of the area's popularity, many changes will likely come as a result of further development—with mixed reviews from residents. Regardless, its dog park is one of the city's best and is one solid reason to visit or live here.

DOG-EAR YOUR CALENDAR

Annual Trick or Treat Street: If you have a dog and kids, this is a don't-miss Halloween event. Manayunk's Main Street retail stores dole out candy to the kids in costume and biscuits to the pups. Plus, there's a kids costume contest, a pet costume contest, and a pet parade. All of the family will, no doubt, have a Yappy Halloween. 215/482-9565.

Hound-o-Ween: Don't miss the ever popular Hound-o-Ween event held at Northern Liberties' Orianna Hill Dog Run. Every year, the community comes together to have a howl with their hilariously costumed doggies. It's definitely a must-do on your list for Halloween dog fun. www.oriannahill.org.

Pug-O-Ween Party: Pug lovers unite: You do not want to miss this Halloween Party. There's no denying that there's something especially charming about a pug, let alone one in costume. Pups who come to this party dress up in everything from black tie and tails to scary bugs and crazy crocodiles. The party takes place around Halloween at Schuylkill River Dog Run. www.phillyfido.net.

PARKS, BEACHES, AND RECREATION AREAS

12 Orianna Hill Dog Run

🐾 🐾 🐾 🐾 🐕 (See Philadelphia County map on page 16)

If the dogs who played at this excellent park were people, they'd probably belong to co-op grocery stores, eat organic foods, and wear t-shirts that read something along the lines of "Free to Be (Naturally) Leash-free." That's because this truly is a community-run dog park. In fact, it's quite the puptopia, tucked away in the most unsuspecting spot in this Northern Liberties neighborhood.

Orianna Hill Dog Run is actually the only truly legal dog run in Philadelphia because the members own the land on which the dogs play off leash. Community ownership protects the park from the sale, development, or other loss of land to the city, now or in the future.

Getting to this point for the Friends of Orianna Hill Park (the membership group) has been anything but easy. In fact, it took close to 20 years for the park to get established through petitions, lobbying, and negotiation with the city's Redevelopment Authority. On September 14, 2000, the city sold the park to the Friends of Orianna Hill Park for $1. It's been a barking success ever since.

At this dog park, you'll find dogs that are friendly and fun, and people who are interesting to talk to—you might even go so far as to say eccentric. The best time to come with puppies and older dogs with not as much pep in their step is when it's not as crowded, during the morning or midday. Late afternoons tend to be busiest.

The park has a double-gated entrance to prevent escape artists, and the run is covered in wood chips, with a water drum, poop bags, trash cans, chairs, and some trees lining the perimeter. There's even a community garden here. Lighting is provided for nighttime use, and the Friends are working on installing more. One of the park's best features is the striking mosaic on the wall of the bordering building.

If you're planning on frequenting the park, it's encouraged that you join the nonprofit corporation, Friends of Orianna Hill Park, for a $20 tax-deductible donation. Money raised from dues goes towards insurance, maintenance, and improvements. Send your check to Friends of Orianna Hill Park, 942 N. 4th St., Philadelphia, PA 19123.

There are no set hours at the park. From 4th Street heading south take a left onto Poplar. The park is on the left-hand corner of Orianna and Poplar between 3rd and 4th Streets. 215/423-4516; www.oriannahill.org.

PLACES TO EAT

Azure: If you're vegan or even if you're not, chances are you'll be happy eating moderately priced "vacation cuisine" outdoors here with your canine carnivore. (Word on the street is that dogs are "sometimes" allowed in the bar area of the restaurant, too.) Azure is known for having an incredible vegetarian menu, as well as similarly delicious entrées, sandwiches, salads, and

soups for nonvegans, with a Caribbean and Greek-isle twist. You might try the vegetarian grilled seitan (meat substitute) tips prepared with soy chipotle aioli sauce or, if you'd like the meat version, the grilled filet mignon tips. 931 N. 2nd St.; 215/629-0500.

700 Club: Want a howlin' good time? Come here with your dog! Since food is not served, you and your pup have basically no restrictions at this hipster bar. The staffers absolutely love dogs and allow them to have the run of the place. Linus didn't even care that I was with him when we came here, he was so happy to see so many friends. Even better is that they have dog biscuits available if your pup is hungry. You, on the other hand, will have to rely on the fun atmosphere and the beers on draft. 700 N. 2nd St.; 215/413-3181.

Standard Tap Bar & Restaurant: One of the darlings of the Northern Liberties scene, Standard Tap is known to locals as a good ol' fashioned bar with exceptional food. Linus would definitely say that the best feature of this place is that you can take your pooch inside with you (to the bar area only). While not open for lunch, only brunch and dinner, the Standard Tap offers everything from crab cakes and venison to duck salad and gourmet grilled cheese sandwiches. It prides itself on the number of excellent local beers on draft. 901 N. 2nd St.; 215/238-0630; www.standardtap.com.

PLACES TO STAY

Conwell Inn: Although not in Northern Liberties proper, the Conwell Inn is not too far from all of the action. Located nearby on Temple University's campus in North Philadelphia, this small, quaint historic inn welcomes "controlled and quiet" pups who are lighter than 30 pounds for a $10 pet fee per night. Rates are $130–150. 1331 W. Berks St.; 215/235-6200; www.conwellinn.com.

West Philly

Don't listen to the locals lament about West Philly. Although it's seen its share of crime and dilapidation over the years, the University City area, especially, is downright gorgeous today. Walking through the streets you'll be floored by the number of stunning, brightly painted Victorian row homes whose window boxes are overflowing with cascading, bold flowers. This is another neighborhood making a comeback in the city, and if you haven't been here in a while, it's worth a trip back to see the transformation in person—or, of course, in dog.

DOG-EAR YOUR CALENDAR

Bark Breakfast at Loews Philadelphia Hotel: Every year in summer, the dog-loving Loews Hotel hosts a Bark Breakfast at its Center City location. Here, you and your pup can learn about the latest trends in pet-people happiness in a social setting. Admission to the event is $20 per human, free for pups and includes breakfast for people and a special breakfast bark-ffet for dogs, as well as a Loews Bark Briefcase for each dog attending. Reservations are recommended and can be made by calling 215/231-7228.

Pet Picnic: The People-Pet Partnership sponsors the Pet Picnic to honor National Homeless Animals Day in August. The picnic is held in the parking lot of 9th and Montrose Streets in the Italian Market from 11 A.M.–3 P.M. Adoptable animals will be available, as well as a pooch picnic at noon. For details, contact the People-Pet Partnership at P.O. Box 63575, Philadelphia, PA 19147; 215/218-9212; www .peoplepetpartnership.com.

Semi-Annual Beagle Party: If you have a Beagle or just love them, you're welcome to hit the Beagle Party at the small dog section of Schuylkill River Dog Run usually held in September. At the last event, nearly two dozen Beagles partied hardy. Lots of fun is sure to be had and treats are available for all hounds. www.phillyfido.net.

Bark in the Park: This annual always-a-blast, free event is held one Saturday in October at Clark Park in University City. Your leashed pup and any and all of her friends are welcome to come. Costume contests, owner look a like contests, loudest bark, shortest legs as well as a variety of other categories make sure every dog wins something. Veterinarians are on hand to answer questions, too. The event is held 2–4 P.M. 215/222-2255; www.clarkpark.info.

PARKS, BEACHES, AND RECREATION AREAS

13 Clark Park

🐾 🐾 (See Philadelphia County map on page 16)

One of the main off-leash areas in University City is a wide-open depression (a.k.a. The Bowl) in Clark Park. Although it's not an official off-leash park, if dogs are well controlled and friendly, off-leash play in The Bowl works quite well.

Yet it can be risky as the park is unfenced and near some busy streets. Plus, controversy remains over whether or not dogs should be allowed off leash here because children at the adjacent tot lot have been terrified by dogs running astray there. The Friends of Clark Park is looking into the option of installing a fenced dog run and/or strictly enforcing the leash law elsewhere in the park.

In the meantime, if you choose to let your dog off leash here, make sure that he stays in The Bowl, and if he doesn't, he must have excellent recall. Also make sure he gets along well with other dogs because The Bowl gets crowded at times.

If puppers is equally happy on a leash, Clark Park is a nice place to come relax together or have a picnic.

A favorite hangout of nearby university students, Clark Park has bike paths, benches, tables, ample shade, street parking, lights, water fountains, and trash cans. To help you clean up after your pup, poop bags are available (donated by local dog lovers).

Interesting tidbit: If you're a fan of Charles Dickens, you'll be happy to know Clark Park is home to the only life-sized statue of the famed writer in the world, erected in 1901. Right next to him is one of his best-known characters, Little Nell of *The Old Curiosity Shop*. Every February, a birthday party is held in this location celebrating the author.

The park is located in University City between 43th and 45th Streets on Baltimore Avenue. Street parking is available. Hours are 6 A.M.–10 P.M. 215/552-8186; www.clarkpark.info.

🖤 Chester Avenue Dog Club

🖤 🖤 🐕 (See Philadelphia County map on page 16)

Definitely one of the most frustrating aspects of sharing your life with a dog is explaining a disappointing situation to him. That's exactly what happened when Linus and I visited this dog park. From the outside it looked great: completely fenced in, wood chip ground cover, toys, trash cans, water bowls, benches, and even a seesaw. But after getting closer to the gate, I realized what we were in for: a padlock on it with a sign about membership, and a sticky situation to explain to my faithful friend.

In order to use the park, you have to get a key and in order to get a key you must become a member and pay the $50 fee that covers maintenance and insurance.

Actually, these dog owners are quite smart and we don't begrudge them. Rather than risk not having a dog park at all, they've opted to lease a piece of land from the neighboring nursing home, which means there are dues necessary to use it. Membership is encouraged among University City residents, and it maxes out at 50 members total.

From University City, take Baltimore Avenue to 48th Street and make a left. Continue for about five blocks to Chester Avenue. Park anywhere along the street. The entrance is at the corner of 48th and Chester. Hours are 7 A.M.–9 P.M. weekdays, 9 A.M.–9 P.M. weekends. 215/748-3440; ottohound079@yahoo.com.

15 Bartram's Garden

🐾 🐾 🐾 (See Philadelphia County map on page 16)

Another jewel within Philadelphia's city limits is Bartram's Garden, the oldest botanical garden in the country. More than 250 years ago, John Bartram, a Quaker farmer, was so taken by the simple beauty of a daisy he found in the fields that he was inspired to spend the rest of his life (with his son, William) exploring, collecting, and attempting to understand all forms of nature. Known as America's first botanist, Bartram grew medicinal plants and treated friends who couldn't afford medical treatment. His lush estate is now known as Bartram's Garden.

Here within its 45 acres, you and your dog can discover the results of his efforts: a wildflower meadow, a river trail, a stone house, and farm buildings overlooking the Schuylkill River. The beautiful historic botanical garden of native plants is the only part of the gardens off limits to dogs. Regardless, there's plenty of natural beauty throughout the whole estate to enjoy with your furry pal. It's such an escape, you won't even notice Philadelphia's skyline across the river or the housing projects in front of the property.

From Center City take 23rd Street south below Market Street and merge right onto Gray's Ferry Avenue just beyond South Street. Take the first left onto Paschall Avenue. Turn left at the next light onto 49th Street and drive around the bend onto Gray's Avenue. Follow the trolley tracks and bear left at the fork onto Lindbergh Boulevard. Just beyond the 54th Street sign and immediately after crossing the railroad bridge, make a sharp left into the entrance (not visible until you've crossed the bridge). Admission is free as is parking in the adjacent lot. Hours are 10 A.M.–5 P.M. daily. 54th St. and Lindbergh Blvd.; 215/729-5281; explore@bartramsgarden.org; www.bartramsgarden.org.

PLACES TO EAT

Green Line Café: Named for the subway line that runs right by it, the Green Line Café is a great place to come on a lazy afternoon. The organic coffee and cappuccino are tasty as are the fresh baked goods, bagels and pastries, sandwiches, and salads. You and your pup can sit on its streetside seating offering a lovely view of Clark Park. 4239 Baltimore Ave.; 215/222-3431.

White Dog Café: With a name like this, of course, they love doggies. This cozy yet upscale restaurant has been around since 1983 and is one of the most renowned in the area—a favorite of Penn alumni. Serving contemporary American cuisine with a conscience, most of the offerings are organic from local farmers and meats are raised in humane ways. Plus, the restaurant is involved in a variety of social change issues; check out its website. We couldn't feel better about dining at such a socially-conscience place as this, even though it's on the pricier side. The restaurant serves lunch, brunch, and dinner, but if you can come for brunch, do so as everything on the menu is fresh and delicious and you don't need a reservation. You and your any-color dog are welcome on its small yet quaint front patio seating. 3420 Sansom St.; 215/386-9224; www.whitedog.com.

Zocalo: Chihuahuas won't have to *"quiero* Taco Bell" if they come to this hip yet understated, rather pricey Mexican eatery. Interesting and inventive Mexican cuisine is hard to come by, but Zocalo does it successfully. One of the best dishes is the shrimp sautéed with jalapeño and habañero chiles, and cooked in tequila. Ay, chihuahua! Dogs are "allowed" to sit on the patio, but, as mentioned, it'd be best if your dog is a Chihuahua because the space is small and big lugs like Linus are welcome only if it's not too crowded. 36th Street and Lancaster Avenue; 215/895-0139.

PLACES TO STAY

Sheraton University City Hotel: A comfy and clean room awaits you and your pup at this conveniently located hotel. Even better, dogs up to 80 pounds are welcome for no additional fee. The staff happily provides your pooch a dog bed, water bowl, and treats. They only ask that you sign a waiver and agree not to leave your dog in the room alone. Rates are $129–259. 3549 Chestnut St.; 215/387-8000.

The Business District

While it's not exactly Rittenhouse Square or Old City, the Business District of the Center City region boasts a plethora of dog-welcoming hotels and restaurants, and dog-friendly shops, all just a few blocks from one great off-leash dog park.

PARKS, BEACHES, AND RECREATION AREAS

16 Schuylkill River Dog Run

🐾 🐾 🐾 🐾 🐕 (See Philadelphia County map on page 16)

Established in 1998, the Schuylkill River Dog Run was the first official dog park in the city. It's definitely one of the most popular, which always makes it a fun spot to take Spot. It is completely fenced in with two sections: one for smaller pups and a bigger section for medium to large dogs. In both sections, you'll be able to access benches, shade, a water fountain for dogs and people, trash cans, and bag dispensers (but not always bags so be sure to bring your own). Recently, the wood-chip ground cover in the dog run was replaced by a gravel/limestone mix to minimize dust and mud.

This park offered one of the best workouts for Linus because all the dogs in the dog run were as big as he was and he was always able to encourage several friends to chase him around like a furry fool. True canine happiness!

DIVERSION

Love Park: Remember the design of the word LOVE that was an icon of the '60s and '70s? Now it's an icon of the City of Brotherly Love. Originally it was a 1964 painting by Robert Indiana, reproduced on everything from postage stamps to jewelry and t-shirts. But in 1976, Indiana loaned a large sculpture of the image for Philadelphia's bicentennial celebration. Although it took a brief jaunt to New York two years later due to interest from a buyer, after much uproar from Philadelphians, it was purchased by a local businessman and donated back to the city. Now it's considered a park, although it's not in our book due to the lack of grass. Love Park is famous as a great skateboarding area since it's mostly concrete, but, sadly, the city has recently outlawed it. The statue sits at the park (also known as JFK Plaza) on the eastern end of the Ben Franklin Parkway not far from City Hall. You and your pup are free to feel the love while admiring its fountain and surrounding flowers.

On weekdays, you're likely to meet grad students from local universities, as well as Center City residents. On weekends, you'll meet dogs and their owners from the city as well as the 'burbs. Many people come from up to 30 miles away just to take their dogs here for a fun run.

The park's only drawback is the licensing regulation that went into effect in 2003. Because a few aggressive dogs made it miserable for lots of others, the park requires that all dogs have a current Liberty Bell tag from the Philadelphia Department of Public Health. Park rules state that it's the first step to making a safer environment for everyone by having law-abiding park users. To get a license, call 215/683-LOST.

If you plan on frequenting the park, you are encouraged to join the Friends of Schuylkill River Park for an annual minimum fee of $20. Send your check to P.O. Box 30246, Philadelphia, PA 19103. However, there's no charge for using the park.

The park is located on 25th Street between Locust and Spruce. From the Center City, take 24th Street south and make a right on Spruce Street. It will dead-end right into the park. Park anywhere on the street. Two-hour parking is available except on Saturdays and Sundays. Hours are 5 A.M.–1 A.M. www.phillyfido.net.

PLACES TO EAT

Bliss: Well, you can't get any dog-friendlier than offering a K-9 Café menu, now can you? This relative newcomer to the Philadelphia restaurant scene, located on the Avenue of the Arts, loves having dogs at its outside seating. Your pup can enjoy gourmet dog biscuits as well as beef tenderloin tips and rice, chopped sirloin burger, and even plain old chicken and rice for those pups with more sensitive tummies. You, on the other hand, can enjoy some fabulous yet pricey contemporary/fusion dishes. The experience for you and your dog, indeed: Bliss! 224 S. Broad St., 215/731-1100; www.bliss-restaurant.com.

Brasserie Perrier: If you're familiar with Le Bec Fin, then you'll know who renowned chef Georges Perrier is. And you won't be surprised that this is another upscale (but not as expensive) French eatery named after the restaurateur, but this one features Italian and Asian influences, and is a little more hip. You and your pup are welcome to eat outside. 1619 Walnut St.; 215/568-3000.

Capogiro: Maybe you've been to Italy recently and fell in love with gelato and the charming gelaterias that serve it. Now you don't have to cross the pond to get some incredibly delicious Italian ice cream. This bright and modern gelateria has streetside seating for you and your dog—just like in Italy. And it's not just the bipeds who order the gelato; four-legged customers devour it, too. Although the store owners don't know if the creamy stuff is good for your pooch, they'll happily serve it and water to your dog on hot days. 119 S. 13th St.; 215/351-0900.

Maggiano's Little Italy: Yes, it's a national chain restaurant, which many foodies might scoff at, but it's one of the best. It's moderately priced, and considering the amount of food you get, it's a definite value. Maggiano's prides itself on a family-style atmosphere and a huge menu touting traditional Italian-American fare. Favorites include angel hair shrimp al arrabiata and the chicken scallopine marsala. It's just a bone's throw from Loews and the Convention Center. 1201 Filbert St.; 215/567-2020.

Marathon Grill: Although there are several locations of Marathon Grill in Center City, our favorite is the one on Market Street because that's the one that welcomes dogs at its outdoor seating. Marathon Grill is a preferred salad and sandwich shop among the nine-to-five crowd. Its Caesar salad is honestly superb. As long as it's not too crowded, the Grill will happily allow you and poochie to sit outside and soak in the bustle on Market Street. 1818 Market St.; 215/561-1818.

PLACES TO STAY

Doubletree Hotel Philadelphia: Known for its exceptional service and clean rooms, the Doubletree invites your pup to stay with you at no additional charge, just a $50 refundable deposit. The only requirement is that your dog not be left alone in the room. For you, there are amenities like a heated indoor pool, hot tub, and fitness center. Upon checking in, you'll be greeted with cookies, and if your pup is with you, he might even get one, too. Rates are $99–249. 237 S. Broad St.; 215/893-1600.

Four Seasons: Regularly rated as one of the top hotels in the country, the Four Seasons welcomes dogs, but none that would voluntarily hang out with Linus. Only dogs less than 15 pounds are allowed to stay here at no extra charge. Your diminutive doggy will be happy to know that the hotel provides treats upon check in. The only restriction is that dogs be crated when left alone. Regardless, this is one elegant hotel that you'll no doubt enjoy together. Rates are $310–470. One Logan Square; 215/963-1500; www .fourseasons.com.

Hampton Inn Convention Center: Centrally located near the Convention Center and relatively inexpensive, this hotel is a definite value. The rooms are clean and spacious, and the staff is friendly. Unlimited coffee, tea, and cocoa are provided in the lobby, and continental breakfast is included. Dogs are welcome, but be prepared to pay a $100 refundable deposit and a $25/per day extra charge. Rates are $89–209. 1301 Race St.; 215/665-9100; www.hamp-toninn.com.

Loews Philadelphia Hotel: If it had been up to Linus, we would have changed our address and just moved in. And it's not just because it's a very hip, art deco hotel (he had quite the eye for design). This is truly a puppy paradise. Loews loves dogs so much that it offers a V.I.P. (very important pet) program. Part of it includes a dog treat given upon check-in and a personal note from the hotel manager welcoming furry and unfurry clientele alike. Each room provides information on local dog walking routes, pet services like grooming and pet shops, as well as nearby veterinarians. Doggy-equipped rooms come with place mats for food and water bowls, toys, and treats. Pet room service is also available offering gourmet and vegetarian cuisine for the choosiest poochies. For those who just want a snack, the hotel offers Puppy Power Bars. In case you couldn't fit everything in your suitcase, the concierge will help out with dog beds, leashes, collars, pet toys, and pet videos. An added bonus is the section of the hotel restaurant that allows your dog to sit with you during yappy hour. Last but not least, the hotel spa offers pet spa treatments while humans receive theirs. No size limit or extra charge for your four-legged friend to stay here, either. Rates are $125–300. 1200 Market St.; 215/627-1200; www.loewshotels.com.

Marriott Philadelphia Downtown: Conveniently located next to the Philadelphia Convention Center and Reading Terminal Market, this friendly hotel offers clean, comfortable rooms. Although they allow dogs here without weight restrictions, there is a $100 nonrefundable fee. One bonus for you is the indoor pool and fitness center. Rates are $179–300. 1201 Market St.; 215/625-2900.

Oakwood Philadelphia: For a longer stay in the City of Brotherly Love, you might want to consider the Oakwood. For a 30-day minimum stay and a $250 nonrefundable fee, you and poochie (no size restrictions here) can enjoy being in the heart of the business district and just a few blocks from

FETCHING NECESSITIES

If you're with your leashed pup in Center City, there are lots of tasks you can accomplish together. Shop for one-of-a-kind items for her at the dog boutique **Pooch** (2020 Locust St., 215/735-0793); check out the great selection of independent films at **TLA Video** (1520 Locust St., 215/735-7887); go antiquing at **Matthew Izzo Shop,** offering high-end home furnishings and art pieces (928 Pine St., 215/922-2570); or browse the chic clothing and housewares at stores like **Anthropologie** (1801 Walnut St., 215/568-2114), **Urban Outfitters** (1627 Walnut St., 215/569-3131), **Petulia's Folly** (1710 Sansom St., 215/569-1344), an urban fashion and home accents boutique; visit **Ubiq** (1509 Walnut St., 215/988-0194), purveyors of urban-style sneakers, high-end jeans, and designer tees; and ogle an array of sporting goods at **City Sports** (1608 Walnut St., 215/985-5860). Find interesting gifts at **Hello World** (1201 Pine St., 215/545-7060; 2056 Locust St., 215/545-5207), a quintessential neighborhood gift store.

Rittenhouse Square in this newly renovated building. All rooms come with kitchens as well as washer and dryers. For studio, one bedroom, or two bedrooms rates vary: $2,400–3,700/month. 1601 Sansom St.; 215/568-2188; www.oakwood.com.

Residence Inn by Marriott City Center: A friendly hotel, not far from City Hall, the Residence Inn welcomes pups with no size or weight restriction. However, it does require that dogs be leashed while on the premises. A $150 nonrefundable cleaning fee is charged. Pet sitting and walking can be arranged, too. Since rooms come equipped with kitchens, the staff here has been known to grocery shop for guests if you or Fido is craving a home-cooked meal. Rates are $65–189. One East Penn Square, Market and Juniper Streets; 215/557-0005; www.marriott.com/residenceinn.

Ritz Carlton Hotel: The architecture of the Ritz may be reason enough to stay at this hotel. This former bank building was originally built in white marble as a replica of the Pantheon in Rome, and is just as striking. But more important is that this hotel treats pups as nicely as people. All canine guests are greeted with a smile, a special bowl of water, and a handmade treat from the hotel pastry team. The concierge can also arrange dog walking or a day of beauty at a doggy salon. All pups are provided with a Ritz Carlton bandana, too. There is, however, a $25 nonrefundable fee and only dogs under 60 pounds are allowed here. Sorry, big guys and gals! Plus, your pooch must be accompanied at all times. Rates are $250–3,500. 10 Avenue of the Arts; 215/523-8000; www.ritzcarlton.com/hotels/philadelphia.

Rittenhouse Square

A gorgeous square in a vibrant and upscale neighborhood with striking architecture is what you'll find in this neighborhood of Center City. Lucky for your dog and you, the popular park, its annual spring festival, and many of the area's eateries and hotels are happy to include you both.

PARKS, BEACHES, AND RECREATION AREAS

17 Rittenhouse Square Park

🐾 🐾 (See Philadelphia County map on page 16)

Named after America's first astronomer, David Rittenhouse, this square is one of William Penn's original planned squares. Mostly a passive-use park, the six-acre area is a favorite of Center City workers, residents, and visitors for kicking back and absorbing the sights and sounds of city life in a peaceful setting. Interesting tidbit: The park is full of animal sculptures including two dogs (which appear to be Italian Greyhounds) who welcome you to the park on the southwest corner. Linus loved to sniff their feet for some reason.

Springtime is our favorite time to be in the square because it is alive with activity, dogs, and the area's breathtaking beauty. But because dogs must be leashed here and balls are not to be thrown (so say the posted, often ignored park rules), this park is not a leading contender for puppy playtime.

From the Benjamin Franklin Parkway take 19th Street south to the park on the left. Try to find an ever-so-coveted street parking spot anywhere in the neighborhood. Hours are sunrise–1 A.M. 215/683-0200.

PLACES TO EAT

Alma de Cuba: This cutting-edge Cuban restaurant is located in a Walnut Street townhouse and led by celebrity chef Douglas Rodriguez. I doubt your dog will be impressed, but you might be taken with the fried oysters, a signature dish, and the colorful ambiance the restaurant provides even in its outdoor seating. Much like its trendy counterparts, Alma de Cuba is on the pricier side. 1623 Walnut St.; 215/988-1799.

Bleu: Despite the fun and inviting atmosphere and brightly colored murals inside, you and your pup will be just as happy at Bleu's streetside seating (although service can be a bit slower on busy warm days). Owned by the same restaurateur as Rouge, this is another eclectic, casual, pricey bistro offering French dishes with a little Asian mixed in. The mussels and crème brulee are always good bets. 227 S. 18th St.; 215/545-0342.

Devon Seafood Grill: If seafood is your calling, then Devon Seafood Grill is calling you—and your doggy. This is the epitome of a solid seafood restaurant with delicious steaks and pasta dishes, too. It's on the pricier side, much like its nearby neighbors, but you must try the lobster mashed potatoes.

DOG-EAR YOUR CALENDAR

Chestnut Hill Garden Festival: On the first Sunday in May, Germantown Avenue transforms into a lively, outdoor garden marketplace featuring garden and craft vendors, live entertainment and food, and beer and wine. It draws a huge turnout every year and it's always a ton of fun. Bring your pup to visit with friends or enter her in the festival's canine fashion show, the Bones and Bonnets Pooch Parade. Free admission. 215/247-6696.

Rittenhouse Row Annual Spring Festival: Come rain or shine, you and your pup will know spring has sprung if you hit the dog-friendly Rittenhouse Square area's annual spring festival. The square springs alive every May at this even boasting arts, culture, and city living featuring local bands playing, dancers dancing, and eaters, well, eating. Spanning from the Avenue of the Arts (Broad Street) to Rittenhouse Square along Walnut Street, the festival offers countless family-friendly activities and vendor booths. Lots of freebies and discounted eats are available from nearby chichi restaurants. 215/972-0101; www.rittenhouserow.org.

They're divine. Even better is that they welcome dogs with a nice, cool bowl of water. 225 S. 18th St.; 215/546-5940.

Potcheen: Maybe you and poochie have grown tired of the trendy crowd and you just want to kick back, grab a brew, and some affordable eats. If so, try the outdoor seating of this Irish pub, Potcheen ("potato whisky" in Gaelic), located inside the Sheraton Rittenhouse Square Hotel. Don't expect any over-the-top experience with the food, but the beer's always cold. 227 S. 18th St.; 215/546-9400.

Rouge: Located right on Rittenhouse Square, this fashionable restaurant serves up American food with a French bistro flair. If you're looking for a fun experience, yummy yet pricier food, and a lot of good people watching, go here. Many of the beautiful people and their dogs tend to frequent in warm weather months. Plus, staffers will happily provide your pup with a bowl of water and you'll be able to get one of the best burgers in town. 205 S. 18th St.; 215/732-6622.

Twenty Manning: Named for the intersection of 20th and Manning Streets, this Asian-fusion bistro is a favorite of the yuppy-and-puppy crowd. This is urban chic at its best, but you pay for it in the price of the meals. If you're a seafood lover, try the lobster in coconut water or the swordfish. You and your dog are welcome to sit outside, and the hip staff is happy to accommodate your pup with a bowl of water. 261 S. 20th St.; 215/731-0900.

PLACES TO STAY

Radisson Plaza Warwick Hotel: If your pooch is less than 50 pounds and on the friendly and quiet side, she will be welcome here for a $50 nonrefundable fee. "Aggressive dogs," however, are not allowed, named as Pit Bulls and Rottweilers. If you can get over this detail, the Radisson is a nice option, especially because of its location and its helpful and professional staff. Rates are $89–189. 1701 Locust St.; 215/735-6000.

The Rittenhouse Hotel: If you truly enjoy the finer things in life, or maybe your dog does, this is the hotel for you. Located on the west side of Rittenhouse Square, it's one of the most luxurious hotels in the city. It boasts not just a great view of the square, but also a renovated, elegant, and acclaimed new restaurant, as well as a health club. But even better news is your dog will be treated as well as you are while staying here (sadly, he's not allowed in the restaurant or health club).

The staffers at the Rittenhouse aim to please. Treats are handed out at the concierge desk to all furry guests. In fact, if your pup is super-special she might get a personalized gift. Oprah Winfrey's two dogs, Sophie and Samson, had personalized dog cookies waiting for them when they arrived. Special dog cookies were also awaiting the ever-discriminating Lassie when she recently visited the Rittenhouse on a promotional tour of her latest movie. Let's just say, if Lassie can bark orders for water that had to be boiled, distilled, and chilled to 40°F, and get it with a smile, then the rest of us should be in good shape.

Ever since the hotel opened in 1989, it has allowed dogs of all sizes to stay here. The only restriction is that you not leave Fifi alone in the room. Pet sitting and dog walking can be arranged. Rates are $230–1,800. 210 W. Rittenhouse Square; 215/546-9000; www.rittenhousehotel.com.

The Sofitel: Toy poodles would definitely feel right at home at this modern, friendly, and upscale French-influenced hotel. For an extra fee of $50, dogs under 25 pounds are welcome and must be kept in a crate if left alone in the room. The Sofitel is located in the heart of the business district, just three blocks to lovely Rittenhouse Square. Rates are $149–299. 120 S. 17th St.; 215/569-8300; www.sofitel.com.

The Westin Philadelphia: Again with the weight restrictions, Linus was getting a complex. But if your dog is 40 pounds or under, he will be welcomed with what's known as a "heavenly" dog bed pillow in the room. Just make sure you tell the staff ahead of time that you're bringing him. This hotel is also wonderfully situated right atop the shops at Liberty Place, in the middle of the energy of Center City, and a four-block walk to Rittenhouse Square. The service and rooms are top notch. There are no additional fees, but a pet waiver must be signed. Rates are $100–390. 99 S. 17th St. at Liberty Place; 215/563-1600.

Historic and Waterfront Districts

The area of Independence National Historical Park, Old City, Society Hill, and Penn's Landing couldn't be more historic. It was in this section of the city that our country was both fought for and founded. Just walking the streets of the area with your pup will make you both feel like humming a few bars of "Yankee Poodle Dandee." Sorry, that was Linus's version. You know the song.

Independence Park is often called the most historic square mile in the country. Among other notable sights, you'll find the Liberty Bell, Independence Hall, and the new Constitution Center. Although your doggy isn't allowed in the buildings, the grounds are open to leashed pups.

Old City is an artsy, renovated warehouse district busting with galleries and excellent restaurants—and dogs, too. You'll see them going in and out of shops and restaurants throughout the district.

South of Old City lies Society Hill. Named for the tract given to the Free Society of Traders by William Penn in 1685, Society Hill is a quieter, residential neighborhood with centuries-old homes and cobblestone streets.

Penn's Landing is the waterfront that skirts the Delaware River where William Penn first arrived. In addition to other attractions, Penn's Landing is home to the Festival Pier, which hosts scads of free, dog-friendly summer and winter events and concert series (dogs are not allowed at ticketed events/concerts).

DIVERSIONS

Independence Visitor's Center: Any visit to the Historic District or other parts of Center City should include a stop at the visitor's center. Your pup is allowed in with you while you gather maps and helpful info from friendly Philadelphians for your day in the city together. 215/965-7676 or 800/537-7676; www.independence visitorcenter.com.

Audio Walking Tour: Your doggy probably won't mind if you zone out for a while listening to a 74-minute narrated self-guided walking tour of historic Philadelphia. The tour includes a lightweight CD player and a detailed map featuring 20 important historic sites and 64 narrated segments for $14.95. It's available at the Independence Visitor's Center. 215/965-7676 or 800/537-7676; www.independencevisitorcenter.com.

Horse and Carriage Ride: As long as your pup likes really big doggies (read: horses), feel free to hop a ride in a horse-drawn carriage and get a tour of the historic area. Tours with 76 Carriage Company are completely narrated and start from Independence National Historical Park at 6th and Chestnut Streets. Depending on how much you want to see, prices start from $25 for up to four people and a pooch. 215/925-8687; www.phillytours.com/carriage.htm.

Christ Church—Ben Franklin's Grave: While you're not allowed on the burial ground with poochie, the two of you can see Benjamin Franklin's grave from the street, and throw a penny on it for good luck—in respect to his motto that "a penny saved is a penny earned." The cemetery is located at 5th and Arch Streets.

Independence National Historical Park: You and your pup can't come to Philadelphia without checking out this historic and patriotic area, also known as the birthplace of our nation. Although your pup is not allowed in any of the buildings, he is allowed with you

PARKS, BEACHES, AND RECREATION AREAS

18 Front and Chestnut Park

🐾 🐾 🚶 (See Philadelphia County map on page 16)

Want to soak up some history while giving your pup some much-needed exercise? Then you might be interested in this little park. A fairly popular place among local residents, the Front and Chestnut Park is located along Penn's Landing and is now home to the Irish Immigrant Memorial. Being on leash to explore the grounds our forefathers walked. It's here where you can see the Liberty Bell Center, Independence Hall, and Carpenter's Hall, among other historic sites. You might even see some colonial types walking the streets as they portray life from that era. The historical park is located between Arch Street and Walnut Streets, and 3rd and 6th Streets.

Welcome Park: Named after the ship that William Penn sailed to Philadelphia, the *Welcome,* this small, passive-use park is really not a park. It's more of a plaza covered in concrete and marble outlining the original city plan of Philadelphia. It also has benches and a miniature version of the statue of William Penn that stands on top of City Hall. But you and your doggy should come here for the sheer history that it invokes. It includes a timeline of the history of Philadelphia. Also, a mural depicting a street scene from the early 20th century adorns the wall of an adjacent building. The park is located at Second and Samson Streets.

Benjamin Franklin Bridge: Connecting Philadelphia with Camden, New Jersey, the Benjamin Franklin Bridge has both a south and a north path for walking that flank the roadway in between. If you and your pup are not afraid of heights, this is one unique place to hike together. Not only do you get an incredible view of the Delaware River, but of the Philadelphia cityscape and Camden waterfront, too. From downtown, take 5th Street to 676 heading east to New Jersey. Hours are 6 A.M.–6 P.M.

Riverlink Ferry: Has puppers always wanted to check out the happenin' Camden waterfront with you, but doesn't have the will to walk the Benjamin Franklin Bridge? Then take a ride on the Riverlink Ferry across the Delaware River. The ferry leaves every 40 minutes starting at 10 A.M. Park along Columbus Boulevard and at the Hyatt Regency Hotel parking garage. Fares are $6. 215/925-LINK; www.riverlinkferry.org.

of Irish lineage myself, I found this an added bonus to visiting here with my pup.

The area thought to be a dog park is small and not completely fenced in: There are openings on both sides of the oval-shaped, low-fenced area. It is not a leash-free mecca as are some other areas in Center City. And while many people let their dogs off leash in the fenced area anyway, an attorney for the tenant that controls the area said it is not a dog park. This warning might have stopped some of the suburban dogs from making the trek like they used to, but you won't find many city dwellers deterred. In fact, enforcement of the leash law here is pretty lax. The people are a lot of fun and so are their pups. At one point, a weekly Wine and Cheese night was held for the park users, but as of press time, we couldn't get confirmation on specifics.

From Center City take Chestnut east all the way to Front Street. Street parking is available along Front. Hours are sunrise–1 A.M. 215/683-0200; www.irishmemorial.org.

PLACES TO EAT

Bluezette: If you're a lover of soul food and enjoy upscale dining, you and your pup must try Bluezette. While it sounds like a dichotomy—soul food and an upscale setting—Bluezette sets the standard. Located on Market Street, you and your dog can sit streetside enjoying comfort food favorites like the shrimp and grouper Creole and fried chicken with mac and cheese. Water is available for your pup upon request. 46 Market St.; 215/627-3866.

Cafe Ole: Any time of day, you and your pooch can come here to sip some incredible coffee (or water for the pup) and nosh on delectable pastries and scones. While this proud coffee house boasts their java is the best around, they manage to do an equally good job with breakfast and lunch, too, especially the Mediterranean platter. But be forewarned before you get your hopes up on the weekend: It's closed Sundays. 147 N. 3rd St.; 215/627-2140.

FETCHING NECESSITIES

While strolling along the streets of Old City, your pup may even get a treat if you stop by **Bone Jour** (14 N. 3rd St.; 215/574-1225), a premium pet supply store; **Viv Pickle** (21 N. 3rd St.; 215/922-5904; www.vivpickle.com), a design-your-own purse shop, across the street; **ME + Blue** (311 Market St., 2nd floor; 215/629-2347; www.meandblue.com), an affordable fashion-forward boutique that often has its own pup on the premises, so give a holler on your way up the steps; and **Vagabond** (37 N. 3rd St.; 267/671-0737), an indie designer-clothing boutique. Plus, you and your hound are always welcome at the fun and funky home goods store **Foster's Urban Homeware** (124 N. 3rd St.; 267/671-0588).

If you're in the mood to soak in some culture while in the neighborhood, visit the **Third Street Gallery at Second Street** (58 N. 2nd St.; 215/625-0993; www.3rdstreetgallery.com), the oldest cooperative gallery in the city of Philadelphia showcasing mostly contemporary art; stop in at **Indigo Arts** (151 N. 3rd St.; 215/922-4041) and view its folk and tribal art; or grab a new or used CD at **AKA Music** (7 N. 2nd St.; 215/922-3828).

City Tavern: If you and your doggy truly want a taste of the past with a taste of the past, make sure you put City Tavern on your schedule. During his visit here for the First Continental Congress, John Adams dubbed it "the most genteel tavern in America." You and Fido can sit outside together and pretend you're eating among the Founding Fathers as the servers are decked out in colonial garb. The menu even serves most of the same items it did back in 1774—the lobster pot pie is a definite must. 138 S. 2nd St.; 215/413-1443.

The Continental Restaurant and Martini Bar: One of the hippest spots in Old City is no doubt the Continental. It started out as a trendy martini bar located in a retro diner that attracted lots of young people. But over the years, it's evolved into drawing both a younger and older crowd who enjoy not just a solid martini, but yummy, moderately priced "new" American and Asian cuisine. A few of the crowd pleasers include the Szechwan shoestring fries, seared tuna, and the crab pad Thai. Linus loved all the happenings straight up while sitting with me outside. 138 Market St.; 215/923-6069.

Fork: A fashionable yet affordable American bistro with friendly service is what you'll find at Fork. Newly printed daily, the menu includes some of the best local produce available. The food is fusion cuisine that includes American, Mexican, Italian, French, and Asian influences. If you're a fan of Asian fare, try the striped bass with shiitakes, scallions, and ginger. You and your doggy are welcome to enjoy your cultural cuisine at Fork's streetside seating. 306 Market St.; 215/625-9425; www.forkrestaurant.com.

Lamberti's Cucina: Serving up Italian cuisine in an upbeat and casual atmosphere, Lamberti's Cucina has something for all lovers of Italian food. One of the signature dishes is the chicken maximo marinated and topped with asparagus and mozzarella. You and your pup are welcome to sit on the patio. They love dogs here so much that one four-legged customer comes in on a nearly daily basis with his person and dines on his own serving of chicken parmesan. *Abbondanza!* 212 Walnut St.; 215/238-0499.

Lucy's Hat Shop: You may not come for the food here, specifically, but it's a fun and trendy eatery to frequent in the summertime with your pooch. No hats required to enter—nor are there any for sale—it's just plain old fun. Aside from its party atmosphere, Lucy's delivers some good eats like the beer-battered fries, but its Thai chicken is among the best choices on the menu. You and your furry friend can sit right along Market Street to soak up all the action with or without your own party hats. 247 Market St.; 215/413-1433.

Philadelphia Fish & Company: Famed for its incredibly fresh seafood and close location to Independence Park, Philadelphia Fish & Company consistently serves up delicious, innovative dishes in a fun, fishy-inspired atmosphere. If you try nothing else, taste the award-winning crab cakes and you'll be anything but crabby. You and your pup are welcome on the patio overlooking Chestnut Street. 207 Chestnut St.; 215/625-8605; www.philadelphiafishcompany.com.

Plough and Stars: When picturing an Irish pub in this country, you probably wouldn't envision a place like the Plough and Stars. But that's okay. This restaurant does a great job at imparting the friendliness of a true Irish establishment without all the pretentiousness of trying to be an authentic pub. It's more of an upscale pub, if there ever was such a thing. It's a great place to grab a beer with friends or sit down for a more formal meal. The food can best be described as a current take on traditional Irish fare (read: not your mother's Irish food). The fish-and-chips and the shepherd's pie are always solid choices. They welcome you and your doggy at the streetside seating. 123 Chestnut St.; 215/733-0300; www.ploughstars.com.

Society Hill Hotel Restaurant and Bar: While doggies are not permitted to stay at the Society Hill Hotel, the restaurant and bar welcomes four-footed customers at its outdoor seating. The European-style pub located in a historic building offers one of the best cheesesteaks in this part of the city, as well as other delectable dishes off its classic American menu. 301 Chestnut St.; 215/925-1919; www.societyhillhotel.com.

PLACES TO STAY

Best Western Inn: Maybe because the hotel itself is on the smaller side is why it won't allow dogs bigger than 15 pounds? It's too bad for the larger pups because the hotel has charm not typical of franchise hotels. But if you have a little sweetie to take here, you two will no doubt love the old Victorian hotel and the location, just a few blocks from many dog-friendly restaurants. The only requirement is a $50 nonrefundable fee. Rates are $109–$210. 235 Chestnut St.; 215/922-4443.

Distinctive Historic Inn Bed & Breakfast: Located on Chestnut Street in the heart of Old City is a gorgeous granite structure that houses a small hotel. This B&B, listed on the National Register of Historic Places, has traditionally decorated rooms with both queen- and king-size beds as well as private baths. The breakfast is self-serve continental. You and your doggy can stay for a $50 nonrefundable fee. Rates are $149–169. For more information, contact the Bed & Breakfast Connections of Philadelphia, 800/448-3619; bnb@bnbphiladelphia.com; www.bnbphiladelphia.com.

Sheraton Society Hill: If you're a small-dog lover and looking for a great location at a good price, check out the Sheraton Society Hill. This hotel is a block from Penn's Landing and lots of good restaurants. It allows dogs 40 pounds and under for no extra fee. In case you need them, leashes and bowls are available from the hotel. Best of all, a fluffy dog bed is provided for all pups who stay here—just be sure to remind the staff ahead of time that you're lodging with a canine companion. Rates are $129–260. One Dock St., 2nd and Walnut Streets; 215/238-6000.

Washington Square

The most centrally located of all the Center City neighborhoods, Washington Square is a perfect example of tranquility in an urban setting. It's another affluent neighborhood that includes beautiful homes from the 18th and 19th centuries, Antique Row (Pine Street), and a relatively new off-leash dog park.

PARKS, BEACHES, AND RECREATION AREAS

19 Washington Square Park

🐾 🐾 🔹 (See Philadelphia County map on page 16)

Massive trees shade this park that's steeped in history—it was one of the first squares William Penn planned in his 1692 survey of Philadelphia. Many Revolutionary War soldiers are buried here, the site of the Tomb of the Unknown Soldier, where an eternal flame flickers for an anonymous hero of liberty. Many victims of the 1793 yellow fever epidemic are buried in the park as well, so it's not surprising that the square is believed to be haunted. But if you and your pup aren't spooked by the supernatural, this is a perfect locale to have a picnic on the grass because it's much quieter than other Center City parks.

In the northeast section of the park, be sure to check out the Bicentennial Moon Tree, a sycamore planted to commemorate the nation's bicentennial and grown from a seed carried to the moon by Apollo astronaut Stuart Roosa.

The park is located between 6th and 7th Streets on Walnut Street. Hours are sunrise–1 A.M. 215/683-3600.

20 Seger Dog Park

🐾 🐾 🐾 🐕 (See Philadelphia County map on page 16)

Located in Washington Square West and an underutilized space up until about three years ago, this mini dog park is a great option if your goal is to socialize your dog and exercise her at the same time. It's definitely on the smaller side, but this dog park is completely fenced in with a separate entrance for dogs from the nearby playground. Maybe its size is why it's such a friendly place to come and why there's such a close-knit group of people who volunteer and visit here regularly with their various canine friends.

The dog park is located on a grassy hill that's covered in hay, which is pretty good at keeping mud at bay but not dirt. The Seger Park Dog Owners Association (SPDOA) is raising money for a new surface that will reduce mud and dust, improve the drainage, and enhance the overall beauty of the park. Available at the park are trash bags, trash cans, and benches. Shade is not its strength, so if that's a problem for you or your pup, try not to come during the sunniest times of day.

THINK GLOBALLY, BARK LOCALLY

Dog Blood Drives: Your pooch can make a difference in helping his fellow fluffy and furry friends. Four times a year, the Seger Dog Park hosts a dog blood drive to benefit the (University of) Penn Animal Blood Bank, the oldest volunteer-based animal blood program in the country. The blood bank supports the operation of the Animal Bloodmobile, the only one of its kind.

As long as your dog can be handled by others, is between one and eight years of age, weighs more than 50 pounds, and is in good health and not taking any medication other than flea and heartworm preventatives, he's eligible to donate blood. Your dog's blood type will be checked first to see if it's the appropriate type (universal donor) and tested for any abnormalities in the blood work (you'll be called with abnormal results). All pups who participate get a free gift of food. Seger Dog Park; 215/686-1780; www.segerdogpark.org.

Surrounding the dog park is two-hour street parking. From Center City, take 10th Street south past Lombard and take a right on Rodman Street. The entrance to the park is on Rodman directly behind the Superfresh grocery store. Hours are 6 A.M.–10 P.M. 215/686-1780; www.segerdogpark.org.

If you'd like to become a member of the SPDOA, send a $25 check marked "membership" to Seger Park Dog Owners Association, P.O. Box 1405, Philadelphia, PA 19105.

PLACES TO EAT

Caribou Café: This brasserie is down the road from Brasserie Perrier (see the Business District section), and it's a bit cheaper but not as acclaimed. Although the entrées are not its strong suit, if you're looking to eat some yummy appetizers and drink a few brews with your doggy at a small outdoor café, this could be your place. The fries, for which it's known, are unbelievably good. Plus, the staffers just love dogs and that alone is enough for many to come visit. 1126 Walnut St.; 215/625-9535.

Washington Square: One of the newer cutting-edge restaurants started by a famous Philadelphia restaurateur, this one is actually the first eatery ever on Washington Square (7th and Walnut), hence the name. Many visitors consider it the most spectacular-looking restaurant in town. Although you and your pooch cannot eat inside and view its swanky interior or patio, you two are welcome to dine together at the streetside tables and eat "global street food," playful takes on foods like corn dogs, and red beans and rice. The cuisine is incredibly creative and fresh, and on the pricier side—not exactly what Linus would have called "street food." Translated: free for the taking, in balled-up tissues and napkins. 210 W. Washington Sq.; 215/592-7787.

PLACES TO STAY

Belle Epoque Bed & Breakfast: Located on a charming, historic street not far from Antique Row and the convention and historic districts, and just a block from Seger Dog Park, is Belle Epoque. This enchanting town-house dates back to the early 1800s and has a lovely room with a private bath, kitchen, and entrance to make it convenient for you and your dog. The breakfast is self-serve continental and there's no extra charge for your well-behaved pup. Rates are $125. For more information, contact the Bed & Breakfast Connections of Philadelphia, 800/448-3619; bnb@bnbphiladelphia.com; www.bnbphiladelphia.com.

Pine Street Apartment Bed & Breakfast: A ground-floor apartment in this inviting turn-of-the-century home doubles as a bed-and-breakfast that provides daily and extended stay options. The bedroom with twin beds, a living room, kitchen, and bath is decorated in colonial style and provides a homey feel to the space. In warm weather, the patio opens up outside the room giving you and your pup a nice little outdoor respite. Every day a self-serve continental breakfast is provided. And there's no extra charge for your dog. Daily rates are $95; monthly rates vary. For more information, contact the Bed & Breakfast Connections of Philadelphia, 800/448-3619; bnb@bnbphiladelphia .com; www.bnbphiladelphia.com.

Ten Eleven Clinton Bed & Breakfast: Another B&B full of character and located on the same peaceful street as Belle Epoque is Ten Eleven. Well-mannered canines are always welcome at this Federal period townhouse B&B. You and your pup will enjoy staying in either the studios or one-bedroom suites that come equipped with private kitchens and bathrooms, as well as a courtyard in the back. Every morning an "extended" continental breakfast is provided in your room that includes cereal and breads, coffee, tea, and juice. And there's no extra charge for your furry companion. Rates are $145–175. 1011 Clinton St.; 215/923-8144; www.teneleven.com.

South Street/Queen Village

One of the oldest neighborhoods in Philadelphia, Queen Village is also one of the most unique. Sandwiched between genteel Society Hill and the more ethnic South Philadelphia, it derives some of its character from both areas. Well-known South Street, lined with one-of-a kind funky shops and restaurants, is part of this diverse neighborhood.

PARKS, BEACHES, AND RECREATION AREAS

21 Mario Lanza Park

🐾 🐾 🐕 (See Philadelphia County map on page 16)

Relatively small, quiet, and neighborhoody, Mario Lanza Park was named for the famed Philadelphia opera singer. The dogs who come here don't seem to appreciate its cultural origins but sure have a good time burning off some energy no matter how small the dog run is. The people you'll meet here are as friendly as their dogs, and those dogs that can't play nice are encouraged to leave.

A tight-knit community is what this park is known for. In fact, word has it that one Queen Village resident married another recently and had a wedding reception for the dogs at the dog park while they wedded in a church nearby.

The park is completely fenced in with a separate entrance for dogs, and has a decent amount of shade, water, benches, trash cans, and bags available. An added perk is that the surrounding unfenced area is beautifully landscaped and concerts are held here in the summertime.

From Center City take 2nd Street south to Christian Street. Take a right on Christian to 3rd Street. Follow to Queen Street and take a right. The entrance is located on Queen Street between 3rd and 2nd Streets. Try to find a street spot to park anywhere in the surrounding area. Hours are sunrise–1 A.M. 215/683-0200.

PLACES TO EAT

Azafran: You don't have to travel south of the equator to have a truly South American experience. You just have to travel south of South Street. Azafran is a homey and romantic, moderately priced BYOB restaurant that serves up some of the best tasting, most unique seafood dishes around. Try the calamari served with salsa; it's like no other. If there's any negative about Azafran, it's the fact that dogs are allowed to sit outside with you only on Sunday nights, no exceptions. 617 S. 3rd St.; 215/928-4019.

Bridget Foy's South Street Grill: For more than 25 years, Bridget Foy's has been serving up tasty yet unpretentious food in a casual atmosphere. This is eclectic American that's moderately priced. While the food is good, among the best aspects of this restaurant is the people watching you and your pup can do from its porch on South Street. However, be forewarned that only smaller dogs are welcome as the outdoor seating area is tiny. It's advisable to call first to be sure there's room on busier days. 200 South St.; 215/922-1813; www.bridgetfoys.com.

Creperie Beau Monde: One block south of South Street near Bainbridge lies an enchanting, moderately priced French bistro that specializes in mouthwatering crepes. Try not to become overwhelmed with the options of crepes available, and just focus on what makes you happiest. Choices include everything from cheese and vegetables to gumbo and beef bourguignon. While

FETCHING NECESSITIES

South Street is one of the main destinations for visitors to the Philadelphia area, mostly because of its funky shops and unique boutiques. One of those that loves visiting dogs is **American Pie/ Abode** (718 South St., 215/922-5333, www.americanpiecrafts.com or www.shopabode.com), where you can find handmade crafts and gifts, jewelry, home furnishings and accessories, and Judaica.

In the mood for an interesting movie you probably couldn't find anywhere else? Then be sure to take your pup with you to **TLA Video** (517 S. 4th St., 215/922-3838), where they even have biscuits for your pup to enjoy while you're searching the store. A couple blocks from TLA is a full-service pet boutique, **Chic Petique** (616 S. 3rd St., 215/629-1733, www.chicpetique.com), featuring high-end natural foods and original petware including doggy sweaters, party dresses, and tuxes. (This boutique often partners in events with Loews Philadelphia Hotel.)

the interior of this darling eatery is a must to see (it makes you feel as if you are in a bistro in the northwest section of France where crepes originated), you and your doggy are welcome to eat on the deck of the restaurant. But small doggies would most likely feel most comfortable, as the space is not very roomy. 624 S. 6th St.; 215/592-0656.

Jamaican Jerk Hut: Linus was relieved when he realized we weren't going to a hut filled with rude people from Montego Bay, but to an award-winning, friendly, inexpensive and authentic island BYOB. Here you can order takeout with your pup during colder months, or experience the genuine reggae and tropical ambiance firsthand under the veranda around the back. Some of the most sought-after menu items include the jerk chicken, of course, and the oxtail stew and conch fritters. After our experience here, all we could say was, "Irie, mon!" 1436 South St.; 215/545-8644.

Philadelphia Java Company: A comfy and friendly environment at this charming coffee house makes it conducive to bringing your doggy with you. The inside scoop is that dogs are allowed inside this coffee shop. And you can order some of the tastiest coffee, espresso, and lattes, as well as salads, soups, and paninis. 518 4th St.; 215/928-1811.

South Café: Make yourself at home at this homey coffee house that serves not just great tasting java, but soups, salads, and sandwiches, as well as delicious pastries and cakes. And they love four-legged customers here. If you or your pup is hungry in the morning, definitely add a breakfast sandwich to your coffee order. Both of you are welcome to sit at the outdoor tables, as well as the open-air café tables. 627 South St.; 215/922-6455.

Tattooed Mom: Like its name implies, there's a lot of ink, as well as leather, to be seen at this distinctive bar. Lots of rocker and Harley types make this their home away from home. Doggies are free to roam here at the bar's downstairs tables, but when the clock chimes 7 P.M., you and your pup better high-tail it out of there as that's when dog-friendly hours are over. If you want a little food with your beer, try Mom's Spanish fries. 530 South St.; 215/238-9880.

South Philly

Yo! Rocky made it famous. But South Philadelphia truly is a throwback to the '70s in a very good way. There's a certain understated wholesomeness to this Italian-influenced neighborhood. Many of the businesses are mom-and-pop shops and the Italian market is as authentic as the Italian-American experience gets. Plus, the famous Philadelphia cheesesteak is believed to have been born in this part of town. Linus loved South Philly for the smells (salami and mozzarella to die for), but the people from this area are responsible for much of Philadelphia's unique character.

PARKS, BEACHES, AND RECREATION AREAS

22 12th & Reed Street Dog Park

(See Philadelphia County map on page 16)

If you happen to be in the South Philly area with your pup sharing one of the best cheesesteaks in the world but don't have high dog park expectations, you could check out this little area that we hesitate to call a park or a run. The sad thing about it is that there was much political strife over its location and what it consisted of, and the end result is a small area that's completely enclosed but has no grass, only concrete. There are a couple of squares of dirt for dogs to play in, and trash cans available but no water, bag dispensers, or bags. Basically, it's a sad excuse for a dog park, but at least there's an enclosed area for dogs to frolic freely, right?

From Center City take Broad Street south. Take a left on Wharton Street and follow to a right on 12th Street. The park is located at the corner of 12th and Reed. Hours are sunrise–sunset. 215/683-0200.

23 FDR Park

(See Philadelphia County map on page 16)

In this beautiful, sprawling park covering nearly 350 acres, you'll have a hard time believing it's in the midst of the South Philadelphia industrial area. FDR Park is a perfect place to come for a long walk or to just unwind in this section of the city. At this expansive green retreat, you'll find not just three lakes but marshes, too, along with bike paths, a skate park, picnic tables, trash

FETCHING NECESSITIES

A trip to South Philly with your dog cannot be complete without visiting the lively and authentic **Italian Market,** the nation's oldest continuously operating open-air food market. Situated along 9th Street between Wharton and Federal Streets, it operates much like it did when it opened a hundred years ago. Here, you'll find Italian pastries, cheese, bread, meats, coffee, spices, and service like no other from more than 100 merchants. The bustling, crowded atmosphere might be tricky to maneuver with your pup, but the trip here is worth it for the experience and delicious food. It's open 9 A.M.–5 P.M. Tuesday–Saturday, and until 2 P.M. on Sunday. www.phillyitalianmarket.com.

cans, baseball fields, real working bathrooms, and lots of big, old shade trees. While exploring the park along the paths, be sure to keep your pup on leash as that's what the rules state.

But beware of football Sundays as Eagles fans take over with tailgating since the Lincoln Financial Field is basically across the street. Be sure to yell a hardy "Go, Eagles!" to see the incredible reaction you get.

The park is located at the intersection of Broad and Pattison. From Center City, take Broad Street south to Pattison and take a right. Park near the boathouse. Hours are sunrise–9 P.M. 215/683-0200.

24 The John Heinz National Wildlife Refuge at Tinicum

 (See Philadelphia County map on page 16)

If you can get over the smell of the nearby refineries, this is one amazing inner-city park. Established by Congress in 1972 to protect the last 200 acres of freshwater tidal marsh, the John Heinz National Wildlife Refuge is now home to nearly 300 species of birds as well as fox, deer, muskrat, and turtles—all within the city, which is what makes it so unbelievable (the remaining part of the park is in Delaware County). It's a great spot to take your pup on a long, relaxing hike to truly experience nature in a serene setting.

The refuge has both wooded and gravel-paved pathways along banks of the Darby Creek. And over the creek, you and your outward hound can cross a pedestrian bridge to either the wooded area or the open area. Make sure to keep your dog on leash as that is what the rules indicate.

From I-95 North near the Philadelphia Airport, take Exit 10 (onto Route 291). At the first light, turn left onto Bartram Avenue. At the fourth light, turn left onto 84th Street. At the second light, turn left onto Lindbergh Boulevard and you'll see the main entrance. Hours are 8 A.M.–sunset. John Heinz

National Wildlife Refuge at Tinicum, 8601 Lindbergh Blvd.; 610/521-0662; http://heinz.fws.gov.

PLACES TO EAT

Anthony's Italian Coffee House: Whether you are in the Italian Market area or not, if you want an excellent cup of coffee go to Anthony's. Here you can order some of the best espresso, cappuccino, or plain old joe you'll find in the city. If your tummy's growling, too, try one of their grilled panini sandwiches or a taste of their delectable homemade gelato and pastries. You and your pup are welcome to dine alfresco, relax, and take in the sights of the Italian Market right along Ninth Street. 903 S. 9th St.; 215/627-2586 or 800/833-5030; www.italiancoffeehouse.com.

Geno's: We doubt that you and poochie will be out together at 2 A.M., but just in case you have the munchies, you'll be glad to know that Geno's is open and happy to serve you both 24 hours a day. A definite tourist attraction, and a contender among Philadelphians as the purveyor of the best cheesesteak in town, it is known as one of the leaders. But be prepared and know how to order your steak because the service is speedy and they only accept cash. For example, say "with onions" or "without onions." And specify with provolone, American or—gasp!—cheese whiz. You and your dog pal order your cheesesteak of choice through the window and take your sandwich to the streetside tables and devour them together. 1219 S. 9th St.; 215/389-0659.

Gleaners Café: Located in the Italian Market, Gleaners Café and bakery welcomes you and your four-legged bud to its outside seating and even inside, if it's not too crowded. The ever-popular La Colombe coffee and espresso are served here, as well as bagel sandwiches and salads. The staff here is ultra-friendly and will provide poochie with water. They even sell gourmet doggy treats for that hungry hound of yours. 917 S. 9th St.; 215/923-3205.

Pat's King of Steaks: Similar to Geno's in the setup, offerings, and 24-hour service, Pat's has been in business since 1930 and touts being "the original." Heated debates will arise among locals as to whether its steaks are better than Geno's. It's a tourist attraction, too, of course. Celebrities including Senator John McCain and even Larry King have been known to "tro a few cheesesteaks down der troats." You and your pup are welcome at its picnic tables out front. 9th and Wharton Streets; 215/468-1546.

PLACES TO STAY

Residence Inn Philadelphia Airport: An option when needing to stay near the airport, the Residence Inn allows pups for a $100 nonrefundable fee. If you're really looking for space and a place that feels more like home, this hotel is designed to meet that need—it's like a townhouse community, and it even has a picnic area on the premises. It also provides services like check cashing, grocery shopping, and daily maid service that will even take care of dishes. Rates are $69–189. 4630 Island Ave.; 215/492-1611.

Sheraton Suites Philadelphia Airport: It's hard to fathom an airport hotel as a respite, but this one does a good job at handling the noise from all the air traffic. Plus, it's moderately priced and welcomes dogs less than 40 pounds at no extra charge. This hotel also offers a fluffy pillowy dog bed for all poochies who stay here. For you there is an indoor pool and health club, as well as your own fluffy, comfy bed. Rates are $129–289. 4101 B Island Ave.; 215/365-6600.

68

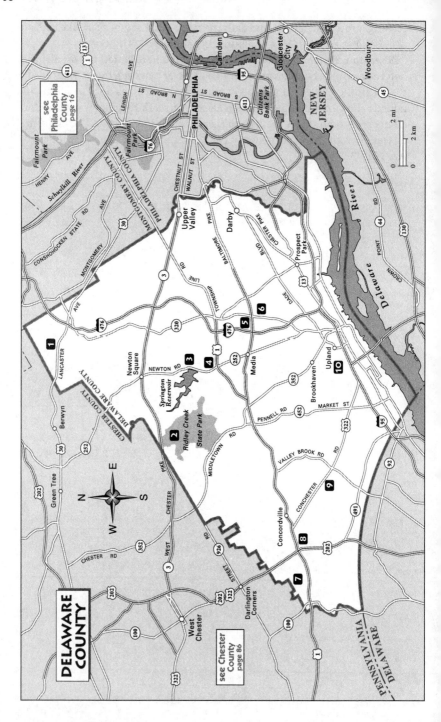

DELAWARE COUNTY

see Chester County page 86

see Philadelphia County page 16

CHAPTER 2

Delaware County

When I am wrong, he is delighted to forgive. When I am angry, he clowns to make me smile. When I am happy, he is joy unbounded. When I am a fool, he ignores it. When I succeed, he brags. Without him, I am only another man. With him, I am all-powerful. He is just my dog.

Gene Hill

If you think towns like Chester, Chichester, and Chester Heights are in Chester County, you're not alone. Surprise! They're actually in Delaware County. Good thing that Delaware County borders the state of Delaware or we'd all be frantic trying to find it. Actually, Delaware County wasn't created until 1789 (much later than the other surrounding counties), when it was formed from part of Chester County and named for the Delaware River that it also borders.

PICK OF THE LITTER—DELAWARE COUNTY

BEST DOG PARK
Harford Park Dog Park, Radnor (page 71)

BEST PLACES TO EAT
Roux 3, Newtown Square (page 76)
Feasts of Fairville, Chadds Ford (page 80)

BEST PLACES TO STAY
Hamanassett Bed & Breakfast, Chadds Ford (page 80)
Sweetwater Farm B&B, Glen Mills (page 84)

BEST EVENT
Dog Days of Summer, Chadds Ford (page 82)

Delaware County is most famous for the Battle of the Brandywine, which took place along the Brandywine River in Chadds Ford in 1777. Lucky for you and your pup, you can see it together first hand. The county is also known for its Brandywine River Museum (sadly, poochie isn't allowed inside) showcasing works from the prolific artistic Wyeth family, including N. C., Andrew, and Jamie.

Delaware County's affluent "Main Line" suburbs (the towns that were along the route of the Pennsylvania Railroad's Main Line), including Radnor, Villanova, and Wayne, are highly sought-after yet expensive places to live. Sadly, though, if you're a Main Liner and you step into another area of the region, it's not uncommon for others to poke fun at your neighbors by imitating them with a stiff, protruding jaw while talking about Buffy and her dog Fluffy.

In general, though, people and dogs who live or visit Delaware County are fortunate since it borders Philadelphia and it's quite convenient to jaunt to the city for work or play.

Although Delaware County is one of the smallest suburban counties in land area and lacks a plethora of space for parks like some of the larger counties, it rates fairly well on the dog-friendliness chart. In fact, all four county-run parks allow dogs, and many others do, too. There's even an excellent off-leash dog park in Radnor. An off-leash dog park may also be included in the Haverford State Hospital redevelopment effort (for up-to-date info visit www.mainlinecanine.org).

Dog-friendly restaurants abound in Delaware County. Plus, the bed-and-breakfasts located in this part of the Brandywine Valley are some of the Philadelphia area's most gorgeous and they love dogs.

Radnor Township

More than 300 years old, Radnor Township was settled by Welsh Quakers who purchased the land from William Penn in 1681. Located in the heart of the Main Line suburbs, Radnor Township is a thriving area that prides itself on its tremendous community spirit and a growing multicultural population. Wayne, the township's main business district, has a main street with quaint little eateries and shops. Radnor Township's off-leash dog park, the only one in the county, is a must-see.

PARKS, BEACHES, AND RECREATION AREAS

◻ Harford Park Dog Park

🐾🐾🐾🐾🐕 (See Delaware County map on page 68)

If you can picture Doggy Heaven in your mind, you might just picture this park: wide-open, hilly fields, a creek, beautiful big trees, and tons of delighted canines playfully cavorting about. There is no fence at the dog park—one is not needed since it sits back in a nook surrounded by woods, not near any traffic or visible homes. Nellie never had a better time at a park with me. At one point, I couldn't find her because there were at least five other Golden Retrievers, including two others with the same collar as hers. She finally appeared after she said had hello to a half-dozen other people and dogs. Speaking of humans, they couldn't be more welcoming. Everyone seems to have the same (read: right) idea. Relax and let your pooch burn some energy with furry friends in a beautiful yet laid-back environment. Some of the amenities here include a doggy and person water fountain, bags, picnic benches, and, of course, excellent scenery. The best time to visit is on weekends as that's when it's loaded with pooches, and the park area is big enough to support all the activity.

From I-476, take Route 30/St. Davids exit. Take a right on Route 30 heading east. Then take the first left onto King of Prussia Road. Follow it until you pass the schools on the right and take a right onto Biddulph Road. At the end of Biddulph, take a right onto Gulph Creek Road and a quick right into the Harford Park entrance. Hours are sunrise–sunset. 260 Gulf Creek Rd., Radnor; 610/688-5600.

PLACES TO EAT

Station Café and Juice Bar: Although there's no where for you and your pup to sit here, if your looking to grab some great food to go, visit this small eatery

FETCHING NECESSITIES

The Bone Appetite K9 Bakery & Boutique: If Milkbones just don't cut it anymore for your picky poochie, or maybe that old collar or dog bed needs some stylish updating, then get your paws over to Wayne and visit this dog lover's boutique and bakery. All biscuits are homemade and are good enough for you to eat, too. And the selection on custom pet furniture and collars is doggone incredible. They host several events a year from fashion trunk shows to adopt-a-pet programs. Best of all, your pooch can get some water and a treat just for visiting. 122 E. Lancaster Ave., Wayne; 610/995-2663; www.theboneappetite.com.

Braxton's Animal Works: A definite favorite among Main Liners, Braxton Animal Works has been around since 1938. This pet store welcomes you and your doggy to check out all of the wares including doggy clothes and sweaters, beds, premium dog food, and memorials. Here, you can find health-related items for your pooch as well as more fun items like freshly baked canine cannoli. Your doggy is always welcome here. 620 W. Lancaster Ave., Wayne; 610/688-0769; www.braxtons.com.

Whiskazz and Pawzz: Located in Chadds Ford as well as online, this pet store extraordinaire offers gifts and gourmet treats for pups and their people. You and your doggy are always welcome here and are great company for the sweet, resident canine consultant, Cappi, the beagle. Here you'll find everything from hand-painted pillows and mugs to gourmet dog biscuits and aromatherapy for your pooch. There are even cute doggy drawer pulls for that dresser you've wanted to update. Chadds Ford Shops, Bldg. #1, Routes 1 and 100, Chadds Ford; 610/388-7010; www.whiskazzandpawzz.com.

located in the Wayne Train Station. The friendly place offers breakfast muffins, scones and pastries, as well as sandwiches, and grilled paninis. All types of coffee drinks can be made to order, too. But if you're there in the warm months, try some incredible fresh fruit smoothies and fresh-squeezed lemonade, or in the colder months, you might like the scrumptious hot chocolate. 135 N. Wayne Ave., Wayne; 610/687-1931.

Teresa's Café Italiano: Serving contemporary Italian cuisine, Teresa's Café Italiano dishes up yummy antipasta, brick-oven pizzettas, pasta dishes, and specialty desserts. No outdoor seating is available, but takeout may just fill the bill for you and your dog. 124 N. Wayne Ave., Wayne; 610/293-9909.

The Wild Onion: The friendly manager of this Rosemont staple hated to tell me there was no outdoor seating because he loves dogs, and shares his life with one, too. But you can be assured that the takeout option is worth your while because anything and everything from the eclectic menu is available to go. From seafood and steaks to veggie dishes, sandwiches, and salads, you'll definitely find something you like. The wings are delicious, but the wild onion soup is among the restaurant's signature dishes. 900 Conestoga Rd., Rosemont; 610/527-4826.

Media

The county seat, Media is a friendly town where people still say hello to each other. This town even has a trolley still running through its center. And since it's in the center of the county, Media is near just about everything good in Delaware County, including some great parks and nice places to eat with poochie in Media and nearby.

PARKS, BEACHES, AND RECREATION AREAS

2 Ridley Creek State Park

🐾🐾🐾 (See Delaware County map on page 68)

This 2,600-acre hilly, wooded park is one of the Philadelphia area's most beloved, maybe because it's centrally located in Delaware County and offers more than 12 miles of hiking trails? Or maybe it's the five-mile paved trail for dog walkers, joggers, cyclists, and even cross-country skiers? Or possibly it's the scenic and rumbling Ridley Creek that bisects the park? Whatever the reason, you'll find yours.

Nellie enjoyed the hike along the multi-use trail as it was both hilly and flat at different intervals. Plus, there are dog bowls of water along the way right next to benches. But her favorite part was spotting some sweet deer babies nibbling away at weeds nearby.

On your first visit here, don't be alarmed about how huge the park is and how hard it is to navigate. You'll no doubt run into other dog walkers or even some anglers to ask for directions. The worst part about the park is that entrances to certain areas are not well marked. Hiking trails are also somewhat confusing. To alleviate any concerns, be sure to pick up a map at the park office or at any park kiosks you come across.

One good place to access the multi-use paved trail is near picnic area #17. It's shaded and there's parking and a playground here, so it's easy to remember.

From Media take Route 1 North to 252 North (Providence Road) and take your first left onto Gradyville Road into the park entrance. The park is located between Routes 252 and 352. Hours are sunrise–sunset. Ridley Creek State Park, Sycamore Mills Road, Media; 610/892-3900.

❸ Hildacy Farm

 (See Delaware County map on page 68)

If you're in Media and want to check out some beautiful flora and maybe a little fauna if you're lucky, come here. This farm is actually all that remains of a 300-acre 1683 land grant from William Penn to a local tanner and his family. Through the 1800s only one small grove of large oak woodlands survived harvesting for agriculture. A family bought the farm in the meantime, and in 1981 donated it to the Natural Lands Trust with instructions to conserve and preserve it.

Since then, the woodlands and meadows have been restored to a more natural state. Wetlands were created here to help prevent storm water runoff to Crum Creek. Now the preserve consists of 55 acres of woodlands and meadows with striking wildflowers and provides homes to wildlife like deer, rabbits, and fox, as well as amphibians, birds and fish. Although your pup is welcome here on a leash, dogs are not allowed during spring bird nesting season April through June. However, the rest of the year, you and your pup can hike the two-mile trail that takes you by Crum Creek and other tributaries and ponds. Although they might look refreshing on a hot day, your pup is not allowed to get her feet wet here.

While there are fences up at the mowed-grass trails, you and your doggy can walk around them to access the trails. They were installed to discourage rebellious teenagers from partying on the property.

From Media take Route 1 North and head north on PA 252. Cross the dam at the reservoir and immediately turn right onto Palmers Mill Road. Enter the preserve via the first driveway on the right. Hours are sunrise–sunset. 1031 Palmers Mill Rd., Media; 610/353-5587.

❹ Rose Tree Park

 (See Delaware County map on page 68)

Yet another park that's not marked very well (you might just drive past it; if so, turn around if you see the reservoir on your left), it's worth a visit if you're in the area. Consisting of open fields, rolling hills, woodlands, and a small hiking trail, this 120-acre park is beautiful even if it's not entirely shady, like Nellie would prefer. Many people take their dogs about a quarter-mile from the parking lot to a large open area straight ahead and let them run. There's no danger to them in this area except getting caught by a park ranger who might hand you a hefty citation for letting your dog off leash. The park rule is to keep your dog on a leash six feet long or shorter. When we've visited, there's always at least one dog running off leash in this remote area. Ironically, there is a completely fenced-in equestrian area and Nellie wondered why it simply couldn't double as an off-leash dog park? Hmmm…something to ponder.

DOG-EAR YOUR CALENDAR

Delaware County Summer Festival: People and their pups in Delaware County are truly lucky dogs as they can partake of about 50 free outdoor concerts June–August at Rose Tree Park's amphitheater. All events begin at 7:30 P.M. Don't forget your lawn chair and a blanket for puppers as well as any snacks and drinks you both might need. 1671 N. Providence Rd., Media; 610/565-7410.

Smithbridge Summer Concert Series: Your leashed doggy is invited with you to bring a picnic dinner, kick back, and relax with some of the nation's finest singer songwriters on Friday evenings, June–September. Showtime is 7–9 P.M. outdoors on the deck and adjoining canopy of the cedar-sided 18th-century winery, with beautiful views of countryside and covered, reserved seating for 50. Dogs are welcome as long as they're picked up after. Admission: $10 advance purchase, $12 at gate, includes wine-tasting before the show. 610/558-4703; wines@smithbridge.com.

Old Ridge Village Concert Series: Starting in June, you and your pup can have fun together checking out the Summer Concert Series in Chadds Ford's Old Ridge Village at the gazebo. Different types of music are offered throughout the summer but three things remain the same: it's free, it takes place every Thursday, and runs 6:30–8:30 P.M. You're welcome to bring a lawn chair and a picnic supper—Pagano's boxed supper is a delicious treat. 610/494-4035; www.oldridgevillage.com.

At Rose Tree Park, you'll find picnic areas but no creek or river to take a dip in. Lucky for us, doggy water fountains are scattered throughout the park, as well as some benches, trash cans, and bathrooms.

What's most exciting about Rose Tree Park is that it hosts the popular outdoor concert series called the Summer Festival. Almost every night from June through August, the ampitheater's grassy hill is packed with people and pups. The free series attracts thousands of spectators. In December, the park's Festival of Lights illuminates the surrounding trees.

From Media take Route 1 North to Route 252 (Providence Road) and take a right on Rose Tree Road. Follow it to the left and park in the main parking lot. Hours are 8 A.M.–sunset. Providence Road, Media; 610/565-7410.

PLACES TO EAT

D'ignazio's Towne House: Like stepping back in time, this family-dining restaurant has sincere service and very good food that's big in quantity and

THINK GLOBALLY, BARK LOCALLY

Bark in the Park: Your pup can run, walk, and bark in the park to help raise money for the Delaware County SPCA. Ridley Creek State Park hosts the walk and related events such as animal behavior demonstrations and pet contests with prizes. Adoptable animals will be featured, too. An entrance fee of $10 is collected upon registration. Delaware County SPCA; 610/566-1370.

Chesco Greyhounds Annual Pupnic: Whether you share your life with a greyhound or a basset hound, you are more than welcome to join in on this tailwagger held at Ridley Creek State Park one weekend day in September. It's free but food and raffles are for sale. All funds are donated to greyhound adoption. a.menn@verizon.net; www.chescogreyhounds.com.

quality. The owner of this landmark restaurant has pugs, so is happy to see dogs on the outdoor deck enjoying their time with diners. The menu includes Italian pasta favorites as well as dishes like crab au gratin and lobster tail, and veal marsala. 117 Veterans Square, Media; 610/566-6141.

Barnaby's: Known for its friendly atmosphere, vast menu, and new outdoor deck bar, this fun eatery welcomes you and your dog to enjoy it all together. On the deck you can have anything from a sandwich or a salad to a pizza and a full entrée, as well as an array of beer and frozen drinks. 5501 Pennell Rd., Media; 610/558-1929.

Roux 3: With a name like Roux 3, you might expect French Bulldogs to feel right at home here. But this upscale restaurant actually serves a new take on mostly American continental cuisine with a little French influence. The name is actually poking fun of the street it's located on, Route 3 (a.k.a. West Chester Pike). French Bulldogs are, indeed, welcome to sit outside with you but so are good ol' American Bulldogs, or any dog as long as she's well behaved. Some of the tastiest items on the menu are the calamari appetizer, any of the seafood dishes, and the pork. 4755 West Chester Pk., Newtown Square; 610/356-9500.

Teikoku Restaurant: If it's scrumptious sushi or delectable pad Thai you're looking for, you'll find it on a huge menu combining moderately priced Japanese and Thai cuisine here. Although there was no outdoor seating at Teikoku by the time we went to press, it's on its way. Dogs will most certainly be welcome to sit outside with you to enjoy miso salmon then, but in the meantime, try the takeout version. 5492 West Chester Pk., Newtown Square; 610/644-8270.

Swarthmore and Wallingford

Towering tree-lined streets to walk with puppers and a downtown filled with independent stores and restaurants are just part of what makes Swarthmore so special. Although Swarthmore College, a small, Quaker-founded liberal arts school, is what anchors the town and its Scott Arboretum is a definite gem, this storybook-like town is a jewel in its own right, as is its neighbor, Wallingford. You and your pup could easily spend a whole day in the area, walking through the towns and the Swarthmore College campus. Two winning parks and dog-friendly restaurants are located in this area as well.

PARKS, BEACHES, AND RECREATION AREAS

5 Smedley Park

🐾🐾🐾 (See Delaware County map on page 68)

This park was named after the founder of Delaware County's Park & Recreation, Samuel L. Smedley. Just about anything you and your pup want to do, you can do within the 120 acres of this serene setting. Play fetch in some of the open fields, hike along the trails and over the creek, in and out of the woods, or let your dog take a dip in the water. It's an ideal suburban park with lots of space and shade. There are various picnic areas with trash cans. The most convenient way to access the park is the playground area. This spot has picnic areas as well as bathrooms and easy access to the trail and water. The only drawback is that it's right near the trolley tracks, so it can get loud at times.

From I-476, take Exit 3 (Baltimore Pike/Route 1) and take a left toward Swarthmore. Take the first left onto Paper Mill Road and to the park entrance. The playground parking lot is the second lot on the left. Hours are 8 A.M.–sunset. 521 Avondale Rd., Wallingford; 610/565-7410.

6 Scott Arboretum at Swarthmore College

🐾🐾🐾 (See Delaware County map on page 68)

The campus of Swarthmore College could not be any greener and its beauty is largely the result of its Scott Arboretum, which encompasses 300 acres and includes more than 4,000 kinds of ornamental plants and trees. Most plants are labeled with both their scientific and common names, and grouped in collections to make them easy to identify. The best part is that you and your leashed doggy are welcome all over the campus to experience the different gardens and landscape attractions of the arboretum.

Among the most eye-catching attraction is the Scott Amphitheater, an outdoor theater built into a heavily wooded, steep natural slope covered by grass. The theater's columns are formed by the trunks of tulip poplars, providing a shade ceiling. The amphitheater is used for graduations and summer concerts.

More nose-catching are the Teresa Lang Garden of Fragrance, which features highly fragrant plants and flowers, and the Dean Bond Rose Garden which includes more than 200 varieties of roses. The roses grown here are traditionally pinned to a Swarthmore senior on graduation day.

But if you and your pup are looking for a long hike, check out the hiking trails at the arboretum's Crum Woods, 200 acres of woodlands bordering Crum Creek. While it's not advised, some dog owners do let their dogs roam leash-free here. Use discretion since it's against campus rules.

Take I-476 to Exit 3, Media/Swarthmore. At the bottom of the exit ramp, follow sign for Swarthmore by turning left onto Baltimore Pike. Stay in the right lane on Baltimore Pike and in less than .25 mile turn right onto Route 320 South. Watch turns on Route 320. Proceed to the second light; turn right onto College Avenue into the Swarthmore College campus. Hours are sunrise–sunset. 500 College Ave., Swarthmore; 610/328-8025; www.scottarboretum.org.

PLACES TO EAT

The Cheese Court: Specializing in catering and gift baskets, this cute little shop also serves lunch and fresh, gourmet coffee. Poochie and you are welcome to sit outside and enjoy whatever you love most at one of the tables in front of the store. 1 Park Ave., Swarthmore; 610/328-4140.

Salvucci's Cucina: You and your doggy will love to munch on the homemade and creative Italian sandwiches, pastas and salads, and finger food while you sit outside together. Some of the best are the chicken cutlet sandwiches served with broccoli rabe. And after your main meal, you and your pup can have water ice or ice cream together. What a treat! 417 Dartmouth Ave., Swarthmore; 610/543-4339.

Chadds Ford

A small, quaint community, best known as the site of the Battle of the Brandywine and the home of the artistic Wyeth family, Chadds Ford has a long, rich history. Ironically, though, it wasn't until 1996 that this town became a township in Delaware County. Previously it was known as Birmingham Township and was shared with Chester County. Visiting here will put you at peace, no doubt. It's a quiet, affluent community with an appreciation for dogs, as they're welcome at select wineries, bed-and-breakfasts, and stores.

PARKS, BEACHES, AND RECREATION AREAS

7 Brandywine Battlefield

🐾🐾🐾 🐕 (See Delaware County map on page 68)

American history buffs and their "ruffs" will not want to miss this highly significant battlefield that spans 50 acres. But even if you don't consider your-

DIVERSIONS

As the Brandywine Valley is known for its wineries, Nellie thought that's where the name for the valley came from. Silly pup! Regardless, they're a great escape with your pooch from the hustle and bustle of everyday life, and you might even get a sample or two while visiting on a weekend.

Chaddsford Winery: This award-winning winery, very well known throughout the area, usually does not allow pups inside or out. But in very limited circumstances during less busy times, they are allowed leashed on the grounds. Call first before making the trip and disappointing your eager doggy in the car. 632 Baltimore Pk., Chadds Ford; 610/388-6221; www.chaddsford.com.

Smithbridge Cellars Winery: Located in an 18th-century bank barn in the middle of a 200-acre nature preserve, this winery affords miles of trails for you and your four-legged nature lover to explore. Smithbridge Cellars is a small winery focusing on barrel-aged Chardonnay and blends of classic Bordeaux grape varieties. The owners of the winery love dogs and have one of their own, but they also have a cat, so there are some rules that need to be followed. All dogs should be on a leash and cleaned up after; no jumping on people or chasing the winery cat, since she's a working mouser. Other than that, they welcome you and your poochie for a spectacular visit. 159 Beaver Valley Rd., Chadds Ford; 610/558-4703.

self a history buff, you'll learn about the incredible pursuit of the American spirit while visiting here. It was at this battlefield where the British defeated American forces in one of the largest land battles of the American Revolution on another fateful September 11, in 1777. Although we lost the battle, we won General Marquis de Lafayette's allegiance to America as he attended this, his first American battle. This allegiance secured America's friendship with France. It was here also that General George Washington faced British General Howe for the first time on Pennsylvania soil.

What you'll gain from your visit is more firsthand knowledge of our history and a great walk with your pup on a leash in the area's hilly woodlands. You'll also see the two farmhouses Washington and Lafayette used as their quarters, which look much like they did during the battle. Also on the grounds are trees, a graveyard site, an old church, and a creek. Picnic areas are scattered throughout, too. Be sure to check out the kiosk map near the visitor's center. Maps are available inside for $1.50.

If you'd like a driving tour of the battlefield and other important military sites nearby, check out the website for detailed information including how long to spend at each site and how long the tour might take you. There are three different tours to choose from.

From Media, take Route 1 South, cross over Route 202, follow Route 1 and look for the park about a mile down on the right. Hours are Tuesday–Saturday 9 A.M.–5 P.M., Sunday noon–5 P.M.; closed Monday. 610/459-3342; www .ushistory.org/brandywine.

PLACES TO EAT

Feasts of Fairville: Not only is your pup able to join you outside here, she will likely be warmly welcomed with water and dog treats. This creative little catering business features great food for carryout to its outdoor seating, including boxed lunches and dinners, soups, salads, and entrées. If you're unsure of what to order, try the chicken club salad as it's always fresh and distinctively yummy. 518 Kennett Pk., Chadds Ford; 610/388-4570.

New Orleans Café: An extensive menu with a Cajun emphasis, this upscale BYOB is a relatively new local favorite. You and your pup are welcome to sit outside and taste such mouth-watering dishes as Southern fried chicken and macadamia-encrusted crab cakes. 101 Olde Ridge Village, Chadds Ford; 610/361-9030.

PLACES TO STAY

Brandywine River Hotel: Although "hotel" is in the name, the friendly staff and personal touches make this hillside colonial establishment feel more like a bed-and-breakfast, especially since a hearty breakfast is included. The rooms here are clean and comfortable and come with private bathrooms. Dogs weighing less than 20 pounds are allowed to stay crated for an extra $20 per night. Best of all, the Whiskazz and Pawzz Pet Boutique is located in the shops adjacent to the hotel. Rates are $125–169. Routes 1 and 100, Chadds Ford; 610/388-1200 or 800/274-9644; www.brandywineriverhotel.com.

Hamanassett Bed & Breakfast: If you and poochie would like more space or privacy, you might want to stay here. This two-bedroom English carriage house has 1,200 square feet to stretch out in and can sleep six. Plus, it has its own kitchen and a fenced-in back yard. The owners of this B&B are dog lovers themselves, with two of their own (a doberman and a mixed breed), and provide all furry guests with biscuits and silver dog bowls. A $25 one-time pet fee and a $500 refundable cleaning deposit are required (no deposit has ever been kept, according to the owners). Rates are $275–350. 725 Darlington Rd., Chadds Ford; 610/459-3000; www.hamanassett.com.

Pennsbury Bed & Breakfast: Provided you have a nice, friendly dog on the smaller side and you clear it with the owners before your visit, you two are welcome to stay in this gorgeous, historically significant home dating back to 1714, listed on the National Register of Historic Places. All dogs who stay here must have written proof of shots and must be crated if left alone in the room. Most rooms come with a private bath, which is a plus for you. For your pup, there are loaner bowls, leashes, and towels, as well as a bedtime snack. Plus, a cute, small poodle named Teddy lives here. There's a one-time pet fee of $10–15. Rates are $72–225. 883 Baltimore Pk., Chadds Ford; 610/388-1435; www.pennsburyinn.com.

Concord Township

Because of the harmonious feelings settlers felt here, this township was named "Concord" when it was established in 1683. You and your doggy will likely feel good, too, when you visit its famous Newlin Grist Mill and county park. Plus, the gorgeous bed-and-breakfast and restaurants mentioned here are not just friendly, but dog-friendly, too.

PARKS, BEACHES, AND RECREATION AREAS

8 Newlin Grist Mill

🐾🐾🐾 🐕 (See Delaware County map on page 68)

Dating back to 1704, the Newlin Grist Mill is believed to be the only original, fully functioning colonial grist mill left in the United States. Nicholas Newlin obtained a grant of 500 acres from William Penn in 1683 to build two mills along the Chester Creek. His son, Nathaniel, built a third mill, in 1704, which is now the Newlin Grist Mill park, where wheat, corn, oats, buckwheat, and rye were ground.

While your pup can't go inside the grist mill itself or any of the buildings, she is allowed to tour the 150 acres of the surrounding park on a leash. Three miles of hiking trails are here for you to enjoy together. On your walk you'll see the original mill race, hand-dug in 1704 to redirect water from the west branch of Chester Creek to power the Grist Mill, as well as a barn, a miller's house, a stone springhouse, a log cabin, a blacksmith's shop, a railroad bridge and dam, a small waterfall, and fishing ponds. These sites are on both sides of Cheyney Road.

The entire setting is extremely shaded and peaceful, except for traffic noise from Route 1. You and poochie can picnic here, too. But as tempting as the mill race is to jump in, poochie is not allowed to wade in the water.

Be sure to stop at the visitor's office (hours 9 A.M.–4 P.M.) for a map of the park, or download a map from the website, which also features a video of how the mill actually works.

From Media, take Route 1 South, past the town of Wawa. You can see the burgundy visitor's center from Route 1. Take a left on Cheyney Road and park

DOG-EAR YOUR CALENDAR

Dog Days of Summer: Maybe you missed your local Independence Day parade, and your pup has been begging to be dressed up in red, white, and blue. If you attend the Dog Days of Summer in Old Ridge Village, Chadds Ford, he can participate in the Patriotic Puppy Parade (provided he's under the age of three). Or maybe people always tell you how much you and your dog look alike? Then enter the Look-alike Contest. Still, if Rex loves being dressed up in that bunny suit, then enter him in the Canine Costume Contest. All three of these events are part of the Dog Days event that takes place at the gazebo in the village. The event is $3 to enter (benefiting the Chester County SPCA) and takes place one Saturday in August 10 A.M.–2 P.M. 610/494-4035.

Pennsbury Balloon Fest: Although your pooch may not be too keen on sitting inside a hot-air balloon, he is welcome at this fun festival that has live entertainment and all sorts of family fun including real hot-air balloon rides, games, and pony rides. Festivities are held one Saturday in September 2–6 P.M. Adults $10, children 6–12 $5, under 6 free. pennsbury-lt@comcast.net; www.pennsburylandtrust.org.

Chadds Ford Days: Experience a glimpse of the past with your canine companion at the Chadds Ford Historical Society's annual Chadds Ford Days event in September. You'll be in the midst of an open-air colonial fair displaying colonial crafts and Brandywine Valley art. There's also live music, yummy food, and rides and games for the little ones. Admission is $5 per adult, $1 for children 6–12, free for kids 5 and under. 610/388-7376.

on the immediate right. Hours are 8 A.M.–sunset. 219 S. Cheyney Rd., Glen Mills; 610/459-2359; www.newlingristmill.org.

🐾 Clayton Park

(See Delaware County map on page 68)

Although the biggest Delaware County park, consisting of 170 acres, it's probably best for golfers since a nine-hole golf course is part of the park. But since Nellie doesn't know the difference between a birdie and those cute little, feathered tweeters that flit around her back yard, it wasn't the best dog destination for her. The golf course was well manicured, but it's too bad the same can't be said for the rest of the park. Yes, there are lots of areas to walk in the woods and the walking path is paved, and there are even several shaded picnic areas. But the park itself isn't very inviting and

Braxton's Harvest Festival: One weekend in September Braxton's holds its pet fair featuring freebies from all sorts of vendors, as well as dog health information, canine good citizen testing, and dogs available for adoption. Proceeds benefit a different nonprofit rescue group each year. 610/688-0769; www.braxtons.com.

Blessing of the Animals: Your pup can join Delaware County SPCA alumni pets in getting blessed by a priest one weekend in October near the holy day, the Feast of St. Francis, as well as meet adoptable animals and enjoy some refreshments. The event is located at the Delaware County SPCA at 555 Sandy Bank Road, Media. 610/566-1370.

Newlin Grist Mill Fall Festival: One October Saturday a year, the Newlin Grist Mill welcomes everyone including leashed doggies to its grounds for a fun fall festival. Here, you and poochie can enjoy colonial paper-making demonstrations, cooking and craft events, live music, artisan stands, and rides for the kiddies. The best part is that it's all free! 610/459-2359; www.newlingristmill.org.

Festival of Lights: From December through early January, Rose Tree Park invites you and your pup out to get in the holiday spirit and see its Festival of Lights. The display features multicolored lights draped throughout the park's trees in different wintry scenes. Some scenes include America's favorite pooch, Snoopy, Frosty the Snowman, and Santa and his reindeer. 1671 N. Providence Rd., Media; 610/565-7410.

it's not easy to find. Lucky for you, Nellie sniffed around and found the right way to access the park.

The main entrance is not the golfing area, where the sign to the park is located. In fact, you can't get to the picnicking area or the trail from that section. You have to pass the golf course and drive around the back side of the park and park your car at a picnic grove. It's horribly marked and there are no maps to make it easier. Once you arrive you can have a picnic or walk around the shaded area.

From Route 1 take 322 East past the golf course. Take a sharp right on Garnet Mine Road. Parking is about a quarter-mile down on the right. Hours are 8 A.M.–sunset. 610/891-4663 or 610/891-4664.

PLACES TO EAT

Big Cheese Pizza: This family-owned pizza joint serves a selection of delicious pizzas, strombolis, pasta, hoagies, salads, calzones, and steaks. The best part is there's outdoor seating for you and your dog, or you can take your Italian treat home with you. 331 Wilmington, West Chester Pk., Suite 8, Glen Mills; 610/358-0800.

Boxcar Café Inc: If you or your furry companion love pancakes, especially those "as big as your head" (the eatery's tagline), you'll want to stop at the friendly, family-owned Boxcar Café and enjoy them outdoors together. They specialize in pancakes but offer lots of other breakfast and lunch items. Everything on the menu is made from scratch. Other interesting foods to try are the scrapple fries that are like steak fries but crispier, and the clam chowder. 264 Baltimore Pk., Glen Mills; 610/358-0255.

PLACES TO STAY

Sweetwater Farm B&B: Located on 50 beautiful Brandywine Valley acres with resident horses and goats, this estate includes a 1734 Quaker farmhouse with five pet-friendly cottages. All cottages come equipped with private bathrooms, air conditioning, and cable TV, and some have their own kitchens. No matter what room you stay in at the B&B, you'll have access to the outdoor pool, heated whirlpool, and surrounding hiking trails. Every morning a gourmet breakfast is served at the Manor House. The extra daily charge for dogs is $35. Rates are $100–275. 50 Sweetwater Rd., Glen Mills; 610/459-4711 or 800/SWEETWATER; www.sweetwaterfarmbb.com.

Upland

Upland, a small community of fewer than 3,000 people, is not a dog-lover's paradise, per se, but it does offer a county park. Although the park isn't exactly stellar, it is an option if poochie needs a potty break. The hotels listed below are not in Upland but in Essington, a town about seven miles away that borders the Philadelphia International Airport. The restaurants are in neighboring towns as well.

PARKS, BEACHES, AND RECREATION AREAS

10 Upland Park

(See Delaware County map on page 68)

A former Salvation Army camp for underprivileged children, this park was purchased by the county in 1968. It's too bad, according to Nellie, since it probably was a lot better when it was a camp. Basically, this is an active park with a nice playground, trash cans, and ball fields, but not a lot to offer poochie except a place to squat. There isn't a lot of shade here, nor is there any water source. Plus, the surrounding neighborhood is not the friendliest place to be, especially after sundown. Still, if you're traveling in the area, it's fine for stretching your legs during daylight hours.

Take 476 to Route 1 South to 352 toward Brookhaven. Take a right onto Brookhaven Road, which eventually turns into Bridgewater Road. After you pass the 7-11, you'll soon see the brown county-park sign on the right. The park is located on Sixth Street in Upland Borough. Hours are 8 A.M.–sunset. 610/891-4663 or 610/891-4664.

PLACES TO EAT

Bruster's Ice Cream: If you want sinful and delicious ice cream, come here, but if you or your pup is watching your carbs, then this is still an option as Bruster's has low-carb items on its menu. Still, there's nothing better than the home-baked waffle bowl sundae. The best part of this Bruster's (it's a franchise) is that your doggy can get a Dog Cone of his own with ice cream and a biscuit inside. How doggone thoughtful! There are picnic tables and benches for you and poochie, too. 3630 Concord Rd., Aston; 610/859-7868.

New Station Pizza: You can't go wrong with one of the pizzas or strombolis here; the cheese is top grade and the crust is thick and downright yummy. Although there's no place to sit with your doggy here, they friendly staff will happily deliver to Upland or prepare takeout. 3304 Edgmont Ave., Brookhaven; 610/874-0707.

PLACES TO STAY

Comfort Inn: Staying at this hotel, conveniently located near the Philadelphia Airport, can alleviate the need to park at the airport as daily shuttle service to the airport is available and parking is free. Plus, you'll find a friendly and helpful staff as well as a clean room. The only drawback is that only dogs 25 pounds or less are allowed to stay here for an extra $10 per night. Rates are $75–99. 53 Industrial Hwy., Essington; 610/521-9800.

Red Roof Inn: This is another option if you need to be near the airport and are looking for shuttle service and free parking. However, this hotel is not the cleanest place you'd ever stay. The good news is that dogs up to 75 pounds can stay here for no extra charge. Rates are $80–88. 49 Industrial Hwy., Essington; 610/521-5090.

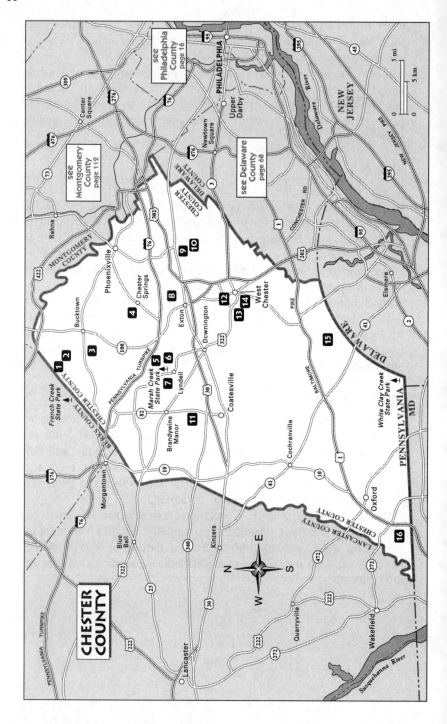

CHESTER COUNTY

see Montgomery County page 112

see Philadelphia County page 16

see Delaware County page 68

French Creek State Park

Marsh Creek State Park

White Clay Creek State Park

PENNSYLVANIA TURNPIKE

BERKS COUNTY / CHESTER COUNTY

MONTGOMERY COUNTY

CHESTER COUNTY / DELAWARE COUNTY

LANCASTER COUNTY / CHESTER COUNTY

PENNSYLVANIA / MD

DELAWARE

NEW JERSEY

PHILADELPHIA

Delaware River

Susquehanna River

NEW JERSEY PIKE

CONCHESTER RD

BALTIMORE PIKE

Rahns
Center Square
Bucktown
Phoenixville
Chester Springs
Exton
Downingtown
West Chester
Upper Darby
Newtown Square
Elsmere
Lyndell
Coatesville
Brandywine Manor
Morgantown
Cochranville
Oxford
Blue Ball
Kinzers
Quarryville
Wakefield
Lancaster

5 mi
5 km

CHAPTER 3

Chester County

Dogs are not our whole lives, but they make our lives whole.

Roger Caras

Rolling hills, crackling creeks and rivers, and stone farmhouses adorn the rural Chester County landscape, the heart of the Brandywine Valley. It's gorgeous, peaceful, and pristine. Visiting with your pup may make her think she's gone to doggy heaven as the open spaces beckon her to run.

But not all Chester County is lush countryside equipped with great open spaces; a good part of it is suburbanized and growing at a rapid pace. Many strip malls and mega stores exist here just like in every other part of the country. Yet its quaint suburban towns like Kennett Square and West Chester are solid reminders of the county's uniqueness.

Chester County, founded in 1682, is one of William Penn's original three counties. Named after Cheshire, England, ironically, this county prides itself

PICK OF THE LITTER—CHESTER COUNTY

BEST PARK
Stroud Preserve, West Chester (page 105)

BEST PLACE TO EAT
Four Dogs Tavern, West Chester (page 106)

BEST COMMUNITY GROUP
Chester County Canine Hiking Club (page 93)

BEST DIVERSION
Linda's Dog Pool, Spring City (page 93)

BEST TOWN
West Chester (page 103)

on playing a major part in the founding of our nation, including roles in the Battle of Brandywine, the Paoli Massacre, and the Valley Forge encampment.

It's known not just as mushroom country, being home to Kennett Square, "the mushroom capital of the world," but also as horse country, as horse farms dominate the rural areas. Plus, it's home to the annual spring Devon Horse Show, the nation's oldest and largest multibreed horse competition.

This dynamic county also boasts several vineyards and wineries—some of which even let you bring your pup.

The hard part to fathom is that Chester County is only 30 miles from Philadelphia.

Equally difficult to understand is that, despite all the open space, sadly, as a whole, Chester County is not a dog and dog lover's paradise. Although public parks allow dogs on a leash, there are no specific off-leash dog parks in the county (read: no four-paw destinations). Nor is there a variety of eating establishments that allow dogs, even though many have outside seating.

But there are talks in West Goshen of starting a dog park as part of a new municipal park near Pottstown Pike and Greenhill Road. And the county does have lots of dog-friendly activities, especially the Chester County Canine Hiking Club, an informal group that organizes hikes to give pups the opportunity to socialize. The perpetual optimist, Nellie seems to be just as happy with that aspect.

But if you can visit no other location in the county, make it West Chester. This incredibly charming and friendly town has lots of yummy spots to eat with poochie and some amazing parks nearby.

Elverson

Many of the most scenic areas with rolling hills and farmland in Chester County are in Elverson. It's highly rustic and undeveloped with fantastic parks making it a perfect place to visit with your dog. While the recreation areas are in this borough, the featured places to stay are in nearby Pottstown and St. Peter's.

PARKS, BEACHES, AND RECREATION AREAS

1 French Creek State Park

🐾🐾🐾 (See Chester County map on page 86)

Driving here might make you feel like you're headed toward the earth's edge as civilization seems to get farther and farther behind you. That's not to say it's not lovely. On your travels, you'll see several manicured farms and old farmhouses with huge front porches that will compel you and your pup to kick back and sip some lemonade with the locals. The area is rural and desolate, which makes it an ideal place for a giant park like French Creek State Park, which encompasses 7,475 acres of land and 201 campsites. While your dog isn't allowed to camp in the cabins at the state park, he is allowed to stay at pet-designated campsites and visit the day-use areas, where you'll find more than 30 miles of well-marked trails to conquer, picnic areas, a playground, and two lakes for boating and fishing. Nellie loves to walk the trails here, but if she had her way, she'd be swimming in the lakes with the geese, possibly trying to retrieve a few. Sadly, swimming is not an option for pups or their human companions.

Take Pennsylvania Turnpike to the Downingtown exit. Take Route 100 North to Conestoga Road (401 West) toward Elverson. Follow 401 West to 345 North until it leads to the park entrance. Hours are 8 A.M.–sunset. 843 Park Rd., Elverson; 610/582-9680; www.dcnr.state.pa.us/stateparks/parks/frenchcreek.

2 Hopewell Furnace

🐾🐾🐾 (See Chester County map on page 86)

Adjacent to French Creek State Park and situated on more than 800 acres of its own land, Hopewell Furnace is a National Historic Site. This remarkably preserved "iron plantation" is a predecessor of today's iron and steel industries. Between 1771 and 1883, charcoal-fueled iron furnaces produced iron goods ranging from cannon and shot to stoves and pots.

DOG-EAR YOUR CALENDAR

Chester County Evenings of Music: What could be better than spending a summer evening outside enjoying live music with your pup? Featuring a wide range of musicians from folk to jazz to country rock, the annual Evenings of Music concert series takes place May–September in Hibernia and Warwick County Parks and Springton Manor Farm. A total of 11 free concerts are set against a backdrop of historic mansions, open fields, and a ceiling of stars on a warm summer night. Blankets and lawn chairs are encouraged, and picnic suppers are welcome. The only restriction is that dogs must be on leashes. 610/344-6415; www.chesco.org/ccparks.

Turks Head Music Festival: For the past 20 or more years, the ever-popular Turks Head Music Festival takes place the third Sunday in July in Everhart Park in West Chester borough. Featuring cool live music, tons of food, crafts, and family entertainment, it's a blast for the whole family, including, of course, the furry members. All that's required is a leash for your pup. 610/436-9010; www.west-chester.com.

Malvern Movies: You and your leashed pup are welcome to join the community for family movies in Burke Park after dark on Thursdays July–August. The park is located between Warren Avenue, Channing Avenue, and Roberts Lane. 610/644-2602; manager@malvern.org.

While your pup is not allowed in any of the buildings, she is welcome to peruse the grounds, footpaths, dirt roads, fields, and woods on a leash and soak in some history from afar. You can visit the website for a virtual tour before you embark on your personal journey.

Take Pennsylvania Turnpike west to the Downingtown exit. Take Route 100 North for about nine miles, turn left onto Route 23 West for about seven miles, then turn right onto Route 345 North. The park will be on your left after about four miles. Hours are 9 A.M.–5 P.M. The entrance fee is $4 for adults, free for children under age 17. 2 Mark Bird Ln., Elverson; 620/582-8773; www.nps.gov/hofu.

🐾 Warwick County Park

🐾🐾🐾 (See Chester County map on page 86)

About seven miles southeast of French Creek State Park, located in the hills of Knauertown, you'll find this impressive county park. It's got many of the same amenities as French Creek, but on a much smaller scale. This 455-acre park includes two miles of the French Creek running through it and offers several miles of hiking trails. One of them, Horse-Shoe Trail, is a 130-mile trail that stretches from Valley Forge National Park to the Appalachian Trail, north of Harrisburg. It's marked with yellow blazes. At Warwick County Park you'll always see an active doggy or two who like to hit the trails. Dogs have to be on a leash but they love it anyway. What's not to love? It's got hills, water, open spaces, and tons of shade, especially along the trails. Poop bags are available as well as trash cans. You and your family will appreciate the picnic tables, pavilion, soda machines, restrooms, and new playground.

For more information on Horse-Shoe Trail, contact the Horse-Shoe Trail Club, Inc., P.O. Box 182, Birchrunville, PA 19421-0182.

From Route 100 North, take a left heading west on Route 23. Drive about four miles and take a left on County Park Road. You'll see the entrance to the park up on the left. Hours are 8 A.M.–sunset. 382 County Park Rd., Pottstown; 610/469-1916.

PLACES TO EAT

Sonny's Pizza & Pasta House: Although there's no outdoor seating here, Nellie is just as happy eating lasagna to go from this local favorite. Everything from pizza to pasta and salads, sandwiches, strombolis, and hoagies is yours for takeout. 18 W. Main St., Elverson; 610/286-7376.

PLACES TO STAY

Comfort Inn: An award-winning hotel that's friendly and clean, the Comfort Inn makes you and Fido feel like it's name says: comfy. One of the best parts, according to Nellie, is the make-your-own waffle station offered during the deluxe continental breakfast. Although she can't actually design her own waffle, or eat them at the restaurant, she's happy as heck that everyone else can...well, sort of. Plus, there's no extra charge for your pet, just a $50 refundable deposit, and no weight restrictions. The only requirement is to keep your doggy crated while in the room and not alone for long periods of time. Rates are $85. 99 Robinson St., Pottstown; 610/326-5000.

Days Inn: Inexpensive with few frills, the Days Inn is a good option for the budget-conscious dog-loving traveler. If your pup is a fan of Animal Planet, you'll both be happy to know that cable with HBO is free. A free continental breakfast is provided too. And while there is no weight limit on your pooch, there is an extra $10 per night per pet fee. Rates are $44–69. 29 High St., Pottstown; 610/970-1101.

Econo Lodge: A bit on the bare bones side of hotel options, it is less expensive than the alternatives. Your pup is able to stay with you for an extra $10 per night, no weight restrictions. The only requirements are that your pup be caged when you're not in the room, and out of the room while housekeeping is cleaning. Complimentary continental breakfast is included, too. Rates are $49. 387 Ben Franklin Hwy., Douglassville; 610/385-3016.

French Creek State Park Campsites: At French Creek State Park your pup is not allowed to stay in any cabins but is welcome to stay in the pet-friendly campsites known as Loop B, 1–11, and Loop D, 1, 43, 45, and 47–51. Rates are $10–19. French Creek State Park, 843 Park Rd., Elverson; 610/582-9680; frenchcreeksp@state.pa.us; www.dcnr.state.pa.us/stateparks/parks/frenchcreek.

Motel 6 Pottstown: Another inexpensive option that doesn't charge pet fees or impose any weight restrictions, is Motel 6. The only stipulation is letting the front desk know that your well-behaved pup is accompanying you. While this new, clean facility doesn't offer much in the way of amenities, it does have free cable with HBO. Rates are $50–60. SR 100 at Shoemaker Road, 78 Robinson St., Pottstown; 610/819-1288.

Warwick Woods Campground: Your doggy is welcome to camp here for no additional charge at one of the more than 200 large campsites spread out over 100 acres. Each site has a picnic table and fire ring. Water and electric and sewer hookups are also available. Plus, the campground has a pond, hiking trails, and an outdoor pool for humans. Hosted events include everything from crafts for kids to picnics and bingo. Although there are cabins and trailers for rent here, dogs aren't allowed in them. Rates are $29–41. P.O. Box 280, St. Peters, PA 19470; 610/286-9655.

Phoenixville

Phoenixville is known for its old-fashioned charm with many covered bridges in the area as well as its 19th-century-looking downtown accented by elaborately carved cornices and wrought-iron railings. This homey feel could be why there are a couple of dog-friendly B&Bs here. Although there are no featured restaurants or parks here, Valley Forge National Historical Park is just three miles away, across the Montgomery County border.

PLACES TO STAY

The Manor House: This warm and inviting English Tudor B&B on a quiet, tree-lined street will happily accommodate you and your pooch for no additional fees or restrictions on your pup's size. A full breakfast is served daily. Rates are $55–80. 210 Virginia Ave., Phoenixville; 610/983-9867.

Morningstar Bed and Breakfast: If you have what's considered a well-behaved "hair dog" rather than a fur dog, meaning curly coated poodles and the like, you're welcome to stay at this historic 1820s home for no extra charge and no weight restrictions. The restrictions on fur dogs are due to the allergens on their coats. Rates are $105. 610 Valley Forge Rd., Phoenixville; 610/935-7473 or 866/261-3289; www.morningstarbandb.net.

DIVERSIONS

Chester County Canine Hiking Club: About three years ago, a local dog enthusiast and professional pooper-scooper, Miriam Hughes (a.k.a. Miss Poop), and her dog-loving friends, started this canine hiking club as a way to bring people and their dogs together in Chester County. The hikes are sporadic throughout the year (sometimes monthly, sometimes not), never last more than 1.5 hours, are low-intensity, and usually take place in large preserves or parks. All ages and abilities of humans and dogs are welcome. The best aspects about the hikes are that dogs can walk, swim, or run alongside their own canine companions, and treats are served afterward. Plus, they're free. Woof! 610/933-1506; misspoop@comcast.net.

Linda's Dog Pool: No doubt your dog will make a splash and flip if you take him to this one-of-a-kind dog pool. Whether your pup has arthritis and needs swimming therapy, or he's a young sprightly pup and simply needs to expend some energy, he'll have the time of his life here. The Dog Pool is actually two heated, indoor lap pools that are open 365 days a year. Dogs jump in and out of the pool and play rousing games of "monkey [dog] in the middle." You must sign a waiver before your first visit, and it's best to call ahead before arriving the first time. There's a $10 fee per visit. Hours are 8 A.M.–8 P.M. 723 Saylors Mill Rd., Spring City; 610/495-7247.

Chester Springs

Located in northern Chester County, Chester Springs is a small town that neighbors some very developed areas but holds its own when it comes to history and charm. Here you and your pup can enjoy some of its history together, stay overnight, and grab a bite to eat, too.

PARKS, BEACHES, AND RECREATION AREAS

🖪 Historic Yellow Springs

🐾🐾🐾 ◀▶ (See Chester County map on page 86)

If you and poochie are looking for a little enlightenment with your hike, look no further than Historic Yellow Springs, an inviting 145-acre historic village that dates back 275 years. This "living museum" village invites you and your pup to explore the grounds together and learn about its fascinating Revolutionary War history as well as involvement in the Civil War. If your dog is anything like Nellie, she will delight in the sights, sounds, and smells of the

DIVERSIONS

Fifi loves to gobble grapes and you love to sip shiraz, so why not visit a few local establishments that farm the delicious fruit?

Eagle Crest Vineyard: You and your pup are invited to visit this unique winery together. Here, you'll find not just a large vineyard to explore, but also a farm, a petting zoo, and a wildlife sanctuary. You'll also be able to get up close to a bunch of alpacas, fluffy cousins of the llama. An animal rescue is also located on the grounds of this huge estate that strives to be an escape from day-to-day life and a place to appreciate nature. The staff here is in the process of making their first wine, which may not be ready yet for sale, but may be for sampling. 1853 Eagle Farms Rd., Chester Springs; 610/458-1595; laura.soto@eaglescrestvineyard .com; www.eaglescrestvineyard.com.

Folly Hill Vineyards: This four-acre vineyard welcomes well-behaved pups to peruse the grounds with you. If you have the opportunity, stop at the wine shop and tasting room—it's such a treat. But since there is a very busy road next to the entrance of Folly Hill Vineyards, dogs need to be supervised. They love dogs here and welcome them as long as they're under a watchful eye. 700 Folly Hill Rd., Kennett Square; 601/388-5895; sherrysowers700@comcast.net.

Kreutz Creek Winery, Inc.: On weekends 11 A.M.–6 P.M., this award-winning winery welcomes you and your pup to check out the eight acres of vineyards and even sample the hand-crafted regional wines. All that's required for the fun is a leash for your pup and your own poop bags. 553 S. Guernsey Rd., West Grove; 610/869-4412; www.kreutzcreekvineyards.com.

Oriental Bog Garden, featuring ponds and a footbridge resembling a dragonfly, or the sulphur spring located in the Jenny Lind Spring House.

Plus, there are miles of great hiking trails that pass through meadows and woodlands. Stop by the lobby of the Lincoln Building to pick up a self-guided tour map or purchase a trail booklet and audio tour.

From Route 202 South, take the Route 401/Frazier Exit and turn right onto Route 401 West. Continue for about six miles to Route 113. Turn right onto 113 North and follow through the village of Chester Springs. Take a left on Pikeland Road and then a left on Art School Road. Follow to the village for about a half-mile. Hours are sunrise–sunset. 1685 Art School Rd., Chester Springs; 610/827-7414.

PLACES TO EAT

The America Bar & Grill: Definitely not the typical generic suburban eatery, this charming bar and grill has one of the most extensive and interesting menus around, offering everything from the usual soup, sandwiches, and pastas to Asian-inspired salmon, meatloaf, and filet mignon. The friendly staff warmly welcomed Nellie and me to the patio seating. Shops at Lionville Station, Route 113, Chester Springs; 610/280-0800.

PLACES TO STAY

Inn at Chester Springs: Spending time with your pup at this full-service hotel that provides complimentary bottled water and a newspaper, as well as amenities like an indoor and outdoor pool, will definitely be a treat. There's no weight restriction on your pup, but there is a one-time fee of $50. While you can check in and out with your dog in the lobby, the hotel asks that you use another designated entrance when taking your pup out for potty breaks. Rates are $129. 815 N. Pottstown Pk., Exton; 610/363-1100.

Downingtown and Exton

Dating back to 1716, Downingtown was first known as Milltown as it was the last milling village on the edge of the unsettled western frontier. In 1958, it served as the site of the science fiction movie classic *The Blob.* Today Downingtown and nearby Exton are a developed suburban area that offers many conveniences and recreational escapes for you and poochie.

PARKS, BEACHES, AND RECREATION AREAS

🟥 Marsh Creek State Park

🐾🐾🐾 (See Chester County map on page 86)

Lucky duckies, is all Nellie and I could collectively think while watching the ducks float by on the 535-acre lake in this gorgeous park. Sure, the lake is manmade, but who cares? A view of the lake, the park, and its surrounding countryside will likely put you and your pup at peace. Marsh Creek State Park is a popular spot to take your doggy on leash, especially during the summertime. You and puppers can gaze at a variety of canoes, rowboats, and sailboats glide across the lake. While your dog can't swim here, and neither can you, he can accompany you to the water's edge and lap up a drink or soak his toes. Hiking trails are available to check out with your pup, and when you're tired, you two can take a break and have a picnic. There's also a playground and restrooms.

Take Route 100 North and go through the town of Eagle, following signs directing to the park. Take a left when you see the park sign and continue until the road ends at the park. Hours are 8 A.M.–sunset. 675 Park Rd., Downing-town; 610/458-5119.

6 Robert G. Struble Hiking and Biking Trail

🐾🐾 (See Chester County map on page 86)

This trail is a 2.6-mile stretch of pathway that connects Downingtown to Marsh Creek State Park. It's nice for walking your pooch because it's mostly paved, gen-

DIVERSIONS

Veterinary Natural Pharmacy: You know the drill. Rex hears the pill jar and runs for the hills. Or he pretends to take his medicine, only to spit it out when you're not looking. Have no fear: Lionville Natural Pharmacy and Health Food Store is here. The veterinary specialists compound a variety of dosage forms to make giving meds to your pup easier (e.g., chewable treats, flavored liquids, and transdermal creams). More problematic doggy behavior can be helped by the staff's certified Bach flower practitioner, who works with homeopathically prepared plant- and flower-based essences used to promote emotional well-being in both humans and animals. 309 Gordon Dr., Lionville; 610/363-7474; info@lionrx.com; www.lionrx.com.

Canine Care and Community Center: You know you want to spend as much time with your pooch as possible, but it can be difficult when the weather won't cooperate. One of the first facilities of its kind, slated to open in the spring of 2005, will serve as a one-stop-shop to dog and person happiness. Here, you'll be able to drink coffee and hang out with your pooch, use the Internet, participate in a dog playgroup, watch your pooch frolic in the swimming pool, and sign up for obedience training, freestyle dancing, and rally, flyball, agility, and tracking training. A veterinarian will be on site, as well as a dog-friendly retail section. This giant undertaking will be located in Malvern. The leaders of this center are also the renowned trainers of What a Good Dog training school in Villanova. 610/688-2400.

Veterinary Acupuncture: Of course, your *chi* (or energy) can get out of whack. Well, so can Fido's. When this happens you might consider acupuncture to help restore him to good health. Dr. Leah L. Whipple, VMD, CVA, is a certified veterinary acupuncturist who for years has been treating dogs afflicted with everything from orthopedic problems to gastrointestinal issues. Rates are $95 for initial consult and $50–60 for weekly treatments that typically last six to eight weeks. Berwyn Veterinary Center, 1058 Lancaster Ave., Berwyn; 610/640-9188.

erally flat, and provides plenty of shade and scenery since it skirts Brandywine Creek. You'll often pass other pups and their people, fishermen, and beautiful lush landscape and trees. Picnic areas are scattered throughout, and poop bags are available at various locations along the trail. The trail is a work in progress that will eventually span 16 miles to Honey Brook Borough.

It is located near the intersections of US 30 and 282 on Norwood Road in Downingtown; parking is available. Hours are sunrise–sunset. Questions about the park should be directed c/o Springton Manor Farm, 860 Springton Rd., Glenmoore, PA 19343; 610/942-2450 or 610/344-6415.

7 Springton Manor Farm

🐾🐾🐾 (See Chester County map on page 86)

If you're looking for a quiet spot to take your pup, with some outstanding landscape featuring friendly farm animals, then by all means make the trek to Springton Manor Farm, about five miles from Downingtown. Here you and poochie can walk the grounds of this meticulously cared for 300-acre farm, part of a William Penn manor that's been in agricultural use since the early 1700s. Being nestled among the hills and woodlands of Glenmoore gives the farm true tranquility. You and your doggy will love it. On the flip side, hopefully your pup isn't afraid of farm animals because you'll likely hear the soft bleating of the sheep the minute you step outside of the car. You can view the animals from afar, but up-close animal visiting is off limits to doggies. In addition to the farm, you two might want to check out the lake with picnic areas, and about six miles of marked hiking trails that surround the entire area.

From Downingtown take Route 100 South. Turn right onto Route 113 South and follow to Route 30 Bypass. Pick up Route 30 Bypass West exiting onto Route 322 West. Follow Route 322 West through Guthriesville. Take a soft right onto Springton Road at the traffic light. Cross Highspire Road and continue about a half-mile to the park entrance on the right. Hours are 8 A.M.–sunset. 860 Springton Rd., Glenmoore; 610/942-2450; www.chesco.org/ccparks.

8 Chester Valley Trail

🐾 (See Chester County map on page 86)

While the rating for this trail isn't great, it doesn't mean the future of this trail isn't promising. The Chester Valley Trail is actually a work in progress. Apparently the currently opened 1.4-mile trail will grow to stretch from Exton to the Montgomery County line in Norristown. It will follow a now-abandoned railroad line and will eventually connect Chester County's Struble Trail in Exton with Montgomery County's Schuylkill River Trail in Norristown.

However, as of press time it's simply a straight trail with no shade, nor is there much scenery except for the Church Farm School's backside and some telephone wires. Plus, it gets quite hot here in the summertime. But check back in a couple of years when the rest of the plans are completed, and it might be the local outdoor hot spot. The expected completion date is fall 2007.

From Downingtown follow Route 100 South to Swedesford Road. Go left on Swedesford Road approximately 2.75 miles to Phoenixville Pike. Go left on Phoenixville Pike and travel about a quarter-mile to trailhead parking at Battle of the Clouds Township Park on the right. Hours are sunrise–sunset. Chester County Parks Development, Government Services Center; 601 Westtown Road, Suite 160, West Chester; 610/344-6415.

PLACES TO EAT

Rita's Water Ice: With locations throughout the Philadelphia area, Rita's serves exceptionally good water ice and gelato. When we're visiting friends in Downingtown, Nellie and I like to stop at this Rita's, and, if we're lucky enough to score some bench space, eat here. Otherwise, it's to go. 43 Yellowwood Dr., Downingtown; 610/380-1101.

Victory Brewing Company: Sadly, this fun, moderately priced eatery does not have outdoor seating, or you and your pup would be more than welcome here. But Victory does have takeout that features pizzas, sandwiches, and salads. Try the Heartland or Napa Valley pizzas and you'll feel like you just scored a victory yourself. 420 Acorn Ln., Downingtown; 610/873-0881; www.victorybeer.com.

PLACES TO STAY

Hampton Inn: Nellie couldn't have been more relieved to hear that this smart hotel doesn't have a weight limit for poochies, nor does it charge any extra fees to have your furry traveling companion with you. The only stipulation is that you don't leave your pup in the room alone unless she's crated. Hampton Inn provides rooms that are quiet and comfy, as well as a complimentary breakfast and use of an outdoor pool in the summertime. Rates are $79–99. 4 N. Pottstown Pk., Exton; 610/363-5555.

Holiday Inn Express: Reasonably priced rooms that are clean and comfy are available at the Holiday Inn Express. The best part is there's no weight limit for your pooch and a one-time nonrefundable pet fee of only $25. Your pup will enjoy his stay with you here, but the rules don't allow him to be left alone for significant chunks of time. Niceties for you include an outdoor pool and daily complimentary breakfast. Rates are $79–116. 120 N. Pottstown Pk., Exton; 610/524-9000.

Residence Inn by Marriott: Whether you're staying a day or a month, Residence Inn rooms come equipped with a kitchen, appliances, and utensils to make your stay more like home. Also available are a hot breakfast buffet, grocery shopping service, and an indoor pool. Your pup weighing less than 50 pounds is welcome to stay with you for a $25–200 nonrefundable fee depending on the length of stay. The staff here enjoys dogs and has been known to spoil resident pups with special treats from time to time. Rates are $90–160. 10 N. Pottstown Pk., Exton; 610/594-9705.

Malvern

Located along Philadelphia's Main Line, Malvern is a small yet thriving community with a busy main street. No, the parks aren't the best for dogs seeing as how there's only three acres of parkland in the borough, but Valley Forge National Historical Park in Montgomery County is only a few miles from Malvern out Route 202. At least there are several dog-friendly hotels in this locale.

PARKS, BEACHES, AND RECREATION AREAS

9 Burke Park

😸 (See Chester County map on page 86)

Since only about 3,000 people live in the borough of Malvern, this little one-acre town park that welcome dogs on a leash serves a purpose. Here, you'll find walking paths, a few shade trees, and a gazebo that hosts outdoor concerts in the summertime. It is nicely landscaped and it has trash cans, as well as a small playground area. But, seriously, that's about it.

From Route 202 take 252 south to Paoli. Follow that to Route 30 East. Get off Route 30 East after you pass a Wendy's and see a side street on the left named King Street. Take a soft left onto that. Follow it to the city center. Take a left turn on Warren Avenue. You'll see the park up on your left at Roberts Avenue. Park along Roberts Avenue. Hours are sunrise–sunset. www.malvern.org.

10 Horace J. Quann Memorial Park

🔥 (See Chester County map on page 86)

It really pains Nellie to give a park a hydrant rating, but she just had to do it. This park, although it's apparently the most frequently used in Malvern, doesn't offer much for dogs except those who can shoot hoops like Air Bud. The park features a basketball court, a ball field with a portable toilet, and a couple of trashcans, and that's it. Dogs could possibly run on the ball field when not in use, but it's not totally fenced so we wouldn't recommend it.

From Route 202 take 252 south to Paoli. Follow that to Route 30 East. Get off Route 30 East after you pass a Wendy's and see a side street on the left named King Street. Take a soft left onto that. Follow it to the city center. Take a left turn on Warren Avenue. Follow it until you see First Avenue and the park on your right. Park along First Avenue. Hours are sunrise–sunset. www.malvern.org.

PLACES TO EAT

Berwyn Coffee Company: Serving delicious coffees as well as some of the tastiest salads and sandwiches around, the Berwyn Coffee Company welcomes you and your pup at its outside tables. Try the scrumptious turkey wrap. 720 Lancaster Ave., Berwyn; 610/640-4545; www.theberwyncoffeecompany.com.

THINK GLOBALLY, BARK LOCALLY

Easter Bunny Fun: Every spring, the Easter Bunny is ready and willing (amazingly) to have pups sit on his lap and bark cheese. Have your pet's picture taken with the Easter Bunny for a $5 donation to whatever rescue is sponsoring the event, held at Petco in Malvern. 181 Lancaster Ave. (Route 30), Malvern; 610/644-9959.

Walk for Paws: For a pawticularly fun way to spend a Sunday with your dog and benefit our fellow furry friends, the annual Walk for Paws & Spring Music Festival takes place the first Sunday in May, rain or shine. The event, which spans a couple of miles (you can walk or just hang out), features live entertainment and scads of food vendors. Prizes are awarded for the largest dog, smallest dog, most precious puppy, owner/pet look-alikes, best tailwagger, best singing dog, best dressed, and best dog trick. Registration begins at 9 A.M. at the Brandywine Valley Association's Myrick Conservation Center, 1760 Unionville-Wawaset Road (Route 842), West Chester. The registration fee is $20 for adults and $8 for children over 5, free for kids 5 and under. All proceeds benefit the Chester County SPCA. To be in the walk, dogs must wear I.D., be current on vaccines, be on a leash at all times, and be at least six months old. Poop bags will be provided for clean up. 610/692-6113, ext. 222.

Benefit Horse Show: Chester County is horse country and, lucky for homeless animals, and the annual Benefit Horse Show raises money for their cause. The show welcomes you and your leashed doggy to join in on the fun. The Chester County Society for the Prevention of Cruelty to Animals usually holds the event the third Sunday in September 8 A.M.–dusk at the Radnor Hunt Pony Club, Providence Road, Malvern. 610/692-6113, ext. 222.

Photos with Santa: Of course, if the Easter Bunny welcomes pups for photo ops, Santa is in on it, too. That jolly ol' elf is usually on hand one December Saturday at PetsMart. Whatever amount is charged (usually $5) is donated to the sponsoring rescue group. 1010 East Lancaster Ave., Downingtown; 610/518-0250.

Caffé Craze: This little coffee shop just loves four-legged customers at its outdoor seating and will happily give your pup some water while serving you hot, delicious coffee and breakfast breads. 13 W. King St., Malvern; 610/644-0829.

Rita's Water Ice: From straight Italian water ice to gelato, Rita's serves up some of the best in the area. You can never go wrong with the lemon, but Nellie seems to enjoy mango most of all. Rita's also provides water for doggies while you sit outside and enjoy your treats together. 430 Lancaster Pk., Malvern; 610/644-2920.

PLACES TO STAY

Homestead Studio Suites Malvern: A nice comfy room with a kitchen, work and bedroom area, and an on-site fitness club are what this "homestead" provides. Nellie was happy to learn there was no weight restriction for pups, but there is an extra charge of $25–75 per night. Management assures that every room is disinfected after each guest with a pet stays here. Rates are $120–135. 8 E. Swedesford Rd., Malvern; 610/695-9200.

Homewood Suites By Hilton: This place is just as homey as its neighboring hotel listed above. It features a friendly staff, an indoor pool, and a complimentary breakfast served every day. No weight limit for dogs is stipulated, but there is a pet charge of between $25–150 depending on how long you stay. Rates are $90–160. 12 E. Swedesford Rd., Malvern; 610/296-3500.

Residence Inn Berwyn: Newly renovated and only 2.5 miles from Valley Forge National Park (see the Montgomery County chapter for park info), the Residence Inn gives you and up to three dogs (no weight limits) a home away from home. Some suites even come with fireplaces, but all have access to the outdoor heated pool and picnic facilities. There is a $150 nonrefundable pet fee regardless of length of stay. Rates are $89–189. 600 Swedesford Rd., Berwyn; 610/640-9494.

Staybridge Suites: Another great suite alternative in Malvern, the Staybridge offers clean, quiet rooms, a very professional staff, and a complimentary breakfast served every day. If you're here during the summertime, you're in luck because the outdoor pool will be open. Dogs are welcome at the hotel but a waiver must be signed and a $75 nonrefundable fee paid. Rates are $99–209. 20 Morehall Rd., Malvern; 610/296-4343.

Coatesville

While Coatesville itself isn't exactly a tail-wagging travel destination, there are some great spots to camp with poochie and its Hibernia County Park is downright tranquil.

PARKS, BEACHES, AND RECREATION AREAS

11 Hibernia County Park

🐾🐾🐾 (See Chester County map on page 86)

Although Chester County may not be a bastion of dog freedom, it boasts some beautiful county parks, like Hibernia. This 800-acre park has plenty of shade as much of it is woodlands, as well as huge open meadows that beg for your pup to frolic leash-free. And while we do see dogs off leash here, it's not advised. Hibernia includes miles of trails, the west branch of Brandywine Creek, a children's pond, and a 90-acre reservoir available for boating (but not swimming, sadly). Plus, there are restrooms, pavilions, and even an amphitheater that hosts summer concerts and events.

From Downingtown take Route 100 South to Route 113 South. Then take the Route 30 Bypass West to Route 82 North. Proceed two miles to Cedar Knoll Road at the crest of the hill. Turn left on Cedar Knoll Road and follow the park signs. Hours are 8 A.M.–sunset. 1 Park Rd., Wagontown; 610/383-3812.

PLACES TO EAT

Dairy Queen: Who doesn't love good ol' fashioned soft serve? Nellie prefers it over scoopable ice cream any day, but can't understand why it's often left on her nose. After a long, hot day at the park, you and poochie will feel so much cooler after ordering some of the frosty stuff either dipped or not. If you're really hungry, this joint also serves a burgers and dogs (you know the kind). Picnic area seating is available. 1620 E. Lincoln Highway, Coatesville; 610/384-2761.

PLACES TO STAY

Beechwood Campground: With more than 300 utility campsites, an open pavilion, ample shade, a recreation hall, an outdoor pool, a playground, and hayrides every Saturday night, Beechwood is a happening place to camp. While your pup is welcome to stay with you, he must be kept on a leash at all times. Rates are $22–32. 105 Beechwood Dr., Coatesville; 610/384-1457; beachwoodc@aol.com; www.beachwoodcampground.com.

Berry Patch Campground: Dogs are always welcome at this family-owned campground, as long as they're relatively quiet and on a leash. All sorts of activities are planned throughout the May–September season. Plus, there's a pool and a fishing pond. Rates are $20–36. P.O. Box 370, Honey Brook, PA 19344; 610/273-3720; www.berrypatchcampground.com.

Hibernia Campground: Considered "primitive" with no electric or water hookups, Hibernia Campground welcomes you and your pup to stay at the tent and trailer campsites in the park featured earlier in this chaper, but only

on weekends. Rates are $10 for campsite or small RV space. 1 Park Rd., Wagontown; 610/383-3812.

Philadelphia/West Chester KOA: Located along the Brandywine River, this KOA is a great spot for fishing or canoeing. Your doggy is welcome to stay at the campsites with you but, unfortunately, not in the cottages or cabins. There is no extra charge for your furry friend. Also there is an outdoor pool and activities for humans are planned throughout the season. Rates are $23–45. 1659 Embreeville Rd., Coatesville; 610/486-0447; campkoa@comcast .net; www.philadelphiakoa.com.

West Chester

They just don't make towns like this anymore. A Mayberry of sorts with a tree-lined main street, West Chester exudes the sugary sweetness of a Norman Rockwell painting. But mix in sophistication and the state's second-largest university, and you have a hip and happening town. Art galleries and upscale eateries abound. The small downtown district is listed on the National Register of Historic Places. Its High Street is a showcase for Greek Revival architecture; within the borough limits, more than 3,000 structures date back to the colonial period. Most importantly, as far as Nellie is concerned, pups are truly a part of life here as you'll see them all over downtown as well as in the parks, enjoying the beautiful scenery with their humans.

DOG-EAR YOUR CALENDAR

Family Fun Day: Looking for a free day of fun for the whole family, including poochie? Then head down to Kennett Square's Anson B. Nixon Park in July for the annual Family Fun Day, featuring a dog jumping contest, pony rides, nature programs, and a reptile show. Jumping dogs must be registered with the appropriate category prior to the contest start (10–10:30 A.M.). All dogs at the fun day must be leashed. The event takes place 10 A.M.–2 P.M. For more information, contact Anson B. Nixon Park, P.O. Box 1121, Kennett Square, PA 19348; kapa@kennett.net.

Chester County Restaurant Festival: This annual event, typically held the third Sunday in September in West Chester, gives you and your leashed furry friend the opportunity to sample the offerings of more than 45 of the county's best restaurants. Plus, there are three stages offering family entertainment, as well as a wine and beer court. 610/436-9010; www.west-chester.com.

Halloween Costume Contest at Four Dogs Tavern: Do you want your dog to have the best Yowl-o-ween ever? Then come to West Chester for the Four Dogs Tavern's annual Halloween party and costume contest, established in 1996. Typically the festivities are held on Halloween unless it falls on a weekend, in which case the event is rescheduled on the closest weekday. Prizes are awarded for a variety of categories, and photos are taken of each entrant. Judging usually runs 5–7 P.M. and takes place at the tavern's outdoor, heated patio. There's no entrance fee, just bring that party animal of yours. 610/692-4367.

West Chester Halloween Parade: Speaking of West Chester and Halloween, the town will be alive with its own parade that apparently isn't just for the kids. Usually held the Thursday before Halloween, here you'll see greyhounds, among other breeds, all decked out in costume along with their costumed people. You see, the Chester County Greyhound group (ChesCo Greyhounds) makes this an annual get-together. You should, too. 610/436-9010; www .west-chester.com.

Old Fashioned Christmas in Historic West Chester: An annual event held the first weekend in December, you and your pup are invited to partake of this Victorian-style holiday celebration—no corsets required, just a leash. The four-day event starting Thursday features more than 40 events ranging from singers to jugglers. But the highlight is the parade held on Friday night with Santa lighting the tree in the center of town. 610/696-4046; info@gwcc.org; www.gwcc.org.

PARKS, BEACHES, AND RECREATION AREAS

12 Everhart Park

🐾🐾 (See Chester County map on page 86)

If you're in downtown West Chester, don't miss the opportunity to stroll through Everhart Park with your leashed doggy. This darling neighborhood square has walking paths and bridges, with a creek running below, a gazebo, and picnic areas and playground equipment. Basically, it's just a friendly, little town park. You'll always catch fun-loving dogs and humans here no matter what time of day you come. Hours are sunrise–sunset.

From Route 3 heading west, take a left on Brandywine Street. The park will be one block down on the right. 100 S. Brandywine St., West Chester; 610/436-9010.

13 Stroud Preserve

🐾🐾🐾 (See Chester County map on page 86)

An excellent escape and just a few minutes' drive from West Chester, Stroud Preserve is a stunningly beautiful, privately owned area open to dog lovers and their dogs. Upon entering you'll meet rolling hills and sprawling fields connecting to mature woodlands. You'll also encounter many a doggy and human traversing the more than 500 acres of fields and trails. Formerly known as Georgia Farm, the owner of the land, Dr. Morris Stroud, bequeathed it to the National Lands Trust in 1990. Because of its farming origins, the area is a mix of once-pastured grassland, farmland, and woodlands that is now a natural wildlife habitat that doubles as a research and educational site. Although this gorgeous preserve clearly stipulates keeping your dog on leash, many a pup have been known to take a leash-free dip in its streams and ponds. Nellie has even done it on occasion, but please use discretion if you unleash your beast.

Heading west out of West Chester, take Route 162 about two miles to Creek Road. Make a left and go a half-mile to the Stroud Preserve entrance on the right. Hours are sunrise–sunset. 464 North Creek Road, West Chester; 610/696-6824.

14 Myrick Conservation Center

🐾🐾🐾 (See Chester County map on page 86)

Your canine companion will think this park, located about six miles west of West Chester, is "pawsome" as it encompasses 314 acres of open fields, trails, streams, and rolling countryside. But as much as poochie would love to run free here, leashes are required. Still, puppers will be just as happy taking a dip in the Brandywine Creek that runs through the park. On your hikes through the park, you may catch other pups off leash in the creeks and trails. Although it's doable, it's not advised especially if there are school children in attendance at one of the many programs that take place at the center, as it serves as an outdoor classroom. (Myrick is also known as the key component of education through the Brandywine Valley Association, the first small watershed association in America.) Hiking here might also bring you and your furry friend across the paths of an assortment of wildlife that includes deer, turkeys, and pheasants, just one more reason to keep the leash on if your pup loves the chase like my gal, Nellie. Poop bags are provided at the entrance; however unpleasant, you must take it with you since there are no trash cans.

In West Chester take West Miner Street, which is one block south of Market Street, and follow West Miner Street (Route 842) out of town. Cross two bridges and after the second bridge, cross the railroad tracks; the center is about one mile beyond the tracks. The offices are on the left and the Browning Barn is on the right. If you pass a big red barn (Northbrook Orchards) you've gone a quarter-mile too far; turn around and go back. Hours are sunrise–sunset. 1760 Unionville-Wawaset Rd., West Chester; 610/793-1090.

PLACES TO EAT

Brew HaHa!: A perfect spot to grab a satisfying and steamy cup of java, a morning pastry, or a sandwich, Brew HaHa! allows you to people watch with poochie along West Chester's main drag. The coffee is divine, especially the Brew HaHa! Latte: a mix of mocha, espresso, raspberry, whipped cream, and chocolate shavings. 9 W. Gay St., West Chester; 610/429-9335; www.brew-haha.com.

Four Dogs Tavern: Is it any wonder that this canine-inspired tavern loves pooches at its patio three seasons a year? Here you and your pup will enjoy ample servings of some of the best city bistro food in a country village inn this side of the Brandywine. Moderately priced and eclectic, the menu offers everything from hot wings to catfish with cheddar cheese grits to fried calamari. Puppers will be pleased with the water and dog biscuits. No matter what you try, this tavern is definitely something for both of you to bark about. 1300 West Strasburg Rd., Rt. 162, West Chester; 610/692-4367.

Iron Hill Brewery: This award-winning brewery offers traditional yet delicious "bar food" as well as sandwiches, wood-oven pizzas, salads, seafood, and steak. If undecided, you can't go wrong with the marinated Mediterranean chicken sandwich served with provolone and roasted garlic mayonnaise on focaccia. You and your doggy are welcome to sit at the outside seating and enjoy your moderately priced meal. 3 W. Gay St., West Chester; 610/738-9600; www.ironhillbrewery.com.

Kildare's: Although the interior of this casual Irish pub really does mimic its Dublin counterparts, Kildare's welcomes you and your pup at its outside seating. The moderately priced menu is Irish-influenced, including both traditional and modern dishes. You might enjoy the likes of Irish stew or boxty (stuffed potato pancake), and if your pup is like my friend she will be equally

DIVERSION

Northbrook Canoe Company: If your pup loves quiet times on the water and so do you, you're both welcome to rent a canoe and glide down the scenic Brandywine River together. As long as your dog is leashed and under control during the trip, there's no problem for him to enjoy the ride, too. He's just not allowed on the private property that parallels the waterway. Depending on how long of a trip you want to take, rates are $30–60 and trips span 1–6 hours. 1810 Beagle Rd., West Chester; 610/793-2279 or 800/898-2279.

pleased with the dog biscuits and water provided by staffers. If the day is brisk, don't forget to leave room for a piping hot cup of Irish coffee. 18-22 W. Gay St., West Chester; 610/431-0770; www.kildarespub.com.

Penn's Table: A cherished greasy spoon, this inexpensive diner is a favorite among students and locals for breakfast on weekends. You and your pup are welcome to chow down omelets and pancakes at its streetside seating along the main drag of Gay Street. But if breakfast food isn't your thing, definitely try the spicy chicken cheesesteak or any one of the tasty burgers. 100 W. Gay St., West Chester; 610/696-0677.

Senora's: Although there's no outdoor seating for you to dine with your furry friend, this authentic, casual Mexican joint does have a takeout option. And the best part is it's priced right. Everything here is good whether it's the enchiladas, burritos, or tacos. But we highly recommend the chorizos and chicken mole. 505 E. Gay St., West Chester; 610/344-4950.

Turk's Head Inn: While it looks like a pub from the outside, the inside of this pricier restaurant is bright and more formal with white tablecloths. You guessed it: Your pup can't eat in that section. But on the lovely outside patio both of you can dine on eclectic American food, including everything from sushi to some game dishes. The service is good and friendly. However, dogs are not overly encouraged here. Please call first to let them know you're bringing your pet. 15 S. High St., West Chester; 610/696-1400.

Vincent's: While it's known as an excellent jazz club, the food and service at Vincent's are equally good. This treasured West Chester establishment has something for everyone on its menu. You and your pup can take in the sights on Gay Street while dining on delicious pastas, seafood, salads, and sandwiches. 10 E. Gay St., West Chester; 610/696-4262; www.vincentsjazz.com.

PLACES TO STAY

Korman Communities Waterview: These furnished garden-style apartments available for short-term stays welcome your pup who's 30 pounds or less for a

DOG-EAR YOUR CALENDAR

Maybe it's because they both have four legs and poop alfresco, but it seems dogs and horses go together, as evidenced by the many Chester County horse events that welcome your pup.

Willowdale: An annual tradition held every Mother's Day, the Willowdale Steeplechase sees jockeys competing for purse money while, if you share your life with a certain bouncy canine, your pup participates in the Jack Russell Terrier Races. In April, the Willowdale Point-to-Point Races (a post-fox-hunting racing tradition) also include Jack Russell Terrier Races. Plus, leashed dogs are more than welcome at Brandywine Polo Club season, Sundays June–September. In addition, a variety of dog agility events are held here throughout the year. Willowdale Steeplechase Office, 101 East Street Rd., Kennett Square; 610/444-1582; director@willowdale.org; www.willowdale.com.

Devon Horse Show and Country Fair: The most renowned horse show in the Philadelphia area, the Devon Horse Show is a century-old tradition. You and your well-behaved, leashed poochie are welcome to watch the horse and pony events on the grounds (but not in the grandstand) at any time over the weeklong run in May. The country fair includes all sorts of carnival-ish food, like hotdogs and cotton candy, as well as kids' rides. The show benefits Bryn Mawr Hospital. General admission is $7 for adults, $3 for kids under 12. P.O. Box 865, Devon, PA 19333; 610/964-0550; dhs@fast.net; www.thedevonhorseshow.com.

nonrefundable fee of $250. The apartments have kitchens, complete linens, and cable TV. Rates are $60–80. 2 Waterview Rd., East Goshen; 610/692-5050.

Microtel Inn & Suites: A great value, the Microtel is a favorite among West Chester visitors traveling with furry family members. No matter how big or small your pup is, he's welcome to stay with you for a $10 per night charge. All rooms have queen-sized beds. Plus, a fitness room and a daily continental breakfast are provided. Rates are $69–84. 500 Willowbrook Ln., West Chester; 610/738-9111.

Kennett Square

An old-fashioned downtown with plenty of character, Kennett Square would be a nice spot to visit with your dog. Sadly, though, no restaurants or shops here allow dogs, and even the Mushroom Festival, which is tons of fun, dis-

Ludwig's Corner Horse Show and Country Fair: For more than 60 years, Ludwig's Corner Horse Show has enchanted Chester County with this event held at the 33-acre Ludwig's Corner show grounds, located in the rolling countryside near Glenmoore. More than 400 horses compete in the show, held over Labor Day weekend. You and your well-behaved, leashed pup are welcome to spectate together. The country fair features entertainment, rides for children, games, yummy food, and distinctive shopping. Plus, for the car enthusiast, antique and classic cars are on display. The show raises funds to preserve open space in the surrounding community. The Ludwig show grounds also host a variety of dog shows throughout the year. 5 Nantmeal Rd., Glenmoore; 610/458-3344; www.ludwigshorseshow.org.

The Laurels at Landhope International Combined Driving Event: Coming to Laurels at Landhope, you won't be surprised to see at least as many dogs as horses. Dogs are encouraged to attend this two-day event (usually the second weekend in September) with their family members. Not something you see every day, you and your pup will be amazed at the skill demonstrated in this world-class international equestrian competition. Combined driving has the added challenge of the carriage attached, rather than just a rider on horseback. At the event, a trade fair sells a variety of equestrian and canine collectibles. The Laurels at Landhope benefits the Brandywine Conservancy, the Cheshire Hunt Conservancy, the Large Animal Protection Society, and the University of Pennsylvania New Bolton Center. P.O. Box 587, Unionville, PA 19375; 610/486-6484; laurelslandhope@aol.com; www.laurelscde.org.

courages dogs. But this affluent town is included here because it's a vital piece of Chester County's history, known as "the mushroom capital of the world." A great restaurant in nearby Avondale is also worthy of mention.

PARKS, BEACHES, AND RECREATION AREAS

15 Anson B. Nixon Park
🐾🐾 (See Chester County map on page 86)
Although Kennett Square isn't exactly Dogtown USA, one place worth stopping that encourages leashed pups is Anson B. Nixon Park. This 80-acre park includes four trails, two ponds, five pavilions with picnic tables, a new entertainment pavilion, as well as a playground and restrooms. Leashed doggies are even welcome at many events that take place at the park throughout the year. Visiting here with your pup, you'll likely run into a variety of local

doggies who range in size and shape. Nellie's a bit biased as she prefers the bigger pooches to pal around with, but she's always amicable to any of her four-footed friends. Apparently, people not picking up after their pets is becoming a problem here, so watch your step and take your poop bags.

From Route 1 South (Baltimore Pike), take the first Kennett Square exit and continue straight on Old Baltimore Pike (once in the borough, it changes names to State Street) down the hill to Walnut Street. Turn right onto Walnut, go two blocks, and look for the park entrance on the left. Hours are 7 A.M.–sunset. N. Walnut St., Kennett Square; kapa@kennett.net; www .kennett-square.pa.us/kapa.

PLACES TO EAT

The Grille & Pub at Hartefeld National: The setting is an outdoor patio with a gorgeous view of the golf course, Hartefeld National, and surrounding countryside. This award-winning restaurant serves mostly continental cuisine with outstanding soups, salads, and sandwiches as well as fresh fish, crab cakes, and beef. You and your pup can dine alfresco and even listen to live music if you're here on Friday and Saturday nights. 1 Hartefeld Dr., Avondale; 610/268-8800.

Taqueria Moroleón: This incredibly genuine Mexican restaurant located in an uninteresting Acme strip mall does not have any space for you and your doggy to eat, but it does have takeout which is highly worth your while. The prices are reasonable and the food is spicy and authentic. 15 New Garden Shopping Center, Kennett Square; 610/444-1210.

PLACES TO STAY

Allemann's Tiptree Lodge Suites: Planning on being in the Kennett Square area for a month or more? Then you might want to check out this long-term stay option that's fully furnished. The outdoor deck overlooks the private woodlands and a stream. Pet sitting and even grocery shopping services are available. The nonrefundable fee for your pup depends on the length of stay and ranges from $50–100. Rates are $1,500–2,850. 302/893-2102; www .allemannventures.com.

Oxford and Nottingham

Oxford is a small community that still very much prides itself on its rolling fields, vast farmland, and many covered bridges that date back to the 1800s. Close by is Nottingham, which is equally charming and the location of one of Chester County's great parks.

PARKS, BEACHES, AND RECREATION AREAS

Nottingham County Park

😊😊😊 (See Chester County map on page 86)

Another wonderful Chester County park is at the southwestern tip of the county, almost to Delaware. But if you visit here, you'll be glad you did as the ride here is scenic countryside and the park itself sits on top of one of the largest serpentine stone barrens on the East Coast. Plus, the park has everything you and your leashed pup need: MacPherson Lake to take a drink in and watch the fish and birds, open spaces to play in, 10 trails to hike, rustic-looking picnic facilities with pavilions, trash cans, restrooms, and playgrounds if you have kids in tow. All in all, it's a great spot for the whole dog-loving family or for just the two of you.

From West Chester take Route 202 South to Route 1 South past Kennett Square and Oxford. Make a left onto Route 272, Nottingham; proceed .25 mile to Herr Drive. Take a right on Herr Drive, a right onto Old Baltimore Pike, and another right onto Park Road. Follow signs to the entrance on the left. Hours are 8 A.M.–sunset. 150 Park Rd., Nottingham; 610/932-2589.

PLACES TO EAT

Mansion Café: This café situated in the Ware Presbyterian Village retirement community is not the most typical of places to take your dog, but the staff will welcome both of you to sit at one of the few tables outside. In cooler weather, you can get your food to go. Serving everything from soups and salads to sandwiches and wraps, they are open for lunch only Monday–Friday. Oxford Manor, 7 E, Locust St., Oxford; 610/998-2629.

PLACES TO STAY

Hopewell Hill Farm Bed & Breakfast: Listed on the National Register of Historic Places, this lovely house dating back to 1832 sits atop 92 acres of a working farm. A large back yard is available for your pup to play in, a creek is nearby for swimming, and there's no extra pet charge. The B&B, just a few minutes' drive to Nottingham County Park, is located in a historic district featuring a two-mile walking tour, on which leashes are required. 1012 Hopewell Rd., Oxford; 610/932-4769; hopewell@epix.net.

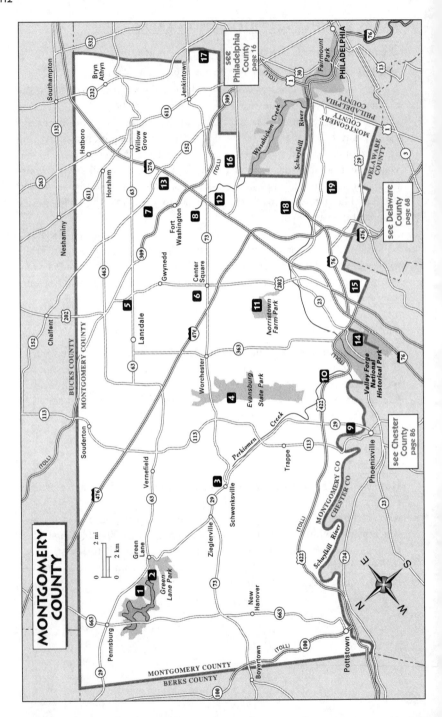

MONTGOMERY COUNTY

see Philadelphia County page 16

see Delaware County page 68

see Chester County page 86

MONTGOMERY COUNTY
BERKS COUNTY

MONTGOMERY CO
CHESTER CO

PHILADELPHIA COUNTY
MONTGOMERY COUNTY

BUCKS COUNTY
MONTGOMERY COUNTY

PHILADELPHIA

Fairmount Park

Wissahickon Creek

Schuylkill River

Valley Forge National Historical Park

Norristown Farm Park

Evansburg State Park

Green Lane Park

Perkiomen Creek

Schuylkill River

Bryn Athyn
Jenkintown
Southampton
Hatboro
Willow Grove
Horsham
Neshaminy
Chalfant
Souderton
Lansdale
Gwynedd
Fort Washington
Center Square
Worchester
Vernefield
Zieglerville
Schwenksville
Trappe
New Hanover
Boyertown
Pottstown
Phoenixville
Pennsburg
Green Lane

0   2 mi
0   2 km

532
232
132
263
611
611
276
309
152
152
202
113
463
63
63
63
73
73
202
23
202
363
477
477
113
113
113
29
29
29
29
663
663
473
476
422
422
724
100
100
1
30
76
13
3
611

CHAPTER 4

Montgomery County

Dogs laugh, but they laugh with their tails.

Max Eastman

"People who live south of the Schuylkill don't go north and people who live north don't go south…unless they have to," a friend once told me when I was a new resident to the area nearly 12 years ago. Odd but true. Similarly silly, when the Blue Route (I-476) opened in the early 1990s, which passes through Montgomery County and over the Schuylkill River, bridging the two areas of the county, another friend said, "It's like a whole new world opened up."

While the cause for the provincial attitude may be unknown, if dogs had something to say about it, they'd be begging you to cross that river as much as you had to to visit some of the destinations in this chapter.

Currently the third-most-populated county in the state, Montgomery County borders Philadelphia. Although much of the northern and western rural areas are under development, the southern section of the county has

PICK OF THE LITTER—MONTGOMERY COUNTY

BEST PARK
Montgomery Township Bark Park, North Wales (page 120)

BEST NATURE WALK
McKaig Nature Education Center, King of Prussia (page 139)

BEST PLACES TO EAT
The Back Porch Café, Skippack Village (page 119)
Maya Bella, Conshohocken (page 145)
Spring Mill Café, Conshohocken (page 145)

BEST PLACES TO STAY
Best Western Inn at Towamencin, Kulpsville (page 120)
Residence Inn, Conshohocken (page 145)

BEST DIVERSION
Doggie Wash N' Go, Fort Washington (page 134)

already seen major development. Neighborhoods with big old trees abound, and big and little parks alike beckon you and your furry friend to come for a walk or romp. Not the least of these is Valley Forge National Historical Park.

But Linus could not tell a lie: Montgomery County is not as dog-friendly as we'd hoped.

In fact, two county-run parks—Lorimer and Upper Schuylkill Valley Park—don't allow dogs at all. Other townships and boroughs like Abington, Upper Moreland, Upper Dublin, and Whitemarsh prohibit dogs in most or all of the parks.

Now for the good news: One truly excellent off-leash dog park does exist in the county, and three townships are working on developing off-leash areas for doggies to play.

Montgomery County also prides itself on the Schuylkill River Trail and the newly completed Perkiomen Trail, together providing more than 40 miles of hiking in the area. Even more exciting, more than 160 miles of trails are slated for the future, with nearly 60 miles already in the planning or design stages. And with a new open space preservation and trail funding initiative proposed in 2004, Montgomery County may become the Philadelphia region's leader in trail development.

In addition to developing parks and trails, Montgomery County contains some truly breathtaking, lesser-known parks that are terrific for a tranquil hike with your four-footed friend. Also, there are some great places to eat with your pooch, especially in Conshohocken, Skippack, and Ambler, and lots of dog-friendly places to stay in Horsham.

So, as Linus would attest, "It's all good" in Montgomery County.

Green Lane

Quiet and scenic with a community that's small (fewer than 600 live here) and close-knit, the town of Green Lane is like a postcard from the past. With its lovely county park and nearby dog-friendly restaurant, you and your pooch will feel like you're away from it all—and still be less than 50 miles from Philadelphia.

PARKS, BEACHES, AND RECREATION AREAS

1 Green Lane Park

🐾🐾🐾 (See Montgomery County map on page 112)

How refreshing it is to visit a county park that offers such an excellent mix of beauty, fun, and relaxation. When Linus was younger, we'd come to this park (then called Green Lane Reservoir) and he'd take a dip when no one was look-ing. Now the park encompasses both the reservoir and what used to be the Upper Perkiomen Valley Park, spanning nearly 3,400 acres of woods, fields, and three lakes: the Green Lane Reservoir (805 acres), Deep Creek Lake (38 acres), and Knight Lake (26 acres). The park is truly better than ever. All trails except the Hemlock Point Trail are open to you and your pooch on a leash. The biggest and most widely used trail, 10-mile Red Trail takes you through fields, cedar stands, wooded areas, and scenic views of the lake. But the big-gest trail news is the completion of Perkiomen Trail, which now serves as the northernmost trailhead. (To access Perkiomen Trail, park on Snyder and Deep Creek Roads.)

A word of warning: You'll share some of these trails with horses. Please use caution when passing behind or in front of these spookable creatures. It's advised to call out a friendly hello and wait for the rider to signal you to keep moving or step aside.

The always-handy poop-bag dispensers and trash cans throughout the park make cleaning up after your darling easy. The picnic areas and camp-grounds are the only areas of Green Lane where dogs are not allowed.

In one area surrounding Deep Creek Lake, you and your pup can sit along the beach and enjoy the stunning scenery and watch the boats float by. You can even take a walk across the lake via a bridge/reservoir wall. No matter what you and your furry friend decide to do, there's a lot of space to do it here. Hours are sunrise–sunset. 215/234-4528.

To get to the Deep Creek area of the park, from Green Lane, take Route 63 West until it dead-ends into Route 29. Take 29 South to Snyder Road and take a right. Go over the green metal bridge to the park.

2 Perkiomen Trail

🐾🐾🐾 (See Montgomery County map on page 112)

Using the original railway bed of the Reading Railroad, the Perkiomen Trail is part of the Rails-to-Trails movement that's creating a nationwide network of public trails from former rail lines and connecting corridors. Linus, always happy to reuse resources (his favorite blanket was an old family one), couldn't think of a better idea to start a trail network.

Although the county originally purchased the land for the trail in 1978, the project didn't get off the ground until about 1999 due to litigation regarding surrounding properties. The trail was officially completed in November 2003—in a record-breaking 3.5 years for the state of Pennsylvania. And what a magnificent trail it is.

Spanning from Green Lane south to Oaks, 22-mile Perkiomen Trail hugs the scenic Perkiomen Creek and connects three county parks: Green Lane, Central Perkiomen Valley Park, and Lower Perkiomen Valley Park. (Restrooms and water fountains are available only in these areas of the trail.) You can hike as much or as little of it as you like with your pup, of course. Along the way you might find yourselves in a quiet, untouched area, a busy town center, or the middle of suburbia. You're likely to be in the company of many other dogs and their humans, equestrians, and bikers. Most of the trail is packed cinders, but in the southern section, the surface is paved macadam. Poop-bag dispensers are located at various spots along the trail.

Parking to access Perkiomen Trail at Green Lane Park is on Snyder and Deep Creek Roads. Hours are sunrise–sunset. 215/234-4528, 610/287-6970, or 610/666-5371.

PLACES TO EAT

Murzillo Bistro: Homemade pasta, made-from-scratch focaccia, and even handcrafted mozzarella—all this and more are available for you to *mangia* with your mutt at this European-influenced bistro's outdoor seating. A native of Naples, the chef was once the Pope's personal chef and cooked for the Rat Pack back in the '60s, too. Everything here is fresh and delicious, especially the seafood. You can't go wrong with any of the specials. Plus, it's just down the street from Green Lane Park. *Mangia! Mangia!* 116 Gravel Pk., Green Lane; 215/234-4242.

Schwenksville

If you say the name of this town with a southern twang, it sounds like it's a glamorous destination where only the poshest pups might congregate. Oh contraire, said my boy Linus. This town is best known as home of the wildly popular Philadelphia Folkfest. Although dogs are not permitted at the festival, which is truly a shame, you can head over to Schwenksville any time of year to experience the love and peace.

PARKS, BEACHES, AND RECREATION AREAS

🔢 Central Perkiomen Valley Park

🐾🐾🐾 (See Montgomery County map on page 112)

Located along Perkiomen Creek in western Montgomery County, this charming 600-acre park features open fields, woodlands, and wetlands. But Linus thought the best feature of all was Perkiomen Trail (the 22-mile trail mentioned above), in this section a gravel trail almost completely shaded that skirts Perkiomen Creek. Because there aren't a lot of places for pups to take a potty break along this section of the trail, try to unwater your friend near the parking lot before embarking on your hike. Poop bags and trash cans are located throughout the park and along the trail. Shaded picnic areas, a playground, and restrooms are available, too. One of the most unique features of the park is the Old Mill House, a turn-of-the century building that served as a summer retreat for a local doctor and his wife. Of course, dogs are not allowed inside the home, but you can definitely view its charm and beauty from the surrounding grounds.

The park and its headquarters are located on Plank Road, between Routes 29 and 73 in Schwenksville (across from Ott's Greenhouse). Hours are 8 A.M.–sunset. 610/287-6970; www.montcopa.org/parks/cpvp.htm.

THINK GLOBALLY, BARK LOCALLY

Paws Across PA: If you love Labs, or any dogs, for that matter, you and your pup might want to earmark the Paws Across Pennsylvania dog walk fundraiser for Brookline Labrador Retriever Rescue. This annual rain-or-shine event usually takes place in mid-June at Central Perkiomen Valley Park. Registration begins at 11 A.M., and the walk starts at 11:30 A.M. All funds go directly to helping place Labs in their new adoptive homes—including vet care. www.dogsaver.org/brookline.

PLACES TO EAT

Ortino's: While there's no outdoor seating at Ortino's, you may want to opt for takeout here. One of the best menu items, the Chicken Ortino features broccoli and chopped tomatoes in a lemon sauce. The pizza is beloved by locals. 800 Main St., Schwenksville; 610/287-8333.

Skippack Township

If you're traveling through central Montgomery County, you just have to take your pup to Historic Skippack Village. Here is where General George Washington and troops stayed before the Battle of Germantown. But what's most alluring about this village is the village. Renovated 18th- and 19th-century barns and homes double as restaurants, galleries, and shops. Plus, dogs are welcome here, and it's a great place to grab a bite to eat after a brisk hike in Evansburg State Park. One dog-friendly place to stay is just a short drive away in Kulpsville.

PARKS, BEACHES, AND RECREATION AREAS

◪ Evansburg State Park

🐾🐾 (See Montgomery County map on page 112)

While the park's official address is Collegeville, the eastern section is just a few sniffs away from Skippack, so my furry friend preferred this way to the park.

You'd never guess this vast and quiet oasis consisting of more than 3,000 acres existed in this ever-developing and redeveloping area of Montgomery County. But it's here in all its tranquility for you and your pup to enjoy. Here you'll find more than six miles of trails that are relatively easy to hike for the two of you. If you're lucky enough to come in the springtime, the smell of honeysuckle will knock you and your pooch off your feet, it's so fragrant and lovely. Also, the trees here are in various stages of growth, many of them still relatively small, something you don't see often at state parks.

Skippack Creek runs through the park, and if you hike along Mill Race Trail, you'll be able to get up close and personal and get your doggy's feet wet and yours too, if you'd like. Hundreds of picnic tables and a few pavilions are scattered throughout the park. If you have kids in tow, you'll appreciate the relatively new playground in the main park area. But beware of poison ivy as it's common in the wooded sections. Although your pup won't suffer from contact with the itchy stuff, she can transfer the plant's oils onto you. The trash policy here is carry in, carry out.

Although it's an adequate state park as far as recreation is concerned, probably the most interesting aspect is its history. The valley surrounding Skippack Creek was inhabited by Mennonites who powered their industries from the Skippack's water in the early 18th century. Within the park's borders

FETCHING NECESSITIES

From the Past: Your dog doesn't have to be miniature to visit here. If he's well behaved and has good tail control, he's welcome to check out the dollhouses and other cute little things with you here. There's one very cute but not-so-little thing you'll find here, too: a chubby, friendly beagle named Smokey. After your visit, you and your doggy can sit together on the store's patio and enjoy some ice cream from the shop next door, if you so desire. 4039 Skippack Pk., Skippack; 610/584-5842.

you'll see mill remnants, mill buildings, and even homes from the 18th and 19th centuries.

From Route 73 south of Skippack, take a left on Evansburg Road at the traffic light. Follow it and then bear left onto Kratz Road, then bear right onto Anders Road. Follow that to Mill Road and turn left, which brings you to the main day-use area. Hours are sunrise–sunset. 851 May Hall Rd., Collegeville; 610/409-1150.

PLACES TO EAT

The Back Porch Café: The interior of this BYOB eatery couldn't be cozier with its working fireplace, hardwood floors, interesting artwork, and linen tablecloths. Sadly, puppers isn't allowed to see the inside with you, but she definitely can join you on the porch. It was one of Linus and my family's favorite places to go for brunch. Anything you order will be incredibly good; however, we always went for the jumbo lump crab eggs Benedict. Lunch and dinner are equally tasty. 4000 Skippack Pk., Skippack Village; 610/584-7870.

Mal's American Diner: What makes this eatery unique is not that it resembles a '50s diner with its chrome stools, lacquered milkshake bar, and checkered tablecloths, but that it has outdoor seating right along the cutesy Skippack Pike. Linus loved the dog watching here. The food is "diner" through and through with burgers and shakes, pies and cakes. The more unusual fare like the chicken Caesar salad and wraps are worth a try. Of course, breakfast is served any time of day. 4006 Skippack Pk., Skippack Village; 610/584-0900.

Tokyo Japanese Restaurant & Sushi Bar: If you want an eating experience off the beaten path and it's a weekday, you and your doggy are welcome to sit on the deck and enjoy this restaurant's fabulous sushi, tempura, hibachi, or teriyaki. However, weekends it's not advised to bring your pup as it gets quite busy and crowded outside. 4044 Skippack Pk., Skippack Village; 610/222-4777.

Victorian Veranda Cafe & Ice Cream Shop: This friendly little eatery welcomes you and your pup at its outdoor seating. Here you can order fresh homemade sandwiches and soups, hamburgers, hot dogs, homemade desserts, ice cream and yogurt, cappuccino, iced specialty drinks, milkshakes, sundaes and floats, waffles, and ice cream. Takeout is also available. 4039 Skippack Pk., Skippack Village; 610/584-1415.

PLACES TO STAY

Best Western Inn at Towamencin: If the city dog decided to visit his friend in the country, this is where he'd probably feel most comfy staying. He'd love the clean, tastefully decorated rooms, free newspaper delivery (although he might prefer delivering it himself), and dry cleaning available on site. His human would love the indoor and outdoor pool. This hotel welcomes your pup no matter where he's from with no weight restrictions. All that's required is an extra $20 per night and your signature on a waiver. Rates are $99–109. 1750 Sumneytown Pk., Kulpsville; 215/368-3800.

Montgomery Township

One of the fastest-growing communities in Montgomery County, this township is known for its retail center in Montgomeryville, including Montgomery Mall, as well as North Wales. Although the pet stores in this region made Linus drool like one of Pavlov's dogs, nothing made him happier than visiting the county's only established dog park, located in this township.

PARKS, BEACHES, AND RECREATION AREAS

5 Montgomery Township Bark Park

🐾🐾🐾🐕 (See Montgomery County map on page 112)

Linus (and I) could not be more ecstatic than when this first and only off-leash dog park in Montgomery County opened in 2002, only a year after it was proposed to the township (a political miracle). He absolutely loved this park and never left here without a new friend. In fact, since the park opened, hundreds of dogs have visited, friendships have bloomed, and a new sense of community has flourished.

Located in a very hard-to-find spot of North Wales, it's amazing that the park is as popular as it is. At this one-acre, six-foot-high-fenced park, you'll find a secure double-gated entrance, water dishes that are often filled, poop bags, a fire hydrant, trash cans, park benches, toys balls, and, best of all, some shade. The ground cover is mulch wood chips that can get muddy, so avoid visiting after spates of rainy weather. Playful pups who visit here must be neutered/spayed and licensed, and not under six months of age.

Otherwise, a visit here will likely be a very happy one as most of the dogs are friendly, as are their people. If an unpleasant exchange happens between dogs, most of the time the humans will intervene and stop it or leave. But there have been some situations that went ignored, so use caution.

Beautiful days on weekends can get crowded, so keep that in mind, too. Early mornings and late afternoons tend to be prime hours at the park.

At the intersection of 202 and 63, take a left on 63 heading west. Take a right into the first strip mall, Bell Run Plaza. Then take a right and head toward the former Superfresh grocery store. Drive alongside the strip mall, following it until it ends. You'll see a Tudor-style house behind the mall with an adjacent parking lot. Try to park in this area. Search for the *very* tiny wooden stake all the way to the right of the lot that announces Montgomery Bark Park. Follow the path from the stake into the woods and you'll see the park ahead. Hours are 6 A.M.–8 P.M. 215/393-6900.

PLACES TO EAT

Cravings Café: After a romp at the dog park, take your pooch over to the adjacent strip mall and nosh on some incredible food at Cravings Café. Linus loved the huge menu, which offers sandwiches and salads, but nothing run-of-the-mill. Some items include grilled flat breads with everything from fresh salmon to hot sausage, or gourmet wraps with blackened steak or grilled veggies. The salads will surely make your mouth water as you read the menu. 1222 Welsh Rd., Bell Run Plaza, North Wales; 215/855.4500; www.cravingscafe.com.

PLACES TO STAY

Quality Inn Conference Center: Although there's no official size limit on your doggy if you stay here, they did mention "no Great Danes" or other dogs of that size. However, if you call ahead and explain your situation, it's unlikely they'd turn you away unless there's no room at the inn. The hotel offers only a few pet-friendly rooms but charges no extra fee for your furry friend. This bare-bones facility, featuring some renovated rooms, is located in a spot convenient to shopping and just a couple of miles from the Montgomery Bark Park. Rates are $94–99. 969 Bethlehem Pk., Montgomeryville; 215/699-8800.

Ambler

On its own, Ambler is a charming community known for its beautiful Victorian homes with friendly front porches. Ambler's downtown is undergoing a major renovation, making it all the more exciting, and was named one of the best places to live in the Philadelphia area by a prominent magazine. Plus, Ambler hosts a Dog Days event in August with a pet parade and doggy costume contests, it offers a few dog-friendly eateries, and the nearby parks are great for hiking.

DOG-EAR YOUR CALENDAR

MonDaug Bark Park's Dog Walk: To be held annually in the springtime, the first annual MonDaug dog walk in 2004 was a huge success, held in Fort Washington at the Camphill and Highland Athletic Complex (CHAC). The volunteers interested in developing an off-leash dog park in Upper Dublin Township raised $2,000 toward the $25,000 needed. After the walk, dog agility demonstrations and even an animal communicator were on hand for entertainment. www.mondaugbarkpark.com.

Oreland Fourth of July Parade: If you really want a taste of small town America, don't miss the Oreland Lions Club's Fourth of July Parade. Linus never did. War veterans, marching bands, fire trucks, Irish dancers, bagpipe players, antique cars, parade queens, and red-white-and-blue-decorated bikes are just some of the sights you'll see. Plus, there are always lots of patriotic pups watching and even participating. Our favorite: the pup lying atop a piano throughout the parade route—he makes it every year. The parade usually starts at 10 A.M. and travels down Wischman and Twining Roads to the Little League field, at Lyster Road in Oreland. 215/572-6941.

Ambler Dog Days of Summer: Held one Saturday in August, Ambler Dog Days is a whole lot of fun with a costumed pet parade down Butler Avenue. Prizes are awarded for costumes and silly pet tricks. Merchants hold sidewalk sales, and pet rescues, local pet stores, and veterinarians are on hand for questions and info. Registration starts at 9 A.M. and the parade starts at 10 A.M. 215/641-1070.

PARKS, BEACHES, AND RECREATION AREAS

6 Gwynned Wildlife Preserve

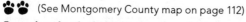 (See Montgomery County map on page 112)

Once farmland, this 240-acre parcel was acquired by the Natural Lands Trust in 1986 to save some of the remaining large open spaces in Montgomery County from development and establish a wildlife refuge. Although it may not be your or poochie's idea of a refreshing walk in the summertime, as the four miles of trails offer little shade, consider what this preserve is trying to accomplish and you might be more willing to visit any time of year. The preserve aims to take this farmland and restore it to a natural state to attract all sorts of wildlife like birds, turtles, and butterflies, to

Ardmore Dog Show: Usually held the first Saturday after Labor Day 10 A.M.–noon, this dog show welcomes you and your pup to participate in this just-for-fun event featuring everything from longest tail and loudest bark competitions to dog/human look-alike contests. It's free and totally fun. 610/645-0540.

Scottish Irish Festival: With as many as 80,000 people attending and 96 dogs participating in the festival's sheepdog trials, this is one popular event that takes place at Green Lane Park one weekend in September. Not only is it a free event with free parking and entertainment, but you can bring that furry lad or lassie along with you. The only places your leashed pup cannot visit are the sheepdog trials, the Falconry, Highland Games, the children's area, and the food areas. But rest assured, there are plenty of dog-friendly areas in this beautiful park. 215/234-4528; fball@mail.montcopa.org; www.montcopa.org.

Skippack Days Craft Festival: Traditionally held the first weekend in October for more than 30 years, the Skippack Craft Festival attracts not just craft lovers but their dogs, too. Pups of all shapes and sizes stroll along Skippack Pike with their families to check out the wares. Plus, lots of fun and food, too. 610/584-5842.

MonDaug Bark Park's Flea Market/Dog Costume Party: Held one Saturday in late October 8 A.M.–noon, this event is a newly annual fundraiser for the Friends of MonDaug Bark Park in Upper Dublin Township. Prizes will be awarded for costumes and the silliest pet tricks. The entry fee is $5. Location may vary. www.mondaugbarkpark.com.

name a few, as well as to create wetlands and wildflower meadows through specified plantings.

It's extremely quiet here. Actually, you and your four-footed nature lover may be the only ones setting foot here on the mowed-grass trails when you visit. And it's a truly natural experience as there's no drinking water available, picnic areas, or restrooms. Although at the time of press no maps were available, there are plans to have some available in a new kiosk once the parking lot has been paved to accommodate 10 cars. That's great news as it's easy to get lost in the surrounding area. In the meantime, you can access the website to download a map.

From Ambler, take Morris Road to 202 North. Take the next left onto Township Line Road and then take the first right onto Swedesford Road. Continue for about a half-mile until you see the preserve entrance on the left. Hours are sunrise–sunset. Parking at main entrance available 8 A.M.–4 P.M. 640 S. Swedesford Rd., Ambler; 215/699-6751; www.natlands.org.

7 Temple University Ambler Campus

☙☙ (See Montgomery County map on page 112)

Throughout the 187-acre suburban campus of Temple University, your pup is welcome to join you on a leash. Much of the campus consists of open, unshaded recreation areas, but many shaded spots near the campus buildings offer peaceful walking areas and picnic tables.

One of the best parts of visiting here is the university's gardens, woodlands, fields, and nurseries, which were recently named an arboretum by the American Association of Botanical Gardens and Arboreta. Among the most impressive are the woodland gardens, formerly an open meadow. Now it's a shady paradise, home to beech, sycamore, tulip trees, dogwood, holly, and rhododendron.

Closer to the campus buildings is the formal perennial garden that showcases striking English-style perennials and shrubs that will no doubt mentally transport you and your pup "across the pond." Hours are sunrise–sunset. 580 Meetinghouse Rd., Ambler; 215/283-1292; www.temple.edu/ambler.

From Ambler's downtown, take Butler Pike West to Meetinghouse Road. Take a right on Meetinghouse Road, and the campus buildings are down on your left. Take a left into the visitor's entrance and park.

8 Four Mills Nature Reserve

☙☙☙ (See Montgomery County map on page 112)

Although this 53-acre jewel is hard to find and poorly marked from the road—you'll likely drive by it at least once—it is well worth the extra travel time for you and your pooch. While Linus's expectations were not very high because so little was heard about this place in the dog community, he was more than pleasantly surprised upon discovering it. In fact, he was doggone shocked at what a tremendous spot this is to frolic in the woods and in Wissahickon Creek. At this nature reserve, you'll find bridges that take you over the creek to islands along the creek. There's a duck pond, a frog pond, and a few marshes along the way. It's completely shaded and the creek is accessible to dogs on leashes. Few people visit during the week, but weekends tend to bring more dogs and people to hike and enjoy the reserve's beauty.

The Four Mills Nature Reserve is also the headquarters for the Wissahickon Valley Watershed Association, which sponsors environmental educational programs. Stewardship programs include reforestation of farmlands and stream banks to prevent excess storm water runoff and the draining of chemicals into the creek. This area is also part of the Green Ribbon Preserve, the land surrounding Wissahickon Creek that stretches from Montgomeryville down through Philadelphia.

From Fort Washington, take 73 West. Take a right on Sheaff Lane. Pass the Highlands Mansion and take a left on Morris Road. The entrance to the Four Mills Nature Preserve is up on your right. (Don't forget, it's hard to see from the road.) Hours are sunrise–sunset. 12 Morris Rd., Ambler; 215/646-8866; www.wvwa.org.

PLACES TO EAT

Ambler Coffee: A town as cute as Ambler just has to have a cute independent coffee house to go along with it. Ambler Coffee is just that, serving what some locals swear is the best coffee in town, as well as delicious cakes, bagels, muffins, and cookies, and frozen drinks in the summertime. You and your canine companion are welcome at the outdoor seating to enjoy your java. 14 W. Butler Ave., Ambler; 215/542-9330.

La Cava: Although the name means "wine cellar," this excellent BYOB doesn't serve any. But it does serve some incredibly good, moderately priced haute-Mexican cuisine. You and puppers are welcome on the restaurant's small outdoor patio, especially if it's not too crowded. The specials here are always extraordinary, like shrimp over white rice served with a tequila sauce, and marinated pork with orange juice and onions. If Linus was a good *perro*, he'd even get a taste and a *perro* bag. 60 E. Butler Ave., Ambler; 215/540-0237.

Trax Café: Maybe you and your doggy are interested in a night on the town starting with a lavish yet not too expensive meal at Trax Café. This tastefully

transformed train station turned BYOB has some of the best-tasting American bistro food this side of the Wissahickon. House specialties include barbeque babyback ribs, herb and pepper crusted rack of lamb, and grilled salmon. 27 W. Butler Pk., Ambler; 215/591-9777.

Horsham Township

Named after the town of Horsham, Sussex County, England, this part of Pennsylvania was one of the original townships delineated by William Penn's engineers. Now it's as busy as suburban towns come, with several friendly places to stay for you and poochie.

Most of the parks in Horsham do not allow dogs at all, which is why there have been efforts to establish an off-leash dog park in the township. But as of press time, a year and a half of garnering support by the Friends of the Horsham Dog Park had still not resulted in a dog park in Horsham. The Friends proposed a one-acre fenced park with poop bags and a double-gated entry. While the parks and recreation department has agreed to the idea, the township management has put a halt on plans until more is learned, apparently because of liability concerns. But it's not a dead issue. For details, visit www .horshamdogpark.com.

Until the final decision is made, the Friends of the Horsham Dog Park asks interested dog lovers, especially Horsham residents, to write a letter requesting the dog park be developed. It would also be helpful if someone well versed in dog park liability would contact the township manager.

Address any persuasive letters about **Horsham Dog Park** to Michael J. McGee, Township Manager, 1025 Horsham Rd., Horsham, PA 19044; horsham@horsham.org.

PLACES TO EAT

Lee's Hoagie House: With several locations around the area, this hoagie shop is a local favorite of suburban Philadelphians. The secret sauce on the hoagies is what makes them so special, and the cheesesteaks are equally yummy. No matter what you choose, you'll get good, cheap food here for takeout. 870-72 Easton Rd., Horsham; 215/674-8000.

PLACES TO STAY

Candlewood Suites Horsham: While the suites themselves are nice, the staff is friendly, and there's no weight restriction on dogs, there are extra pet fees. For up to six days, the nonrefundable pet fee is $75; for 7-29 days, it's $150; for more than 30 days, it's $250 per pet. A maximum of two pets is allowed. The suites have fully equipped kitchens and provide a CD player and a VCR. Movies and CDs are free for you and your furry friend through

DIVERSIONS

Montgomery County has its share of historical sites as it was in the foreground of the Revolutionary War. The following spots, listed in the National Registry of Historic Places, allow you and your pup on the grounds to partake of a little history from the outside.

Hope Lodge: Owned by the Quaker Samuel Morris and built in the 1740s, Hope Lodge is an excellent example of Georgian architecture. While your pup isn't allowed inside the stunning home, which houses period furnishings and accents, the two of you are welcome on the grounds, which offer a picnic table or two. For a virtual tour of the home's interior, visit www.ushistory.org/hope. 553 S. Bethlehem Pk., Fort Washington; 215/646-1595.

Graeme Park: A 1722 Georgian mansion, the Keith House is the only surviving residence of a colonial Pennsylvania governor, Sir William Keith. The house still has the original floor boards, paneling, and paint, but, sadly, you can't see them with your pup. You can, however, take a virtual tour by visiting www.ushistory.org/graeme/keithhouse/tour.htm. However, the 44-acre surrounding grounds making up the park are open for your pup and you to enjoy together. They include trails, picnic tables, and a duck pond. Interesting tidbit: One of the home's residents, Elizabeth Graeme, was a major dog lover for her time; when her beloved pup died, she staged a full-blown funeral and burial ceremony. The park is closed Monday and Tuesday, open Wednesday–Saturday 9 A.M.–5 P.M. and Sunday noon–5 P.M. 859 County Line Rd., Horsham; 215/343-0965.

Pennypacker Mills: A mansion dating from 1720 and 170 acres of farmland await your exploration here (from the outside, if you're with puppers). Inside, the home displays antiques collected by former Pennsylvania Governor Samuel W. Pennypacker reflecting his interests in early Pennsylvania history, German and Dutch settlers, Native Americans, the Revolutionary War, and the Civil War. You can take a virtual tour by visiting www.montcopa.org/historicsites. 5 Haldeman Rd., Schwenksville; 610/287-9349.

Curtis Arboretum: The former estate of the publishing magnate Cyrus H. K. Curtis, this spot includes a lovely 45-acre arboretum with over 50 varieties of trees, two ponds, rolling hills, and a mansion. You and your pup are welcome on the grounds as long as he's leashed. The darling courtyard has benches where you can stop and catch a breather. Church Road and Greenwood Avenue, Wyncote; 215/887-1000, ext 227.

THINK GLOBALLY, BARK LOCALLY

Hatboro Pet Rescue Fair: Animal rescue groups offer pets for adoption (pending background checks and the appropriate paperwork) and a variety of pet products and services at this popular pet fair. Some breeds attending in the past include greyhounds, Great Danes, Siberian huskies, German shepherds, and Labrador retrievers. Dogs and humans are also invited to participate in a Best Dressed Pet Parade at noon. Prizes will be awarded for the most original, cutest, and funniest costumes. The event takes place one Saturday in mid-July 10 A.M.–4 P.M. at Hatboro Baptist Church, 32 N. York Rd., Hatboro; www.hatboro-pa.com.

the hotel's lending library. Rates are $64.99–139.99. 250 Business Center Dr., Horsham; 215/328-9119.

Days Inn Horsham: Newly renovated, this clean hotel has amenities like a fitness room, tennis courts, and a whirlpool. There's even a full, deluxe continental breakfast for you to enjoy (sorry, your pup can't eat in the dining area). But the best news, according to Nellie, is that traveling hounds are welcome here for an extra $10 per night with no weight restrictions. Rates are $89–119. 245 Easton Rd., Horsham; 215/674-2500.

Homestead Horsham: More great news for big doggies: no weight restrictions if you stay here. The only restriction is that the day of cleaning, dogs either stay in a crate or leave the room with you. Otherwise, the rooms at this hotel are studio suites that feature a full kitchen, on-site laundry, and personal voice mail, among other amenities. The nonrefundable pet fee is $25 extra per night up to three nights. After three nights, it's a flat $75. Rates are $99–119. 537 Dresher Rd., Horsham; 215/956-9966.

Residence Inn by Marriott: You can stay for as short or as long as you like with your any-size doggy. The hotel requires a $150 nonrefundable cleaning fee, plus $6 extra per day. You two will likely enjoy your stay here as some rooms come with a fireplace and/or an overhead fan, but all rooms come with a fully equipped kitchen—great for those late-night snacks together. There's even a picnic area outside for daytime snacking with poochie. Rates are $109–179. 3 Walnut Grove Dr., Horsham; 215/443-7330.

Towneplace Suites By Marriott: Horsham certainly loves its canine hotel customers. This is yet another great option in Horsham, with no weight restrictions for poochie in a clean and affordable place. The suites here have fully equipped kitchens and free high-speed Internet access. There's a one-time, nonrefundable pet fee of $100. For shorter stays, the fee can be negotiated. They love animals here as they often give dog bones upon check in. Rates are $84.99–144.99. 198 Precision Dr., Horsham; 215/323-9900.

Upper Providence Township

Another fast-growing community in Montgomery County, Upper Providence Township includes towns such as Oaks, Mont Clare, and Port Providence. Lucky for dog lovers who live here, both the Schuylkill River Trail and the Perkiomen Trail run through this area.

PARKS, BEACHES, AND RECREATION AREAS

◨ Schuylkill Canal Park

🐾 🐾 (See Montgomery County map on page 112)

If it weren't for the history involved with this destination and that it's currently under restoration, it might just warrant a hydrant rating, especially since it's not well marked. But it's a park containing an original canal and canal lock (built in 1846). The Locktender's House is also on the grounds. In the early 19th century, this canal was part of the Schuylkill River navigation system used to move coal via mule barges from the Allegheny coalfields at the head of the river down to the Philadelphia port.

Today Schuylkill Canal Park is undergoing major renovations including a new truss bridge taking you over the canal from the towpath to the Locktender's House in the upper portion of the park. The canal lock also is being fully restored, as is the original toll house. When the lock reopens in April 2005, boaters can experience the lock firsthand and visitors can take a tour of the grounds through the Oakes Reach Interpretive Plan. The plan will feature anecdotes and artifacts from people who grew up playing or living around the canal. The Locktender's House will also be restored as a community and visitor's center.

Additionally, the Schuylkill River Trail is going to be extended into the canal area by 2007.

At the canal park, there's ample parking and you and poochie can hike down the towpath from Lock 60 to its end in Port Providence about 2.6 miles away. Or if you're looking for a shorter hike, the two of you can walk in the paved upper portion of the canal from Lock 60 to the Route 29 bridge, which is about 1.5 miles round trip. But take caution as the towpath trail is paved and cars enter and exit the park via this road.

While visiting here, be sure to check out the Schuylkill Canal Association's information stand at Lock 60, which provides trail maps, brochures, and directions for a nature walk. You'll probably see anglers as fishing is the most popular activity at this park.

From Mont Clare, take Route 29 East. As you're heading over the bridge in the town, take an immediate right where there's a sign for the park. Follow the towpath drive—about one mile all the way to the end where there's parking and Lock 60. Hours are sunrise–sunset. 610/917-0021; info@schuylkillcanal .com; www.schuylkillcanal.com.

🔟 Lower Perkiomen Valley Park

🐾 (See Montgomery County map on page 112)

At the outset, it seems like a wonderful place to take your pup, but this place isn't completely dog-friendly even for those pups on leashes. In fact, dogs are allowed only on the Perkiomen Trail and in the open fields, and must be on a leash not exceeding six feet in length. The picnic and playground areas, which are mostly shaded and very inviting, are off limits to canines. Dogs are not allowed to partake in the summer concert series either. So what's a social yet energetic pup to do? Walk, jog, or run along the trail and in the open fields on a leash, or maybe enjoy a picnic at one of the few picnic tables available here in the upper portion of the park. Linus would have loved the concerts!

From King of Prussia, take 422 West. Get off at the Oaks exit and take a right onto Egypt Road and another right onto New Mill Road. Park in the parking lot in this section. Hours are 8 A.M.–sunset.

PLACES TO EAT

Sunset Grill & Pizzeria: You and your pup are invited to dine alfresco at this great little pizza and sandwich shop. Whether it's the calzones, cheesesteaks, hoagies, or the pizza, you and your friendly quadruped will be happy you stopped here to rest your collective tootsies and dine on some delicious, inexpensive chow. Plus, it's only a mile from Lower Perkiomen Valley Park. 1058 Egypt Rd., Oaks; 610/917-9404.

Norristown

The county seat, Norristown is hoping to revitalize its downtown after falling on hard times for several decades. This town is full of architecturally interesting buildings reminding you and your pup of its long history as a center for commerce, industry, and banking in the 20th century. Surrounding Norristown are some great places to get food and rest like Blue Bell and Jeffersonville. And the borough's Farm Park is one of the newest and nicest additions to the county park system.

There's also a project in the works called the **Liberty Bell Trail,** using part of the former Liberty Bell Trolley route that traveled from Philadelphia to Allentown in the first half of the 20th century. When completed, the Liberty Bell Trail will start in Norristown (at the Norristown Farm Park) and head 25 miles north ending in Quakertown, Bucks County. It's expected that the trail will be interconnected segments of former trolley track beds and segments of on-road facilities (i.e., bike lanes or wide shoulders) coupled with sidewalks.

DOG-EAR YOUR CALENDAR

Looking for a paw-tapping good way to enjoy a summer night with your culture-loving canine? Then head over to a local park for a concert or film, and don't forget the snacks, lawn chairs, and blankets.

Ardmore Outdoor Family Film Festival: Once a week July–August you and your pooch can check out movies on the big screen together in Ardmore. Don't forget your lawn chair and a blanket for puppers. Movies including new releases are shown in the Cricket Avenue parking lot behind Luciano's and Partyland. 610/645-0540.

Cisco Park: About four times in the summer, Springfield Township hosts concerts in the gazebo at Cisco Park in Erdenheim. Erdenheim Parks and Recreation Department, 215/836-7600.

Curtis Arboretum: The serene setting of the arboretum kicks it up a notch about six times a summer for its outdoor concert series. People and their leashed pets gather to enjoy everything from blues and jazz to folk. Cheltenham Parks and Recreation Department, 215/887-1000, ext. 227; http://cheltenhamtownship.org/citp.

Norristown Farm Park: Big bands, folkies, and even Elvis impersonators take the stage in Norristown Farm Park's popular concert series. Several times a month in the summer, locals gather to enjoy the sounds under the stars with their pups. 610/270-0215.

The Schuylkill Canal Park: Twice a month in the summer, the park holds free concerts for all ages in the Lock 60 picnic grove. 610/917-0021; www.schuylkillcanal.com.

If all goes as planned, the Liberty Bell Trail will connect residential areas, employment centers, office parks, shopping districts, historic sites, parks, and schools. It's hoped to provide an alternate mode of transportation for many users. Plus, the trail will offer a gentle grade, built for multiple purposes and for all ability levels.

However, as mentioned, it's still not even a completely workable plan yet. So it may take several years to complete. But when it is ready, prepare for another great escape with your pooch.

For more information, contact David Clifford, Open Space Planner, Montgomery County Courthouse, Planning Commission, P.O. Box 311, Norristown, PA 19404; 610/278-3887; dcliffor@mail.montcopa.org; www.montcopaparks .org/parks/libertybell.htm.

PARKS, BEACHES, AND RECREATION AREAS

11 Norristown Farm Park

🐾🐾 (See Montgomery County map on page 112)

As if its name wouldn't give it away, upon arriving at the park you'll see the barn and silo, and might wonder why you're on a farm walking your dog with crops growing in the background? It turns out this land is actually partially a working farm once owned by the Norristown State Hospital; patients worked the fields as part of their rehabilitation. The farmland was transferred to the Department of Welfare in 1980, which oversaw the hospital, and later to the Department of Agriculture in 1987 to save it from development. Finally it was given to the Department of Environmental Resources, Bureau of State Parks, which manages it in a cooperative agreement with Montgomery County. Norristown Farm Park was officially christened in 1995.

And if the actual numbers say anything, it's that this is definitely a popular place to visit. Nearly 90,000 people and 15,000 dogs visited here in 2003, and it's the second-largest Montgomery county park spanning 700 acres of fields, forests, and streams.

While Linus definitely enjoyed this park, equipped with poop bags and trash cans throughout, and even a doggy water fountain in front of the visitor's center entrance, he was not crazy about the fact that dogs have to be leashed here. Interesting tidbit: Even though more than 400 signatures were secured in a petition to section off a one-acre plot for an off-leash dog park, the farm park advisory committee denied it saying it didn't adhere to the master plan in keeping it a "farm park."

Although there are woodlands within the park, most of the park is not shaded, especially the majority of the main walking trail (a wide, paved path). But the good news is, Stony Creek runs through the wooded area to rest and soak your pup's tired paws. Some dogs swim here, too.

There are three entrances to the park, but the one closest to the doggy water fountain is the main entrance on Germantown Pike.

From Norristown, take Germantown Pike north and take a left on Upper Farm Road, near the Barley Sheaf apartments. Hours are sunrise–sunset. 2500 Upper Farm Rd., Norristown; 610/270-0215.

PLACES TO EAT

August Moon: If you're fond of sushi and other Japanese cuisine, or a fan of Korean food, this place is for you. It's been a fixture in the community for many years. However, August Moon has no outdoor seating, so takeout is the only dog-friendly option, but well worth it. Most of the entrées are moderately priced and very tasty. One of the most popular caused much slobbering in my furry friend: the bibim bap, a delicious combination of piping hot fried egg, veggies, and ground beef. 300 E. Main St., Norristown; 610/277-4008.

Breakaway Café: A little something for everyone, including your pooch, is the theme at this fun and friendly eatery that caters to users of the Schuylkill River Trail. Your pup is invited to sit outside with you and enjoy everything from bagels and coffee to hotdogs and hot roast beef and other sandwiches, as well as ice cream. Healthy snack items are also available and, of course, bottled water. If you're on the trail in Norristown, or even if you're not, don't hesitate to stop here. They love dogs. 620 W. Washington St., Norristown; 610/270-9750.

Moody Monkey: One of the most talked about restaurants in the area, the Moody Monkey serves up some of the best food, albeit eclectic and pricey. Everything from beef stroganoff to Mexican fajitas are on the menu. The portions are large, though, which is never a bad thing. Although The Monkey has outdoor seating, on a rooftop patio, your pup isn't allowed, so takeout is the only option here. 2508 W. Main St., Jeffersonville; 610/631-1233.

PLACES TO STAY

Korman Communities Meadow Wick: If you're looking for a place to stay for a month or more with your pup (or even shorter), there is no size restriction on your dog if you choose to stay at these lovely corporate townhomes. Each private-entrance townhome features a wood-burning fireplace; appliances including washer and dryer, television, and VCR; full kitchen and linens; iron and ironing board; and more. Daily complimentary breakfast is available, as well as access to the clubhouse with swimming pool, tennis courts, sauna, and Jacuzzi. The nonrefundable pet fee is $250 for 30 days or more; it's negotiable for shorter stays. Rates are $80–160. 1707 Meadow Dr., Blue Bell; 610/275-5265.

Summerfield Suites: Another great option for big dogs or little ones is the Summerfield Suites. Here you'll find clean, relatively new one- and two-bedroom suites with full kitchens, a VCR, and even two TVs. For you, there's also an outdoor pool and fitness room, and for your pup there's a pet walk. Even better for your furry friend, it's about four miles from the Farm Park and eight miles from Valley Forge National Historical Park. The nonrefundable pet fee is $150. Rates are $99–229. 501 E. Germantown Pike, East Norriton Township; 610/313-9990; www.summerfieldsuites.com.

Upper Dublin Township

A vibrant township with a welcoming community, it's truly a shame that dogs are allowed in only one of the 26 township parks. The jury is still out as to why, but in the meantime some township residents and residents of surrounding areas are planning a dog park to be located in the only UD park that allows dogs on leashes, Mondauk Manor Park. What they've accomplished so far in

DIVERSIONS

In Montgomery County, here are a couple of opportunities to convene with like-minded humans and canines indoors.

Paws On the Run (indoor dog playgroup): Every week, spayed and neutered dogs (only) get a chance to party with other pooches indoors for up to an hour at Paws On the Run dog training in Horsham. Because this playtime uses the space of the business, humans are charged $7 per dog. Reservations must be made by the Saturday prior to the week's playgroup. 319D Norristown Rd., Horsham; 215/674-4964.

Doggie Wash N' Go (indoor dog wash): If you have a super-hairy dog like I had, you loathe bathing him, and wish you could do it every week, only the messy aftermath prevents you from doing so. Now there is an option. This incredibly friendly, self-described "unique grooming facility" lets you take care of it all away from home. It provides standing-height tubs for baths, towels, hair driers, wipes, and brushes for you to use. But you leave the mess behind and bring home a sweet-smelling pooch! A session at the dog wash, usually about 45 minutes, ranges $15–24 depending on the size of your dog. The shop also sells gift items and pet-care products. An on-site groomer will clip your pup's nails for only $5. One of the best aspects is that it's a great way to meet other dog owners and talk dog. 461 Bethlehem Pk., Fort Washington; 215/283-9525; www .doggiewashngo.com.

The Kennel Club of Philadelphia Dog Show in Fort Washington: This is such a big part of Philadelphia's dog-loving pride and tradition that we decided to mention it, even though you can't bring your pup to it. (Until recent years, it was held at the Pennsylvania Convention Center downtown.) It's a benched show, which means that participating dogs have to be available until the conclusion of the two-day show, instead of going home right after they show. This gives you and your friends and family the opportunity to see the dogs up close and talk to them and their handlers and the many breeders who attend. Plus, the "best in show" segment of the dog show is taped and aired nationally on Thanksgiving Day, a new tradition. While poochie will have to sit this event out, it is doggone fun for you. Just be sure you omit that detail. www .philadogshow.com.

fundraising is remarkable and their dream will likely become a reality fairly soon, thankfully.

PARKS, BEACHES, AND RECREATION AREAS

12 Fort Washington State Park

🐾🐾 (See Montgomery County map on page 112)

Named for the temporary fort built by George Washington's troops in the fall of 1777, before heading to Valley Forge, it's a popular park in this section of Montgomery County. One of the primary uses for this park is dog walking, but that is not to say it is an excellent place to bring your pooch. The park has about 3.5 miles of hiking trails that traverse open fields and the woods. Linus always enjoyed a good walk here, but much of the park is not shaded and there's no easily accessible river, lake, or stream. What does flow through the park is Wissahickon Creek, but it's quite a distance from the main Militia Hill day-use area which is where you'll likely park. Regardless, it's very peaceful here, there are hundreds of picnic tables and a few pavilions, restrooms, a bird-watching deck that you and your pup can access to check out the seasonal migration of raptors to the area, and even an excellent yet unshaded playground for the kiddies. Dogs are not allowed in the campgrounds here.

While there are several entrances to the park, the main one is the Militia Hill day-use area, located at the intersection of Militia Hill and Joshua Roads. From Fort Washington, take 73 West and make a left onto Militia Hill Road, then follow signs to the park. The entrance will be on your left. Hours are 8 A.M.–sunset. 500 S. Bethlehem Pk., Fort Washington; 215/591-5250.

13 MonDaug Bark Park

(See Montgomery County map on page 112)

Talk about perseverance! The woman who came up with the idea for this park proposed it in the beginning of 2004, had a website up within weeks, and by the middle of the year, organized the first major fundraiser: a dog walk. Since then, the dog-lovers group has raised awareness and funds in local flea markets, dog events, and pet fairs. The group's annual dog walk is to be held in the spring, and a flea market and dog costume parade in the fall.

The goal of these fundraising efforts is to raise $25,000 to build a one-acre, double-gated, fenced dog park with two entrances, shade, benches, poop bags, trash cans, and water fountain. Its location is slated to be at the Mondauk Manor Park, located at Camp Hill Road between Highland Avenue and Susquehanna. When you enter Mondauk Manor Park, go to the bottom of the parking lot; on the right is where the fenced dog park is being planned. Also, there are hopes that the trails surrounding the proposed dog park will be improved for hiking.

If you're interested in volunteering or helping in any way, contact the Friends of MonDaug Bark Park at www.mondaugbarkpark.com or mondaug@yahoo .com. If you'd like to make a donation, make checks payable to Upper Dublin Township, write "Bark Park Donation" in the memo section, and send your donation to Upper Dublin Township, c/o Susan Lohoefer, Director, Parks and Recreation, 801 Loch Alsh Ave., Fort Washington, PA 19034.

PLACES TO EAT

Little Italy Pizza: Truly an excellent mom-and-pop pizza joint. Although there's no outdoor seating, getting the pie delivered or for takeout is one of the best things you can do for yourself and your pooch. No matter what pizza you get, it will be fresh and delicious. A favorite of Linus's was the veggie pizza—paws down. It is outstandingly fresh! 416 S. Bethlehem Pk., Fort Washington; 215/628-3845.

Palace of Asia: It's too bad your pup won't be allowed inside because the ambiance is peaceful and the service is great, once you get over the fact it's inside the Best Western hotel. Above all, the Indian food is superb, so make it takeout. It's a great value for the amount of food you get. If you go for lunch, you might try the delicious and filling Tandoori Combination that includes chicken tandoori, seek kabab, and chicken tikka. 285 Commerce Dr., Fort Washington; 215/646-2133.

Upper Moreland Township

Home to bustling Willow Grove, Upper Moreland Township has grown for the past two decades and continues to do so as its downtown is being revitalized. As much promise as the town has for its people, we wish the same could be said for its canines. Leash or no leash, dogs are not allowed in any of the 18 township parks or on school grounds. (And unfortunately, no dog-friendly restaurants are nearby either.)

So what's a taxpaying dog lover to do? If you're like Paw Prints DOG (Dog Owners Group), you make hamburgers out of canned dog food. After the group organized nearly 60 members and came up with a proposal, the commissioners of Upper Moreland Township voted to create a fenced-in, off-leash dog park in the township. At press time, the exact location was yet to be finalized. Estimates for building the dog park are upwards of $40,000 for the fence, ground cover, trash cans, and poop bag dispensers. So Paw Prints DOG is working with the township to raise the money to offset the cost of creating the park. It's no easy task and may take a year or two, but the end result will be fabulous.

The potential area for the dog park may be at Bonnet Lane and Mill Road, but at press time it's still not confirmed.

If you're interested in volunteering or getting more information on fund-raising events for the **Upper Moreland Dog Park,** contact Judy Lamb, the group's leader, at 215/441-4756 or UMDogPark@comcast.net.

Tax-deductible donations are being accepted by the township. Checks should be made payable to The Upper Moreland Township Foundation and should be marked "For Dog Park" in the memo portion of the check. Mail your check to The Upper Moreland Township Foundation, 117 Park Ave., Willow Grove, PA 19090.

PLACES TO EAT

Franconi's: If your hound has a hankerin' for a cheesesteak and you have one for pizza, visit here for takeout and you can bring home both, plus some fries. It's a true Philly local's joint, so you can be assured of the authenticity of the steaks and hoagies. 101 E. Moreland Rd., Willow Grove; 215/659-0900.

Mandarin Garden: If you love Chinese food, chances are you'll love the takeout from here, as there is no outdoor seating for you and your pup. Anything you try is sure to be a hit, but some goodies are the General Tso's Chicken and the Yeh Yang Shrimp. 91 York Rd., Willow Grove; 215/657-3993.

King of Prussia and Upper Merion Township

Why on earth would someone name a town King of Prussia, much less a mall? Legend has it that the town was named for the 18th-century restaurant, the King of Prussia Inn, honoring Frederick the Great, the King of Prussia from 1740 to 1746. General George Washington was rumored to have stayed there. Speaking of our first president, while Valley Forge National Historical Park isn't in King of Prussia, it is located in nearby Valley Forge, Pennsylvania, and is a very popular place to take poochie. And the nearby McKaig Nature Education Center is one of the best-kept nature secrets around.

PARKS, BEACHES, AND RECREATION AREAS

14 Valley Forge National Historical Park

(See Montgomery County map on page 112)

If you're anywhere in the Philadelphia vicinity with your pup, you must make a side trip to Valley Forge. Not only is it an expansive park—more than 3,400 acres making it a great place to walk poochie, but this park offers you the opportunity to learn and see why Valley Forge is so significant to American history. No battle was fought here, but more than 2,000 troops died from bitter cold and disease, with another 10,000 suffering. It's known as a significant milestone in the fight for independence because the remaining troops were transformed back into a major force through the guidance of Baron Friedrich

THINK GLOBALLY, BARK LOCALLY

The Spayed Club Annual Dog Walk: Help prevent unwanted litters of puppies and kitties from being born by participating in the Spayed Club's annual fundraising dog walk, usually held one Saturday in early October. Moneys raised help provide low-cost spay and neuter programs in the Philadelphia area. You and your four-footed friend will have lots of fun if you walk the walk or talk the talk with vendors and animal rescue groups. The event takes place in Valley Forge National Park's Walnut Hill section. The Spayed Club, P.O. Box 1145, Frazer, PA 19355; 610/275-7486; www .thespayedclub.com.

Wilhelm von Steuben, a former Prussian general, who spoke little English. Valley Forge was considered a victory of will, rather than weapons.

Visiting here with your pup should include, if you're organized, download-ing a map off the Valley Forge website. If not, stop at the visitor's center (sorry, dogs aren't allowed inside) to get a park map once you arrive.

Then hop back in your car for a free, fun, self-guided 10-mile auto tour taking you past extensive remains and reconstructions of major forts, the Artillery Park, Washington's Headquarters, quarters of other officers, the Grand Parade where General von Steuben rebuilt the army, and the National Memorial Arch commemorating the patience and fidelity of the soldiers. (An audio tour can also be purchased for $10 in the visitor's center.)

After your tour, park in any area you'd like. There are three picnic areas with parking (Varnum's, Betzwood and Wayne's Woods). Take a hike on a portion of the 18 miles of trail, including six miles of paved multipurpose trail that winds through the park. The multi-use Schuylkill River Trail, which starts in Philadelphia, ends at the Betzwood Picnic area.

Especially gorgeous in the autumn, the park boasts a sea of trees with bold shades of orange, red, and yellow that will take your breath away. If your canine is known as a snow pup, like Linus was, then winter is another oppor-tune time to visit the park, especially for sledding. One strategic spot is the gentle slope near the statue of "Mad" Anthony Wayne.

Any time of year, you'll likely pass lots of walkers, dogs, and bikers, as well as a horse or two. This park is heavily used for its paved trail. If you're here in the late afternoon, it's almost impossible not to spot some deer. Those sweet weed-eaters can't get enough of this park, either!

Take Pennsylvania Turnpike to Valley Forge Exit to the first exit at North Gulph Road. Follow North Gulph Road and take a left onto 23 West, which takes you right into the park. Hours are sunrise–sunset. 610/783-1077; www .nps.gov/vafo.

15 McKaig Nature Education Center

🐾🐾🐾 (See Montgomery County map on page 112)

Upon entering, all Linus could think is that this park is paw-sitively awesome judging from his tail-wagging enthusiasm! And he was right. This little-known park consists of 89 acres of woodlands, rambling streams, and lots of friendly wildlife like white-tail deer, bunnies, and even flying squirrels. You'll no doubt cross the paths of other dogs while visiting here. Because the park is so well shaded, even the hottest summer days can seem cool here. Although your dog is required to be on a leash, many people do let their dogs off leash in the summer to swim in Crow Creek. But the word on the street is that owners of dogs caught off leash and lacking current licenses and rabies certificates have been threatened with $300-plus in fines by the authorities.

On your way in be sure to pick up a brochure, which includes a park map. As there are no poop bags or trash cans provided here, it's advised to clean up and take doggy deposits with you.

From King of Prussia, take 202 South to Warner Road until it dead-ends at Croton Road. Take a left on Croton and follow it to the elementary school. Park on the street in front of the school. The nature area is located on the right side of the road, almost hidden, to the left side of the elementary school. Hours are sunrise–sunset. For more information, contact the Upper Merion Park and Historic Foundation, P.O. Box 60875, King of Prussia, PA 19406; 610/265-1071.

PLACES TO EAT

Marrone's: Sit in Marrone's outdoor patio with your pup and you can enjoy a laid-back atmosphere with tasty Italian-American food. Order anything from burgers and salads to spaghetti and meatballs to chicken parmesan and pizza. If your dog is like Linus was, the most difficult part of eating here will be keeping his nose off the table. 520 Shoemaker Rd., King of Prussia; 610/337-9567.

Starbucks: Café lattes taste much better when you sip them alongside your furry friend. Starbucks' outside tables invite you to savor the flavor of the coffees and bakery items right along Route 202. Sure, it's a less-than-peaceful location, but who cares? You're with your dog. 140 W. DeKalb Pk., King of Prussia; 610/768-5130.

PLACES TO STAY

Homestead Studio Suites: This friendly, comfy and clean hotel welcomes you and your dog with no weight restrictions. The only caveat is a $25 extra charge per night that won't exceed $100. All the rooms come equipped with a kitchen, making those late-night snacks that much easier to whip up for the two of you. Rates are $80–110. 400 American Ave., King of Prussia; 610/962-9000.

Mainstay Suites: Only one mile from Valley Forge National Historical Park, this is another clean and comfy place to rest after a long hike at the park. The nice option here is that up to two dogs are welcome, but they must not exceed 25 pounds each. Sorry, big guys and gals. The hotel charges a $150 nonrefundable deposit for dogs. Rates are $119–139. 440 American Ave., King of Prussia; 484/690-3000.

Motel 6: If price is the ultimate consideration, than you might check out the Motel 6. There are no extra pet fees or size limits, but only one dog may stay here. Your pup must not be left unattended in a room, and must be on a leash outside of the room. However, the adage "you get what you pay for" applies with this motel. Don't expect a super-friendly staff or an immaculately clean room. Rates are $61–67. 815 W. Dekalb Pk., King of Prussia; 610/265-7200.

Springfield Township

One of William Penn's original manors, Springfield Township was given to Penn's wife as a gift. As a result, there's a rich history here, as well as some gorgeous old homes and gardens. Springfield is a place that loves dogs, too, just not off their leashes. Since there aren't too many parks to take your pooch in township limits, you can't drive or walk too far without regularly seeing dogs of all shapes and sizes walking the neighborhoods. Resident dogs even watch and participate in the Oreland Fourth of July Parade.

PARKS, BEACHES, AND RECREATION AREAS

16 Cisco Park

🐾🐾 (See Montgomery County map on page 112)

A nice, friendly little community park is probably the best way to describe the 13 acres comprising Cisco Park (also known to the locals as Hillcrest Pond park). Here, in Erdenheim, you'll find a walking trail surrounding a creek that's somewhat shaded, as well as a few picnic tables scattered throughout and a darling gazebo you and your pup can check out near the fishing pond, a favorite of my furry friend for all the ducks and geese that congregate here. There's also a playground and large playing fields; many dogs go off leash, although it's not advised. If you happen to be here during softball season, you and your pup are welcome to grab some grass and watch as the latest local pubs tackle each other on the baseball diamond. Also during the summer, at least four outdoor concerts are held here. Best of all, we've never met an unfriendly dog owner here.

From Flourtown, take Bethlehem Pike South to Montgomery Avenue. Take a left on Montgomery and the park is on your right. Park in the parking

FETCHING NECESSITIES

Sovereign Bank Drive-Thru: If you're in Oreland and looking to do a little banking via the drive-up teller, stop here, make sure the teller sees poochie's face in the car window, and he will likely get a cookie. The best part is he doesn't even need to make a deposit; in fact, it's preferred that he not. 1401 Bruce Rd., Oreland; 215/887-0475.

lot. Hours are sunrise–sunset. 215/836-7600; www.springfield-montco.org/parks-recreation.asp.

PLACES TO EAT

Halligan's: Springfield Township locals cannot get enough of Halligan's, where the service is great and especially friendly, not to mention how yummy and inexpensive the food is. It's truly a shame there's no outdoor seating here, but the exquisite smells emanating from the takeout bag are almost as satisfying to my furry friend. Some of the best menu items are the hoagies, cheesesteaks, the Portobello mushroom sandwich, the roasted pepper chicken sandwich, and always scrumptious Halligan's Irish Fries (cheddar cheese and bacon on top of French fries). The buffalo wings are spicy and yummy and always a good bet, too. 1619 Bethlehem Pk., Flourtown; 215/836-9597.

Esposito's Italian Water Ice: This superb little mom-and-pop water ice shop has been around for a decade because its water ice is absolutely excellent. No matter what flavor you select, you'll love it. But just in case you're not sure, try the raspberry or the lemon. Linus and I were always torn, so we tended to get both. Although there's no outdoor seating here, it's easy enough to stop off on your way home from Cisco Park. Whether you get a single serving or a quart, be sure to get a shallow cup for your pooch so he can lick it all up. 1050 Bethlehem Pk., Erdenheim; 215/836-4111.

General Lafayette Inn: While not in Springfield, it's worth a short drive to Lafayette Hill just to eat side-by-side with your pup. But call first to make sure it's okay because during busier times, it's not as feasible to bring your pup. Sitting on the patio, you can drink a delicious homemade brew or wine and munch on whatever moderately priced menu item you choose. The menus change with the seasons, but among the old standbys are the crab cakes sautéed with lump crab, and the always excellent seafood bisque. 646 Germantown Pk., Lafayette Hill; 610/941-0600.

Cheltenham Township

Quakers settled this area around 1690, and since a couple of them were from Cheltenham, England, they decided on that as an appropriate name. Cheltenham prides itself on its diverse population and its architecture, with examples representing the major periods of its long history, including the Beth Sholom Congregation Synagogue, designed by Frank Lloyd Wright and built in 1954. You and your pup will be impressed. And while there are no dog-friendly places to stay and eat in this township (those included are in nearby towns), dogs are welcome at all of the parks as long as they're leashed. Even though an off-leash dog park was recently proposed in the township, it was overwhelmingly opposed by residents.

PARKS, BEACHES, AND RECREATION AREAS

17 Tookany Creek Park

🐾🐾 (See Montgomery County map on page 112)

While it's not a major destination, it's a nice place for you and your pup to enjoy a brisk walk along Tookany Creek. A dirt path runs 2.2 miles alongside the creek, and much of it is shaded. There are picnic areas and a couple of playgrounds here (but dogs are not allowed within the playground borders), as well as trash cans and park benches. The most central place to park is about halfway at the Kleinheinz Pond where there's a lovely fountain, park benches, and trash cans.

The bad news is the Tookany Creek and walking path are bordered by Tookany Creek Parkway, a relatively noisy and busy road. But the good news is that five Sundays in the spring and fall, the parkway is closed to traffic making the trail even wider (and quieter) for you and poochie.

Other good news is that the park was recently recognized by the Environmental Protection Agency as a five-star restoration site and awarded $20,000 to plant native vegetation along the streambank to slow eroding and flooding. Additional improvements to the walking trail are in the works, as well.

From Cheltenham, take 73 East to New Second Street and make a right. Pass the school and take a left on Tookany Creek Parkway. The creek and path are on your right. Hours are sunrise–sunset. 215/887-1000, ext. 227.

PLACES TO EAT

AllWays Café: This eatery serves a variety of exotic salads, sandwiches, and pastas, many with a Mexican, Thai, or Indian influence. You and your pup are welcome to sit streetside and munch on your yummy lunch and dinner. If you're in the mood for an excellent treat, you must try the Thai Peanut Salad. 634 Welsh Rd., Huntington Valley; 215/914-2151.

West Avenue Grill: Any place that serves breakfast all day is A-OK in our book, but the friendly service and fresh food make this grill even better. Open for lunch, too, it's an excellent spot to sit outside with your doggy on a sunny afternoon and eat breakfast food or moderately priced sandwiches and salads to your collective hearts' content. 718 West Ave., Jenkintown; 215/886-1540.

Conshohocken and Lower Merion Township

Both of these areas are close enough together that we decided to group them as one.

"Conshy," as it's playfully referred to by locals, is a close-knit community where families reside here for generations in hillside row homes. It's also another area of Montgomery County that's under redevelopment as many new businesses have popped up over the past decade including major hotels and new restaurants, some that allow doggies.

Located across the Schuylkill River, Lower Merion Township doesn't have much in common with its neighbor. It's part of what's known as the "Main Line." Remember the genteel Katharine Hepburn in the 1939 film, *Philadelphia Story*? She was from Bryn Mawr, a town in Lower Merion Township. The moniker "Main Line" actually refers to the stops along the Pennsylvania Railroad line and it just caught on. What the Main Line translates to nowadays is the more affluent, upscale suburban neighborhoods with stately old multimillion-dollar mansion-like homes on rolling landscapes with lush gardens. Still, dogs are welcome at its beautiful nature preserve, Saunders Woods.

PARKS, BEACHES, AND RECREATION AREAS

18 Schuylkill River Trail

🐾🐾🐾 (See Montgomery County map on page 112)

Although the Schuylkill River Trail stretches 23 miles from Lower Perkiomen Valley Park in Oaks to the Philadelphia Museum of Art, Linus preferred

THINK GLOBALLY, BARK LOCALLY

Santa Photos: If puppers loves the Christmas season as much as you, then head down to Bala Cynwyd's Saks Fifth Avenue store for the annual photo op with St. Nick. The jolly ol' elf will happily pose with your pooch one Saturday in early December. Photos are taken digitally and printed on photo paper for a nominal fee. Funds raised from the photos benefit Morris Animal Refuge, a nonprofit no-kill animal shelter in Philadelphia. www.morrisanimalrefuge.org.

accessing the trail at its midpoint in Conshohocken (at the Spring Mill Train Station off Hector Street) since there are some great places to eat not too far from here and free parking after 5 P.M.

In general, the Schuylkill River Trail is a multi-use trail that's mostly flat and paved, except in Manayunk where it follows the Manayunk Canal towpath, which is hard packed dirt. Improvements are underway for upgrading older areas of the trail for bicyclists, which is also good for dog walkers. Also, further development of the trail will extend it the entire length of the Schuylkill River, for more than 100 miles, from the Delaware River to its headwaters in Schuylkill County.

If you and poochie were to walk its entire length, the trail would take you through suburban neighborhoods, heavy industrial sites, and urban parkland. You'll encounter a lot of bicyclists along the way; remember to stay alert so they can pass you safely. Also, the trail provides direct access to the Perkiomen Trail in Oaks.

From Conshohocken, take Hector Street east and look for the Spring Mill Train Station. Take a right on Station Avenue and park in the lot on the left. Hours are 6 A.M.–sunset. 610/666-5371 or 610/278-3736; www.montcopa.org/parks/Schuylkill_RiverTrail/SchuylkillRT.htm.

19 Saunders Woods

🐾🐾🐾 (See Montgomery County map on page 112)

It's always exciting to find a lesser-known spot that has so much beauty. Saunders Woods, a 25-acre preserve managed by the Natural Lands Trust (NLT), includes breathtaking wildflowers in the meadows and woodlands, as well as about two miles of hilly trails and a stream (a small tributary of the Schuylkill River) traveling through the valley.

The NLT loves to see dogs at the preserves as long they're picked up after and leashed to prevent chasing or frightening the wildlife that lives here.

There are poop bags at the entrance but no trash cans, so you must take the bags with you. As Linus would attest, it's a small, smelly sacrifice to enjoy such a natural treasure as this preserve.

From West Conshohocken take Route 23 East for about 1.5 miles toward Gladwyne. Take a right on Waverly Road. The preserve has a very discreet brown sign about a half-mile down on the right.

Also at the entrance, there's a map of the preserve and enough parking for about seven cars in the parking lot. Hours are 8 A.M.–sunset. 1020 Waverly Rd., Gladwyne; 610/520-9197.

PLACES TO EAT

Billy Cunningham's Court: This pub, owned by the former coach of the Philadelphia 76ers, is a terrific spot to meet up with friends for some beers and wings. If it's not too busy, you and your four-footed sports fan can sit at the small outdoor deck. Linus was too big. Be sure to call first to see if it's okay. When you arrive, enjoy the spirited ambiance, grab some wings, or try the yummy chicken Caesar grinder. 31 Front St., W. Conshohocken; 610/834-8085.

Maya Bella: This BYOB loves dogs. In fact, they'll literally roll out the carpet for your pooch—if the pavement is too hot—at its streetside seating. Linus was thrilled to get his own water bowl and dog biscuits. But dog food is available, too. What's great for you is the chef has years of experience working at one of Philly's most famous restaurants, Le Bec Fin, so you can be assured your food will be a delight. 119 Fayette St., Conshohocken; 610/832-2114.

Spring Mill Café: Artsy, interesting, and eclectic describes both the ambiance and the menu at this darling 25-year-old BYOB situated inside an old general store. You and your pup can sit on the front porch or on the deck to enjoy cuisine best described as French provincial with a North African and Cambodian twist. The food is on the pricey side but well worth it. The café is known for its outstanding Sunday brunch, its boeuf bourguignon, and its mouth-watering crème caramel. 164 Barren Hill Rd., Conshohocken; 610/828-2550.

Tango: Located in the Bryn Mawr train station, you and your doggy are welcome at Tango's outdoor tables. The bistro has been known to have erratic service, so keep that in mind if time is pressing. But the pricey haute-American cuisine is tasty, especially for a suburban eatery specializing in seafood and steaks. 39 Morris Ave., Bryn Mawr; 610/526-9500.

PLACES TO STAY

Residence Inn: Located along the Schuylkill River, you and your pup can hit the Schuylkill River Trail right outside the front door and later relax at this comfortable and friendly hotel. The rooms are oversized suites offering full kitchens and high-speed Internet access. Also for you, a daily hot breakfast, exercise room, and indoor pool; there's even complimentary grocery service. While there are no weight restrictions on pups, a $25 per day pet charge will be added, not exceeding $200. Rates are $159–209. 191 Washington St., Conshohocken; 610/828-8800.

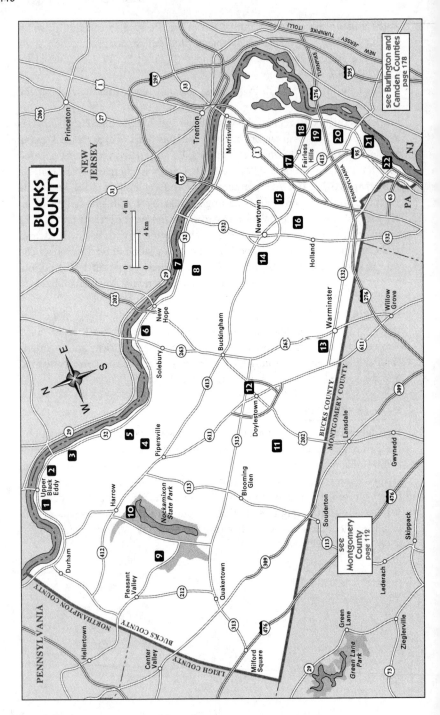

BUCKS COUNTY

NEW JERSEY

see Burlington and Camden Counties
page 178

see Montgomery County
page 112

PENNSYLVANIA

NORTHAMPTON COUNTY
BUCKS COUNTY
LEHIGH COUNTY
BUCKS COUNTY

BUCKS COUNTY
MONTGOMERY COUNTY

PA
NJ

NEW JERSEY TURNPIKE (TOLL)
TURNPIKE

Princeton
Trenton
Morrisville
Fairless Hills
New Hope
Solebury
Buckingham
Newtown
Holland
Warminster
Willow Grove
Lansdale
Doylestown
Blooming Glen
Pipersville
Harrow
Durham
Pleasant Valley
Quakertown
Milford Square
Center Valley
Hellertown
Souderton
Gwynedd
Skippack
Lederach
Zieglerville
Green Lane
Green Lane Park
Nockamixon State Park
Upper Black Eddy

CHAPTER 5
Bucks County

> Sir, this is a unique dog. He does not live by tooth or fang. He respects the right of cats to be cats although he doesn't admire them. He turns his steps rather than disturb an earnest caterpillar. His greatest fear is that someone will point out a rabbit and suggest that he chase it. This is a dog of peace and tranquility.
>
> John Steinbeck

If you've ever met a resident of Bucks County, and ask where they're from, nine times out of 10, they'll tell you the county first, and only if asked, the town. What a difference this is from other areas of Greater Philadelphia, where residents tell you the town they're from before the county.

Obviously, residents take great pride in being from this county because it's so gorgeous as a whole. Traveling through Bucks County you're likely to see some of the most spectacular scenery in the Philadelphia area, especially skirting the Delaware River. Along River Road (Route 32), you

PICK OF THE LITTER—BUCKS COUNTY

BEST STATE PARK
Nockamixon State Park, Quakertown (page 164)

BEST COUNTY PARK
Tinicum Park, Erwinna (page 152)

BEST TRAIL
Delaware Canal State Park, Upper Black Eddy (page 150)

BEST PLACE TO EAT
The Landing, New Hope (page 159)

BEST PLACE TO STAY
Indian Rock Inn, Upper Black Eddy (page 152)

BEST EVENT
Snoopy's DogFest & Canine Education Fair, New Britain
(page 150)

and your doggy will gaze in amazement at the gorgeous old homes on the hillside overlooking the rumbling river and the peaceful and largely undeveloped, rugged landscape. Bucks County also has its share of unusual rock formations and cascading streams. Plus, it is home to four state parks, as well as many county parks.

Is it any wonder that Nellie (and tons of other four-legged friends) love it here? Nellie knows that Bucks County offers plenty to bark about, especially the development of an off-leash dog park in Warminster Township and more than 60 miles of hiking available along the Delaware Canal.

Bucks County also boasts some 26 acres of parkland for every thousand people, making it plentiful in dog-friendly open space. But this, sadly, is not to say Bucks County has been spared development. Many of its beautiful farms are gone or quickly disappearing and giving way to urban sprawl, sparking a lot of controversy among residents.

And with good reason: Bucks is a naturally beautiful and historic area and many residents want to keep it that way.

Originally inhabited by the Lenni-Lenape Indians, Bucks County was later founded as one of William Penn's three original counties in 1682. Named after Buckinghamshire, England, where many of Penn's friends and family were from, Bucks County has a rich past. Not only is the famed Quaker's Pennsbury Manor home located in Morrisville, but George Washington crossed the Delaware River here before a sneak attack on the Hessian soldiers in Trenton, New Jersey (you probably recall the well-known painting of the scene from your history books). Although poochie cannot join you if you choose to visit Pennsbury, you both can see Washington's Crossing and even some gravestones of the soldiers who died there.

Not far from the famed crossing due east is New Hope, an artsy, touristy yet relatively dog-friendly and charming town that you two should check out together. You'll find some friendly places to eat together as well as several options of places to stay.

As much as Bucks is welcoming to pups, ironically it's also strict: dogs are required to be on leashes six feet or shorter at all county parks, and many county parks no longer allow dogs at events like art shows, festivals, antiques shows, or concerts. Too many pups were wandering unsupervised and a public uproar ensued. To be on the safe side, it's best to call the event or festival first to see if it's dog-friendly. Also, dogs are not allowed in camping areas or in the waterways in any county park.

Despite the rigid rules, Nellie would much rather be close by on a short leash than not exploring the beauty of Bucks County at all.

Upper Black Eddy

Upper Black Eddy is a peaceful town right along the Delaware River, home to several scenic areas and at least one excellent place to stay with poochie. It's breathtakingly beautiful no matter what time of year you visit. Plus, the people and pups in these parts are oh-so friendly.

PARKS, BEACHES, AND RECREATION AREAS

1 Ringing Rocks Park

🐾 🐾 🐾 (See Bucks County map on page 146)

You may not come here for the picnicking or hiking, per se, but it's worth a trip just to see the very unique boulder field, about 7 acres wide and 10 feet deep. These boulders will ring like a bell when struck with a hammer, sounding almost hollow. (The mystery is still unsolved but has something to do with the boulders' iron content. However, not all the rocks will ring, which is part of the mystery.) Ringing Rocks also boasts the county's largest waterfall. With only a couple of picnic tables, a bench and a trash can, a few trails, and not much in the way of parking, it's not the most desirable destination to take your dog. But one more excuse to visit Upper Black Eddy is never a bad thing, and the weird science surrounding boulder field is something to see and hear up close. Don't forget your leash, your poop bags, and, of course, your hammer.

DOG-EAR YOUR CALENDAR

Annual Dachshund Picnic: Mark your calendars for the newly annual dachshund meet and greet at Indian Rock Inn in Upper Black Eddy, one weekend in June. This doxie-friendly event doesn't include contests or prizes, just a lot of fun for doxie lovers and their pups. But if you don't have a dachshund, don't be discouraged. Every doggy is welcome, but the focus is on the ever-popular wiener dog. 877/888-7555.

Snoopy's DogFest & Canine Education Fair: Help raise money for the incredible dogs who assist people with disabilities at Snoopy's DogFest. Benefiting Canine Companions for Independence and usually held one Saturday in October at Peace Valley Park in New Britain, the event includes a fundraising walk with the opportunity to receive a Snoopy's DogFest t-shirt, bandana, and goodie bag. Also featured are canine demonstrations, raffles, vendors, pet contests and prizes, various dog rescues, and everyone's favorite animated beagle, the original Snoop Dog. 215/602-2093; www.cciphiladelphia.com.

Paws for Life: Benefiting Gilda's Club of Bucks/Montco (Gilda Radner's nonprofit cancer support foundation), this is one dog-walking event you and the whole family won't want to miss. Usually held the first Saturday in October, Paws for Life includes not just a dog walk but live entertainment including clowns, music, and contests. The entrance fee is $25. Registration 9 A.M.; dog walk 10 A.M. The event takes place at Core Creek Park, Woodbourne Rd., Langhorne. 215/441-3290.

The park is located in Bridgeton Township, two miles west of Upper Black Eddy. Take Route 32 North to Bridgeton Hill Road, then a right onto Ringing Rocks Road. Look for Ringing Rocks Park on your right. Hours are 8 A.M.–sunset. 215/757-0571.

2 Delaware Canal State Park

🐾🐾🐾🐾 🦴 (See Bucks County map on page 146)

Even if you don't consider yourself a granola-eating, Birkenstock-wearing nature lover, a trip to Upper Black Eddy with your dog might make you one. One major reason is the Delaware Canal State Park headquartered here. It's nearly impossible to visit here without a stroll or jog down the canal with your hairy companion. A National Historic Landmark and a National Historic Trail, this 60-mile stretch of canal towpath (which spans from Bristol north through Upper Black Eddy and onward to Easton) retains much of the beauty and features of the canal that existed during its operation in the 19th century. Back then, its primary purpose was transporting coal to and from northeastern cities via mule barges, then a newer and more efficient way of transporting goods. Locks are still intact along the canal today and mule-drawn boat rides in New Hope demonstrate what canal life was like 150 years ago.

In addition to its utility, the canal is a peaceful retreat any time of year with your doggy. In some areas, you'll see breathtaking views of the river, mostly north of Lumberville.

Along the shaded canal towpath, you'll see lots of other cyclists, equestrians, joggers, and dog walkers. Dogs are allowed in all sections of the canal as long as they are on a leash six feet in length or shorter.

Canal-walking etiquette includes yielding to horses and mules to avoid startling them. If you approach from the front, move out of the way about 100 feet from the canal and let the equines pass. If approaching from the rear, make sure you call out about 50 feet away and slow down or stop until you get the clearance from the horse or mule tender.

If it's your first visit to the canal, stop at the park office located in Upper Black Eddy to pick up helpful info, historical literature, and maps. There's limited parking at this location.

An outstanding feature of the canal is that 30 miles of it consists of crushed red-brown stone path excellent for walking or jogging. This area includes Upper Black Eddy but extends from Morrisville to Uhlerstown. Also for 30 miles, the Delaware Canal towpath parallels New Jersey's Delaware & Raritan Canal towpath, separated only by the Delaware River, but six bridges link the two trails.

One of those bridges is a footbridge located in Lumberville, a small village with a few places to grab a bite to eat. If you walk on a stretch of the canal to New Hope, you can stop and refresh with your pup at various eateries there, too. Both of these towns, however, get quite crowded on weekends and street parking is metered. So parking there hoping to make that your base may not be so simple. On weekdays, you're probably in luck.

If you'd rather eat directly on the canal, there are picnic areas located in Erwinna, Tinicum, Lumberville, and Virginia Forrest Recreation Area. The Virginia Forrest Recreation area provides picnic areas, paved parking, and modern restrooms. (Interesting tidbit: Virginia Forrest was the woman credited with getting the park its National Historic Landmark Status.) Another great entry point to the canal with plenty of parking is at Tinicum Park, where you can directly access the canal towpath and easily launch a canoe or kayak with puppers; you might even see a few furry friends floating by, too.

To get to the headquarters of the canal in Upper Black Eddy, take Route 32 North (River Road) to Upper Black Eddy and take a left on Lodi Hill Road. Hours are sunrise–sunset. 11 Lodi Hill Rd., Upper Black Eddy; 610/982-5560; www.dcnr.state.pa.us/stateparks/parks/delawarecanal.aspx.

🖪 Tinicum Park

🐾🐾🐾 (See Bucks County map on page 146)

Probably best known for its regulation disk golf course, Tinicum Park is actually a fabulous place to take your dog for a walk in the park's 126 acres or opt to access the Delaware State Canal, which is right behind the park's picnic area. On our last visit, Nellie couldn't contain herself because she wanted to say hi to a few of the dogs here off leash in the morning hours in the large disk golf field. While it's not "legal" to go off leash here, it seems as though it's a risk these doggies and people thought was worth it. Regardless, Nellie and I opted for a leashed walk along the beautiful and shady Delaware Canal.

The park offers plenty of picnic space and pavilions, restrooms, as well as an impressive playground for the kiddies. It's also the location of the annual Bucks County Kennel Club dog show held each May. Hours are sunrise–sunset. Located off River Road (Route 32), Erwinna; 215/757-0571.

PLACES TO STAY

Colonial Woods Family Camping Resort: As long as your nonaggressive pup is on a leash, he's welcome to stay at the campsites here no matter his size. You and the family can enjoy the pool, playground, mini golf, tennis, fishing, volleyball, shuffleboard, and planned activities throughout the season. Rates for a tent with water are $28–33. 545 Lonely Cottage Dr., Upper Black Eddy; 610/847-5808 or 800/887-CAMP; colwoods@epix.net; www.colonialwoods.com.

Dogwood Haven Family Campground: You and your doggy are welcome to stay at any of the 55 wooded campsites at this campground. An inexpensive alternative to hotel stays, this campground offers electric and water hookups, showers, flush toilets, and dumping facilities. It's located convenient to the scenic Delaware State Canal and the Delaware River. Rates are $17.50–19.50. 16 Lodi Hill Rd. (off Route 32), Upper Black Eddy; 610/982-5402.

Indian Rock Inn: If you truly want a quintessential bed-and-breakfast experience that will welcome your pup with open arms and paws (dachshunds live here), you'll definitely want to check out the Indian Rock Inn. Dating back to 1812 and situated directly along the Delaware, this three-story inn is filled with gorgeous antiques and has river views from its rooms. Its darling front porch allows you and your friendly doggy to sit and enjoy cocktails or dine on French country cuisine. The Inn's back porch is ideal for relaxing and reading. You couldn't pick a more ideal B&B location for you and your well-behaved pup as it's in between the canal and the river. There's no weight restriction for your dog, but make sure to let them know you're bringing her before your stay. A flat $15 cleaning fee per stay will be charged. Rates are $85–235. 2206 River Rd., Upper Black Eddy; 610/928-9600 or 877/888-7555; www.indianrockinn.com.

Point Pleasant

Another picturesque river village situated along the Delaware, it truly is a point of pleasantry. Here, you'll find two fantastic parks as well as unbelievable scenery that include views of the river and surrounding hills and cliffs.

PARKS, BEACHES, AND RECREATION AREAS

4 Ralph Stover State Park

🐾🐾🐾 (See Bucks County map on page 146)

About two miles from Point Pleasant stands the site of a former water-powered grain mill of the late 18th century, known as Ralph Stover State Park. While the name of the park (after the owner and operator of the mill) is a bit dull, Nellie thinks that this park is anything but and could be one of her favorites as it's full of majestic scenery and tranquility. Plus, she's able to walk down to the bubbling Tohickon Creek to soak her tootsies on warm days. Definitely one of the most unique parks in this county, 45-acre Ralph Stover State Park is located along the banks of the creek and adjoins the Tohickon Valley Park. The state park also contains the original mill race that diverted water from above the dam to power the mill. About a mile of trail allows you and your pup to hike along the mill race as well as through various habitats. You'll also get a chance to see some spectacular cliffs and have access to a playground, picnic tables near the water's edge, and picnic pavilions. A scenic vista known as High Rocks is accessible within the park via Stover Park Road and the High Rocks Trail (both closed to traffic). You can also access it by car via Tory Road, a dirt road, a short distance from Tohickon Valley Park.

There's plenty of shade at Ralph Stover, too, as well as water fountains and restrooms. The only drawbacks are the lack of trash cans, so it's carry in, carry out, and dogs must be on a leash no longer than six feet.

From Point Pleasant take Tohickon Hill Road and take a right on State Park Road to the park. Hours are sunrise–sunset. 6011 State Park Rd., Pipersville; 610/982-5560 or 800/63-PARKS; www.dcnr.state.pa.us/stateparks/parks/ralphstover.aspx.

5 Tohickon Valley Park

🐾🐾🐾 (See Bucks County map on page 146)

Don't be fooled when you drive in the entrance of this park (as we were) that it's a rinky-dink little county park. Sure there are some nice, shady picnic areas, a playground, restrooms, and a community swimming pool. But Tohickon Valley Park encompasses not just these day-use areas, but a total of nearly 600 acres on one side of Tohickon Creek. The gorge down to the creek offers spectacular views, especially from the High Rocks vista point (also accessible via Ralph Stover State Park), 200-foot cliffs of red Brunswick shale

DIVERSIONS

If it's between Memorial Day and Labor Day and you're in the eastern portion of Bucks, you're not too far away from the all the action of the Delaware River and canal. Even if you have a water-loving canine, he might be thrilled to trade the doggy paddle for a ride on the water with you.

Canine Canoeing: Although this area may be "the world's river tubing capital," pups and tubes don't mix, for obvious reasons. But there's always the option of taking your furry friend for a relaxing canoe ride along the Delaware. There's no extra fee to take your dog canoeing with River Country, but your pup must be leashed and not allowed on private property along the waterway. Rates are $21–33. 2 Walters Ln., Point Pleasant; 215/297-5000; www.rivercountry.net.

Coryell's Ferry: If you have about 30 minutes and wish to take in some history while visiting New Hope, hop aboard Coryell's Ferry, a narrated paddlewheel ferry boat ride. Well-behaved lap dogs (technically speaking) are usually welcome at no extra charge, but the final decision is up to the captain, based upon space available. The fee for the ride is $7. Interesting tidbit: The Coryell's Ferry Boat Ride company has been partially responsible for the training of guide dogs by providing a place for these working dogs to become accustomed to boats and docks. 22 South Main St., New Hope; 215/862-2050.

that rise above the creek. Especially beautiful in the fall, Tohickon Valley has been the subject of many award-winning photographs.

To access the High Rocks vista, take the main trail in the park (a paved road a short distance from the main parking lot; also known as High Rocks Trail) and it's about a 45-minute hike. There's another short trail that goes behind the pool and parallels Cafferty Road. Both trails will undoubtedly provide you and your doggy with some excellent exercise and scenery.

From River Road in Point Pleasant, take Cafferty Road heading north and see the park entrance on the left. Hours are sunrise–sunset. Cafferty Road, Point Pleasant; 215/757-0571.

PLACES TO STAY

Beaver Valley Campground: If you have two or fewer doggies, you're welcome to stay at the wooded campsites at this family-oriented campground. Some of the amenities you'll enjoy include restrooms, a pool, a playground, a

New Hope Canal Boat Company: As long as your pup is well mannered, he or she is welcome aboard one of the most unique ways to see the canal—a genuine mule-drawn canal boat. The 45-minute ride starts in New Hope and heads north along the canal. On your excursion, you'll get a history of the canal and New Hope, as well as a tune or two from a bygone era sung by a member of the crew. Tickets are $10. 149 South Main St., New Hope; 215/862-0758; www.canalboats.com.

Bucks County Horse Park: If you love canines *and* equines, this is the place for you and your pooch. This park consists of 126 acres with more than 30 acres of trails for hiking and jogging. The park's show rings, polo fields, cross-country courses host more than 50 events spring–fall. So why would it be something a dog would enjoy? Because leashed dogs are always welcome to any and all events (there are even a couple dog shows, too) at the horse park. 8934 Easton Rd., Revere; 610/847-8597; www.buckscountyhorsepark.org.

Covered Bridge Tour: Because of the immense beauty of much of Bucks County, driving it is an event in itself, especially if you and your furry companion choose to see the many covered bridges still standing from the mid- to late 1800s. Get ready to explore some exquisite scenery, as well. Bucks County Conference and Visitor's Bureau, www.bccvb.org/bridge_tours.html.

general store, planned activities, a game room, and even hayrides. Rates are $4–24.50. 80 Clay Ridge Rd., Ottsville; 610/847-5643.

Lumberville

The tiny village of Lumberville is also located directly along the Delaware River. Here, you can access the canal towpath, too. Plus, a footbridge that can take you across the river to New Jersey is also located in this little gem of a town.

PLACES TO EAT

The Lumberville Store: This charming general store that doubles as a deli, a post office, and an art gallery welcomes you and your pup to sample one of the many delicious deli sandwiches or hoagies at the outside tables. The food is top notch and bottled water is sold here for you and your thirsty dog. Route 32, Lumberville; 215/297-5388.

PLACES TO STAY

Black Bass Hotel: The beautiful Black Bass Hotel loves its four-legged guests and has five acres for them to run on. The Federal-style tavern and inn, built in 1740, is furnished with British antiques and affords scenic river views. Seven rooms share baths and three are private suites. Nellie is pleased as puppy punch to hear there's no weight restriction for dogs to stay here, nor is there an extra charge for furry family members. Rates are $65–175. 3774 River Rd., Lumberville; 215/297-5815; www.blackbasshotel.com.

New Hope

A place as special, sophisticated, and picturesque as New Hope just doesn't seem real. This darling riverside village has so much character and is such an escape from the routine, you'll feel like you're on vacation every time you visit. You and your canine will likely get dog tired exploring everything you can in the area including the canal towpath that runs through the town, as well as nearby parks and nature areas. Lots of options for places to stay are in New Hope and environs, as well as places to get a bite to eat with your hungry hound. A word to the wise,

DIVERSIONS

With all there is to do with your pooch in Bucks County, you might want to add one more: wine-tasting. Of course, the two of you combined must be at least 21 in people years in order to taste the fermented goodness. But visiting a couple of these spots will not only give you a taste of the wine but also a taste of where and how it was produced.

Buckingham Valley Winery: One of the first wineries in Pennsylvania and currently one of the largest and friendliest, Buckingham Valley Winery is happy to have you and your dog on the grounds. While your four-legged friend isn't allowed inside the tasting room or winery, you're both welcome to sit on the lawn or at picnic tables and admire the beautiful scenery and munch on snacks and sip cold *vino*. But your pup must be under control as various farm animals meander through the vineyards, too. 1521 Rte. 413, Buckingham (two miles south of Route 202); 215/794-7188.

Chaddsford Winery: One of the best-known local wineries, Chaddsford welcomes you and puppers to its store in Peddler's Village. Here you can buy some of the critically acclaimed wine; even better, you'll able to taste it first. Peddler's Village, Routes 202 and 263, Lahaska; 215/794-9655.

though: It gets awfully crowded here on weekends and since there are only a few streets in town, parking can be fierce. It's metered, so remember your quarters. Also, there's a pooper-scooper law in New Hope, so don't forget your bags. That aside, it's always exciting to visit here.

PARKS, BEACHES, AND RECREATION AREAS

6 Hal Clark Park

 (See Bucks County map on page 146)

This undeveloped 27-acre park is more of a shady trail that leads to the Delaware River than anything else. On the way to the river you can connect with the canal towpath. The walk to the river is nearly a mile and is heavily shaded with a lot of overgrown weeds. But once you get to the river, you'll enjoy the view. Your dog must be on a leash although you're unlikely to see anyone else, since it's such a rugged spot. A trash can is available at the entrance. Still, there's only enough parking for a couple of cars to access this park.

This park is not marked, so to find it you must be on Route 32, one mile south of Centre Bridge, and look for a one-lane red wooden bridge on the river

Fratelli Desiato Winery: Specializing in small-batch blends of hand-crafted Italian-style wines, this winery is located on 12 acres in a rustic hilltop village. Not only is wine for sale here, but also a large selection of authentic, delicious Italian foods like olives, spice blends, vinegars, and pasta. Your Italian greyhound, or any breed pup, for that matter, is welcome as long as you call ahead so the winery owners can make arrangements for their pets. 522 E. Dark Hollow Rd., Pipersville; 215/766-2524.

New Hope Winery: A dog-friendly establishment, New Hope Winery is happy to have you and your pup on the premises. The two of you can check out more than 30 varieties of wines available, some of them award-winning. If you're so inclined, you can also browse the antiques offered in the adjacent Big Red Barn. 6123 Lower York Rd., Route 202, New Hope; 215/794-2331 or 800/592-WINE.

Sand Castle Winery: As long as poochie is on a leash, you both are welcome at this fabulous European-influenced winery located on the banks of the Delaware River in Erwinna. Here, world-class pinot noir, chardonnay, cabernet sauvignon, and Johannisberg Riesling are produced. Events are also held many weekends a year. 755 River Rd., Erwinna; 800/722-9463.

side of the road to take you to the park. Hours are sunrise–sunset. River Road, Centre Bridge; 215/757-0571 or 215/348-6114.

7 Washington Crossing Historic Park

🐾🐾 🐕 (See Bucks County map on page 146)

On Christmas night in 1776, General George Washington led his troops across the icy, choppy Delaware River in a sneak attack on the Hessians in Trenton. It's believed that this move helped boost morale and changed the course of the American Revolution. And it all happened right here in Bucks County. This 500-acre park has two sections: the upper section, the Thompson Mill section about two miles from New Hope, and the McConkey Ferry section five miles south on River Road.

At the Thompson Mill section, you and your curious canine can sniff out the area where the troops camped before the silent crossing. Soldiers' gravesites as well as colonial homes and a gristmill are also on the grounds.

Within the McConkey Ferry section further south on River Road, you'll see the visitor's center, memorials, and several restored historic buildings located here, but your pup isn't allowed inside, sadly. Regardless, she is allowed to explore all of the grounds on a leash at both the upper and lower sections of the park.

You and your pup can't access the river in the upper section, but you can walk along the canal towpath here as well as the wooded trails that surround the area. The area is very wooded. Visiting the upper section of the park is a bit spooky in wintertime because you can't help but get a chill up your spine thinking of what those brave soldiers went through that night.

When turning off of River Road into this section, if you take a quick right there's a parking lot where you can park, or if you're lucky and there are spots available, you can park closer to where history was made over the tiny bridge.

Both sections are on River Road (Route 32). Thompson's Mill is about two miles from New Hope, and the McConkey Ferry section is near the intersection of Routes 532 and 32. 1112 River Rd., Washington Crossing; 215/493-4076.

8 Bowman's Hill Wildflower Preserve

🐾 (See Bucks County map on page 146)

This park would probably grant a three- or four-paw rating if dogs were allowed to smell the more than one thousand species of wildflowers and native plants and hike the trails in the preserve, but sadly, they're not. We don't begrudge the powers that be, especially since they allow dogs all over the grounds before you enter the iron gate that leads to the preserve. And you can always do a virtual tour on the preserve's website if you're curious. On the grounds of the preserve, your dog can run in the meadow (on a leash, of course), access the

Delaware River, or even have a picnic with you. Parking is available, and it's just across River Road from Washington Crossing Historic Park.

From I-95 New Hope Exit 51 (old Exit 31), go north on Taylorsville Road for seven miles (crossing Route 532 at five miles). Turn left (north) onto River Road (Route 32) and go 2.5 miles. The entrance to the preserve is on the left. Hours are 8:30 A.M.–sunset. 1635 River Rd., New Hope; 215/862-2924; www.bhwp.org.

PLACES TO EAT

C'est La Vie French Bakery: If you are in the mood for mouth-watering French pastries, breads, turnovers, and quiches, soups, and sandwiches, then don't forget to stop here. As long as your pup is polite and won't bother the other customers (who might also be canines), you two are welcome here. There are even French dog biscuits available for sale, and the staff will happily provide water for your thirsty pooch. 20 S. Main St., New Hope; 215/862-1956.

Giuseppe's Pizza and Family Restaurant: The second-best thing about this restaurant, after its remarkable, inexpensive menu, is that your pup can sit with you outside during the warm weather. When it's colder, there's always takeout. The same family owns the Giuseppe's in Warminster, offering the same menu and same yummy pizza and cheesesteaks. The beer's always cold and the service is great, too. 473 Old York Rd., New Hope; 215/862-1740; www.giuseppepizza.com.

Havana: Specializing in world cuisine with Caribbean, Latin, and European influences, Havana features a varied, fiery menu, as well as a fun and friendly atmosphere. Some menu items include steak quesadillas, goat cheese salad, and a personal favorite: black beans and rice. While the food here isn't cheap, it is good and the service is great. You and your pup are welcome at the restaurant's outdoor patio bar all year long (there are heaters during the wintertime). 105 S. Main St., New Hope; 215/862-5501; www.havananewhope.com.

Karla's Bar and Restaurant: An old standby in the New Hope restaurant scene, Karla's is one of the best. Even better is that it allows you to bring your pup with you while dining outdoors. It serves mostly pricier American fare with a Greek twist, and its salads and sandwiches are never disappointing, especially the classic hamburger. 5 W. Mechanic St., New Hope; 215/862-2612.

The Landing: A favorite New Hope restaurant among the locals and visitors, like Nellie and me, this eatery serves delicious (albeit pricey) American regional cuisine and welcomes you and your pup on its riverview terrace. For lunch you might try the roasted turkey breast on French bread with Havarti dill and green apple. It's truly scrumptious and worth every penny. Best of all, according to Nellie, the restaurateurs have a Bernese Mountain Dog at home. 22 N. Main St., New Hope; 215/862-5711.

The New Hope Snak Shak: If you're looking for a quick bite without waiting in long lines on Main Street, stop over at this snack shack. The owners of this quaint snackery (the former site of the sadly departed doggy café/bakery) have seven dogs of their own. They invite you and poochie to rest your tired feet and paws on the small outside deck while enjoying your choice of prepackaged snacks, gourmet snack items, ice cream, and a variety of cold drinks. A doggy watering station is available, too, for parched pups. 27A W. Mechanic St., New Hope, 215/862-7087.

The Summer Kitchen: In the days before air conditioning, a summer kitchen was added in well-to-do homes as an alternative way to prevent the main house from getting overly hot. This historic summer kitchen restaurant specializes in contemporary cuisine with a Cuban twist. A couple of the best menu items are the Cuban paella and Havana picadillo. Although not located in New Hope but rather in nearby Penn's Park, the restaurant is worth a mention because it's less crowded, and may even be a nice stop on your way home. However, dogs are not allowed after 7 P.M. on weekends. Route 232 and Penn's Park Road, Penn's Park; 215/598-9210; www.thesummerkitchen.net.

Triumph Brewing Company: This sophisticated yet comfy brewery and restaurant serves moderately priced contemporary, eclectic American cuisine and some of the best handcrafted beer around. Whether you're in the mood for an interesting salad or yummy sandwich, you won't be disappointed. A tried-and-true winner is the Triumph fish-and-chips made with amber ale batter. 400 Union Square, Bridge Street, New Hope; 215/862-8300; www.triumphbrew.com.

Wildflowers Garden Restaurant: A cozy, inexpensive restaurant that's situated right along a quiet creek, Wildflowers' diverse offerings include everything from fondue to barbecue beef and Thai specials. You and your canine companion are allowed on the outside terrace. If you can't decide among the many choices, the sandwiches are always a sure bet. 8 W. Mechanic St., New Hope; 215/862-2241.

PLACES TO STAY

Aaron Burr House Bed & Breakfast: Known for its warmth and hospitality, Victorian beauty, and excellent location, the Aaron Burr House is a nice option for dogs less than 50 pounds. The pet-friendly rooms have a private porch or a separate entrance as well as a main door through the Inn. The Inn is across from a 200-acre field, next to the Delaware Canal State Park, and one mile from Washington Crossing Historic Park. Breakfast is served fresh daily, and of course is complimentary. A $25 per day fee is charged for dogs. Rates are $95–265. 80 W. Bridge St., New Hope; 215/862-2343; http://aaronburrhouse.com.

Barley Sheaf Farm Bed and Breakfast: Right on the outskirts of New Hope in a rural town called Holicong you'll find the Barley Sheaf Farm, the

former home of Pulitzer Prize-winning journalist and playwright George S. Kaufmann. At this true retreat you'll have storybook countryside basically to yourself and likely be greeted by a couple of Bernese Mountain dogs as well as some geese and sheep grazing nearby. The owners are Swiss American so you'll notice a Swiss influence in not just the decor but the incredible breakfast, too. Nellie was so happy to hear there are no weight restrictions for dogs to stay here, but there is a $25 per day fee, and dogs must be crated when unattended. Rates are $115–285. P.O. Box 10, Holicong, PA 18928; 215/794-5104; www.barleysheaf.com.

Best Western New Hope Inn: While it's not as charming as some of the New Hope B&Bs, if you're looking for something less expensive for up to two dogs lighter than 25 pounds each, this may be it. The rooms are adequate and the staff is friendly, and the hotel is located just a short drive to downtown New Hope and Peddler's Village. A $20 pet fee is charged per night. Rates are $73–100. 6426 Lower York Rd., New Hope; 215/862-5221.

1870 Wedgwood Inn: Owned by the same owners as the Aaron Burr House B&B, the 1870 Wedgwood Inn has many of the same amenities like its hospitality, Victorian beauty, and proximity to the center of New Hope. Dogs under 50 pounds are welcome here. This Inn is also across from a 200-acre field, next to the Delaware Canal State Park, and one mile from Washington Crossing Historic Park. A $25 per day pet fee is charged. Rates are $95–265. 111 W. Bridge St., New Hope; 215/862-2570; http://1870WedgwoodInn.com.

Golden Pheasant Inn: If your dog is 30 pounds or less, and you're looking for a romantic getaway with a significant other (other than your dog, of course) or even a family trip, check out the Golden Pheasant Inn, located north of New Hope in Erwinna. Here you and your pup can stay along the river at the Inn's cottage, which comes equipped with a kitchenette, living room, and a charming porch overlooking the Delaware Canal. A fee of $20 per day is charged for dogs and/or children. Rates are $95–225. 763 River Rd. (Route 32), Erwinna; 610/294-9595; www.goldenpheasant.com.

Inn at Stoney Hill: If your dog identifies more with Scooby Doo than Benji in terms of size, you can stop reading this description now. However, if you have a small pup less than 20 pounds, you both will likely enjoy yourselves at this peaceful getaway less than a mile from downtown New Hope. Each room has a private bath, air conditioning, and cable television. Private decks are available as an extra in some rooms. A full breakfast is available on weekends, and a continental breakfast is served weekdays. While well-mannered small poochies are welcome here, all must be flea-dipped prior to arrival. Please bring your own dog bowls, bed, and/or crate. Dogs must not be left unattended. Your $75 pet deposit will be refunded if management finds your room clean and tidy when you leave. Rates are $99–225. 105 Stoney Hill Rd., New Hope; 215/862-5769 or 866/590-9100; http://innatstoneyhill.com.

New Hope Motel in the Woods: Another "you get what you pay for" motel, this modest hotel is nevertheless a dog-friendly option. Although dogs up to 50 pounds are welcome here for a one-time $25 pet fee, there is little to say about the amenities. Dogs are required to be in a crate if you leave the room. Also important to remember is the cancellation policy that charges 15 percent. Rates are $69–149. 400 W. Bridge St., New Hope; 215/862-2800.

Quakertown

Located in Upper Bucks County about 50 miles north of Philadelphia is the small, quiet community of Quakertown. It was here that the Liberty Bell was hidden from the British on its way to its official hiding place in the Lehigh Valley during our nation's fight for independence. A relatively rural area that provides much in the way of recreation for you and your pup, Quakertown is currently revitalizing its downtown, an undertaking that will bring more life and fun into the community. Two of the best parks in the county are located near Quakertown, and lots of nearby spots are waiting for you and your pup to set up camp.

PARKS, BEACHES, AND RECREATION AREAS

🐾 Lake Towhee

🐾🐾🐾 (See Bucks County map on page 146)

Although a golden retriever, Nellie felt like she had the luck of an Irish setter when she could explore two exceptional parks (Nockamixon and Lake Towhee) so close in proximity. Lake Towhee is a 50-acre lake and the surrounding park area is about 552 acres, much smaller than Nockamixon but not any less peaceful and serene. Here you and your pup can picnic in the shade and then walk down to the lake's edge for some refreshment (for your pup, of course). If you have your own boat, the two of you might want to feel the wind in your faces on the quiet lake. Upon entering the park, you will see the lake ahead of you and you can drive down the circular drive to check it out first. Park in the surrounding parking areas near the playground and

THINK GLOBALLY, BARK LOCALLY

The Quakertown Veterinary Clinic Pet Fair: Usually held one Saturday in May or June, the Quakertown Pet Fair is a fun event where you can take your pooch and learn about search-and-rescue dogs, watch agility demonstrations, see horses up close, visit rescue groups, and find out about adoption. Veterinarians and representatives from various dog health and behavior, rescue, and adoption groups are on hand to answer questions. Plus, there are lots of freebies. Shuttles run all day to the clinic since parking is tight. 215/536-6245.

Annual Dog Days of Summer: Whether you have a dog or are looking to adopt one, this annual June event is one you shouldn't miss. Held at the Reigning Dogs & Cats store in Newtown, this pet fair benefiting dog rescue groups and shelters has all sorts of helpful pet care and training info, dog demonstrations, and adoptable dogs from local shelters and rescues available. Your pup will definitely appreciate the day out with you, and you'll have fun and learn a little more, too. Reigning Dogs & Cats, 30 West Rd., Newtown; 215/497-7477; www.reigningdogsandcats.com.

Barctoberfest: German shepherds won't be the only party animals at this festive and fabulous event that benefits various dog rescue groups. Held one Sunday in October, the Reigning Dogs & Cats store puts on the Barctoberfest that includes games, contests, a costume parade, music, food, canine good citizen information, a blessing of the animals, and more. Reigning Dogs & Cats, 30 West Rd., Newtown; 215/497-7477; www.reigningdogsandcats.com.

Pet Fair: Typically held the last Sunday of October at Lick Your Chops store in Richboro, this always well-attended pet fair is a celebration of our furry friends and benefits various animal welfare groups. Some of the excitement includes a blessing of the animals, as well as info provided by rescue groups, dog trainers, and pet sitters. A DJ spins tunes for your enjoyment. Your pup can participate in one of the many contests and even win prizes. Lick Your Chops, 700 Second Street Pk., Richboro; 215/322-5266.

bathrooms. Across from the picnic area is a trail that leads to a big, open field with a trash can and a picnic table. Although it's not allowed, it would be an excellent spot to let Fido run free—at least that's what Nellie was hoping. It's so peaceful at this park, that if you're lucky enough to be here during the off season, you'll only hear birds singing and the trees rustling.

From Route 611 take a left on 563 North to Old Bethlehem Pike. Take a right on Old Bethlehem Pike and look for the park entrance on your right. Hours are 8 A.M.–sunset. Old Bethlehem Pike, Applebachsville; 215/757-0571.

10 Nockamixon State Park

🐾🐾🐾 (See Bucks County map on page 146)

Probably Linus's and my favorite on-leash park of all time, Nockamixon is everything a state park should be: free, beautiful, plentiful in recreation opportunities, and a complete respite from everyday life, sort of like a vacation in Philly's back yard. This park spans 5,300 acres with a 1,450-acre lake. People don't just walk their dogs here (you'll see oodles of them) but also their horses. They also sail on the lake and, in the winter months, cross-country ski, sled, ice fish, and ice skate.

When Linus was just a lad, we'd come here quite often so he could work off some of that young retriever energy. Afterwards we'd have a picnic together. In fact, he learned how to swim here (although dogs and people are not allowed to swim in Lake Nockamixon, somehow we got away with it). This excellent park has four boat launches located around the lake, as well as 300 picnic tables, a playground, and miles of lake- and tree-lined bike and hiking trails. Boats with 18 mph motors or less are permitted. Anglers also love the lake as it's stocked with bass, catfish, and walleye.

Although there are several entrances to the park, the recommended one with poochie is the Tohickon entrance. It's less hectic, provides trash cans, and has more places for blankets than picnic benches. Your pup can get a drink and stick her feet in the lake here, too. If you choose the Haycock entrance, be forewarned: there are no trash cans, so you must bring bags with you and take your trash and your doggy's poop out with you. Aside from that fact, this entire park couldn't be a better spot to come and escape.

The park is located in Quakertown along Route 563 (Mountain View Drive), in between Routes 313 to the west and 611 to the east. Hours are 8 A.M.–sunset. 1542 Mountain View Dr., Quakertown; 215/529-7300; www.dcnr.state.pa.us/stateparks/parks/nockamixon.aspx.

PLACES TO STAY

Hampton Inn Quakertown: While you'll be happy to hear that this hotel has a heated indoor pool and an exercise room, your pup will be pleased to know that there's no weight restriction for him, just an extra $10 fee per day. You'll likely have a comfy and quiet stay here. Rates are $89–145. 1915 John Fries Hwy., Quakertown; 215/536-7779.

Our Farm Under The Mimosa Tree Bed & Breakfast: If you love quiet times, farm animals, and lovely scenery, then this 200-year-old farmhouse B&B may be the one for you and your furry friend. As long as your pup won't chase the animals who roam freely, she's welcome here. If she's not able to restrain herself or is fearful, then a crate is recommended. The B&B is situated on 20 fenced-in acres and there's even a pond that can be used for doggy paddling. The rooms are comfy and the filling breakfast may feature anything from French Toast to omelets. Just be sure to let them know you'll be bringing your dog when making your reservation. Rates are $105–175. 1487 Blue School Rd., Perkasie; 215/249-9420; www.mimosatreebnb.com.

Quakerwoods Campground: The family dog or dogs are welcome at this family-oriented campground featuring events ranging from kids' activities to '50s weekend. The campground has more than 200 wooded campsites that border a creek and a pond. It also has clean, modern restrooms and even a miniature golf course. There's no extra charge for your pet; it's just asked that you clean up after him. Rates are $21–32. 2225 Rosedale Rd., Quakertown; 215/536-1984 or 800/235-2350; www.quakerwoods.com.

Rodeway Inn Quakertown: If roughing it in the great outdoors in one of Quakertown's many campsites isn't your thing, you might want to check out this option. Be forewarned: It's not luxurious, doesn't have many amenities, nor is it extremely clean, so it's a close second to camping. But the good news is there's no weight restriction for dogs and it's only a $5 extra per day pet fee. Rates are $60–75. 1920 SR 663, Quakertown; 215/536-7600.

Tohickon Family Campground: Another fun spot to camp with the family is the Tohickon Family Campground in Quakertown. Here, you and your leashed pup will enjoy more than 64 creekside acres while you and the family will appreciate the fully stocked store, laundry facilities, planned activites playground, and pools. There's no extra charge for dogs nor are there any limits to the number of dogs you may bring. Rates are $30–36. 8308 Covered Bridge Dr., Quakertown; 215/536-7951 or 866/536-CAMP; info@tohickoncampground.com; www.tohickoncampground.com.

Doylestown

More than 250 years old, this little town is giant on charm, culture, and friendliness. Doylestown, the county seat, is home to stunning Victorian architecture and world-class cultural facilities (sadly, they don't allow dogs). In fact, it was recently named as one of a "dozen distinctive destinations" by the National Trust for Historic Preservation. On State Street you can find lots of unique shops and some restaurants that will welcome your pup, and the nearby Peace Valley Park is one of the area's best public parks.

FETCHING NECESSITIES

Having to buy dog food or treats can be a drag on your own, so why not bring along your curious canine to make it fun?

Jake & Elwood's House of Chews: While strolling through New Hope, you and your furry friend must make a stop here. You will find a variety of chewies to chews from...uh, make that choose from. Plus, you two will no doubt have a few laughs at some of the merchandise that includes everything from retro dog bowls to dog sunglasses and party hats. 122 S. Main St., New Hope; 215/862-2533 or 866/285-1800.

Tails of the Village: From gifts to gear, it's all here. This pet shop specializes in representing hundreds of dog breeds in its gift lines. Service here is excellent, and if you can't find your favorite breed the sales associates will. But rest assured, mutts never feel left out as there are tons of toys and treats and even apparel to choose from. Plus, pooches get a free cookie just for visiting. Peddler's Village, Lahaska; 215/794-8292.

P & A Pet Foods: You and your doggy are welcome to shop among 10,000 pet items including dog food, vitamins, and treats; plus, you can even get your dog's nails clipped while you shop (no appointment necessary). This family-owned store also features a dog bakery where you can purchase whimsically shaped homemade biscuits made with everything from carob to yogurt. 826 N. Easton Rd., Doylestown; 215/348-3738.

Lick Your Chops: A pet boutique that specializes in holistic and natural foods, Lick Your Chops is a fun place to find that special something for poochie or for you. Curious canines are always welcome in the store. 700 Second Street Pk., Richboro; 215/322-5266.

Reigning Dogs & Cats: For the discriminating dog lover, Reigning Dogs & Cats has everything you need from food to treats, and beds to apparel. This is a one-stop, best-of-the-best pet shop. Even better, your pup is encouraged to join you while you find everything you need. And if you're wishing for another doggy, every Sunday the shop hosts a "meet and greet" where a rescue group brings its adoptable dogs to find new homes. 30 West Rd., Newtown; 215/497-7477.

PARKS, BEACHES, AND RECREATION AREAS

11 Peace Valley Park

 (See Bucks County map on page 146)

A lovely location to take a long walk with your pooch, Peace Valley is a favorite among Doylestown locals as it once was of Linus and now of Nellie. A hike here could be a walk around the 350-acre Lake Galena on a groomed footpath or on a rugged trail through the woods. Regardless, there are about 14 miles of trails in this scenic park, the biggest county park in Bucks. You'll always see other dogs and their people enjoying the 1,500-acre landscape that includes rolling hills, meadows, woods, and the lake as the centerpiece. Fishing is big here, as is boating. Although boats are available for rent here, they don't allow dogs on them. But if you have your own boat that's 16 feet or shorter with a tiny or no motor, you can bring your pup on the lake. Plus, you and your dog will find shaded picnic areas. Although Peace Valley is fun to visit any time of year, a walk around the lake is most beautiful in the fall when the leaves are changing and it's not too hot. Otherwise, there is minimal shade along the lake path.

Take Route 313 through Doylestown. Take a left on Ferry Road and make a right on Old Limekiln and a left on Creek Road. The main entrance is the second one on the right. Hours are 8 A.M.–sunset. 230 Creek Rd., New Britain; 215/345-7860 or 215/757-0571.

12 Fonthill Park

(See Bucks County map on page 146)

It's too bad that the buildings surrounding Fonthill Park won't let you and your dog in together because the Moravian Pottery and Tile Works (a working history museum that still produces tiles) as well as the Fonthill home are filled with interesting history and were both owned by famed archaeologist, architect, scholar, lawyer and artist Henry C. Mercer. Interesting tidbit: Mercer adored his dogs, who were all Chesapeake Bay retrievers. In fact, one of the dogs, Rollo, left his paw prints in the wet cement of a staircase at Fonthill. If you decide to check it out by yourself, you can see the paw prints and tiles which proclaim "Rollo's stairs" in the Columbus room. Otherwise, the surrounding park isn't much but picnic tables and some woods. Still, the two of you might want to come here to check out the amazing architecture of the tile works and Fonthill home, known to many as "concrete castles."

Take Route 313 (Swamp Road) West through Doylestown and see the park on your left about a half-mile east of Route 611. Hours are sunrise–sunset. 130 Swamp Rd., Doylestown; 215/345-6722 or 215/348-6114.

PLACES TO EAT

Coffee and Cream: The friendliest people own and work at this excellent coffee roastery and ice cream shop. And they love dogs. (The store owners have a super-friendly Labrador mix named Tucker at home.) While you and your pup can't eat inside, you two are welcome to sit on the bench outside the store and enjoy your hot or cold treat. A bowl of water is available for thirsty poochies, too. The coffee here is the freshest around as it is roasted daily. Definitely try the Ethiopian mocha, which ironically isn't chocolate-flavored—just really delicious. 6 E. State St., Doylestown; 215/348-1111.

Siam Cuisine at Black Walnut: If you and your pup are in the mood for a meal on the fancier, pricier side, this French-Thai fusion restaurant welcomes you both outside as long as you call ahead to let them know you'll be eating with your furry friend. Among the tastiest menu items are the shrimp lemon grass soup and the sea bass. 80 W. State St., Doylestown; 215/348-0708.

Stuffits: This friendly café-style eatery welcomes you and your pup at its outside seating. The specialty here is the stuffit, a pizza-crust-filled concoction with your choice of 24 fresh meats, veggies, and cheeses. You can't go wrong with the tomato-basil stuffit. For a sweet treat to your savory meal, try a dessert stuffit yourself, or buy one for your sweet doggy. 16 W. State St., Doylestown; 215/345-4230.

Warminster

Located at the southern edge of Bucks County, Warminster Township is a largely developed, family-oriented suburban community with a nearly 300-year history. Plus, Warminster is the first town in the county to propose and develop a dog park. Although the featured B&B isn't in Warminster, it is worth the short drive to nearby Rushland.

PARKS, BEACHES, AND RECREATION AREAS

13 Kelsey's Bark Park

(See Bucks County map on page 146)

A dog park in honor of Kelsey, a sweet yellow Labrador retriever who worked with her human mom at the Parks and Recreation Department and passed away in 2004, is in the planning stages. It's scheduled to be opened by the fall of 2005, depending on fundraising—more than $20,000 is needed before it can be completed. Still, it sounds like the parks department has its act together as the plans include a fenced area about an acre wide with dual-entry gates, poop bags, benches, young trees, and grass to start with. It will be located at Warminster Community Park, which is off Street Road (Route 132) and Veterans Way. For more information or to make a donation, contact

Kelsey's Bark Park, c/o Warminster Parks and Recreation Department, 1101 Little Ln., Warminster, PA 18974; 215/443-5428.

PLACES TO EAT

Giuseppe's Pizza and Family Restaurant: It's too bad they don't allow doggies inside and don't have outside seating at this location, but you can order takeout from Giuseppe's, one of our favorite inexpensive pizza joints. The plain pizza never disappoints and is exactly what pizza should taste like—fresh and yummy. The meatball hoagie and the cheesesteaks here are equally good. 1523 West Street Rd., Warminster; 215/674-5550.

PLACES TO STAY

The Cottage at Ross Mill Farm: If you happen to have a dog and a pet pig, you'd be in hog heaven staying here. This farm, internationally known for the breeding and care of pet pigs, is happy to have your pup stay as well as or in lieu of a pet pig. While there's no problem if you just have a dog, if you've got a porker, too, there's an outside fenced pen area for pigs; inside a pile of blankets is available for pig beds, as well as complimentary pig feed and treats. The classic 1600s cottage is surrounded by a creek with several hundred acres of conservation land. The fee for dogs is $10 per day and up to two pets are allowed. Rates are $100–110. 2480 Walton Rd., Rushland; 215/322-1539; www.rossmillfarm.com.

Newtown

Founded in 1684 by none other than William Penn, Newtown was initially called New Township, but over the years was shortened to its current name. It's also retained much of its character, with its historic district listed on the National Register of Historic Places. As old as it is, Newtown has all the modern conveniences of American suburbia including some notable places to eat with your doggy.

PARKS, BEACHES, AND RECREATION AREAS

🔟4 Tyler State Park

🐾🐾 (See Bucks County map on page 146)

A former farm known for its dairy herds, with about 25 percent of the land still under cultivation, Tyler State park consists of 1,711 acres. Its roads, trails, and facilities are tastefully embedded throughout the farm and woodland setting. Some of the old stone homes located here date back to the early 1700s. Plus, the Schofield Ford Covered Bridge, the longest covered bridge in the county, stands in the west section of the park (only open to pedestrians and bicyclists).

FETCHING NECESSITIES

Since it's the most wonderful time of the year, shouldn't you have the furriest family member with you helping pick out your next Christmas tree? These farms welcome your leashed pup as long as no deposits are left behind.

Bryan's Farm: "Should it be a Douglas Fir or a Scotch Pine this year?" you contemplate with your pup as you choose and cut your own tree at this farm, open only on weekends during the season. You can come in the fall to pick your own pumpkin with your hairy punkin, too. 2032 Second Street Pk., Richboro; 215/598-3206.

Tuckamony Christmas Tree Farm: About two miles north of Peddler's Village/Lahaska, you can bring your doggy to help pick from more than 30,000 trees, either cut-your-own or precut varieties. Saws are provided and trees are baled and wrapped for you. There's a Christmas shop and bathrooms on site, too. 6320 Upper York Rd. (Route 263), Solebury; 215/297-8447.

The park is a great place to go walking with your pooch, but, considering it's basically in the midst of busy Newtown, it may not be the perfect respite you're looking for. Still, don't discount it. The scenic Neshaminy Creek runs through it, and you and your pup can hike at least 14 miles throughout the park. If you are up for a lengthier hike, cross over Neshaminy Creek to the west side of the park via the causeway at the park's center. Many of the trails provide nice views of the park and the surrounding countryside.

There are tons of picnic areas, many of them shaded, as well as a great playground area and even boating. Sadly, rental canoes do not allow dogs. Regardless, you're welcome to bring your own canoe and your dog and enjoy the creek together after obtaining a launch permit.

We felt the best perks of the park are the poop bag dispensers and trash cans located throughout.

Take Route 413 Newtown Bypass to the Swamp Road entrance of the park and follow the signs. 101 Swamp Rd., Newtown; 215/968-2021 or 800/63-PARKS; www.dcnr.state.pa.us/stateparks/parks/tyler.htm.

PLACES TO EAT

Bagel Junction Deli: Just a quick drive from Tyler State Park, this eatery offers some of the tastiest big, fat, yummy bagels and homemade cream cheese you might ever have. The service is friendly and welcomes you at its outdoor seating with your carb-loving canine. 2826 S. Eagle Rd., Newtown; 215/968-9795.

The Brick Hotel and Garden Grille: Offering a menu that includes mostly gourmet American cuisine, this quaint restaurant is a Newtown favorite. You and your well-mannered pup may eat in the garden seating, but only at the waiter's discretion. It's best to call ahead to be sure. If you get the okay, and it's lunchtime, you might try the filet and spinach salad topped with scrumptious gorgonzola. State Street and Washington Avenue, Newtown; 215/860-8313.

Piccolo Trattoria: This BYOB is known for its good, moderately priced Italian food. While it's located in a generic location (a strip mall), its food and service is anything but. The menu here makes it difficult to decide as it offers everything from wood-oven pizzas to pastas, chicken, fish, and a full page of sandwiches. Your pup is welcome to sit outside with you in warm weather, but takeout is always an option. 30 West Rd., Newtown; 215/860-4247.

Rita's Water Ice: Maybe you and your pup want more than water to cool off on a hot day? Then make a stop for Rita's Water Ice in Newtown. Yes, it's a national chain, but it has a 20-year history and serves some of the freshest Italian water ice in the Philadelphia area. Any flavor is delicious and uses real fruit, but the mango may be the most addictive. You and your pup are welcome to order your favorite flavor and sit on the rocks outside while licking it up. 14 Swamp Rd., Newtown; 215/968-8668.

Langhorne

A relatively small community and home of the ever-popular Sesame Place theme park, Langhorne really does have more to brag about than Muppets, although Nellie can't get enough of them. Langhorne actually has a couple of decent public parks and dog-friendly places to stay and eat in town, as well as in nearby locales.

PARKS, BEACHES, AND RECREATION AREAS

15 Core Creek Park

🐾 🐾 (See Bucks County map on page 146)

If it weren't for the unsightly view of the McMansions and office buildings surrounding it, this would be a solid three-paw park, but Nellie just couldn't bring herself to rating it as such. It's more of an open, flat residential park than a hilly, woodland escape. Regardless, it's a fine place to take your dog and encompasses 1,185 acres including the scenic Lake Luxembourg. At active Core Creek you'll find people walking dogs, running, boating, horseback riding, biking, and hiking lakeside and streamside at virtually any time of day. A one-mile paved bike path encircles half the park; other unpaved trails exist along the water at various points. Many picnic areas and pavilions

THINK GLOBALLY, BARK LOCALLY

Puppy Promenade in Warminster: To help raise money for the off-leash Kelsey's Bark Park in Warminster, the Parks and Recreation Department holds this annual September dog walk at Warminster Community Park. Petco provides doggy treat bags for all pre-registered pups, and pet owners will receive a keepsake photo. Dogs are encouraged to dress up for a costume parade or just come for a 2.3-mile walk on leash. It's advised to bring poop bags, and pre-registration is required to walk. The event kicks off at 10 A.M. The fee is $5 per dog. 215/443-5428.

Walk-A-Thon: The annual Hope for the Animals Walk-A-Thon invites you and your four-legged hiking friend to help rescue animals by raising pledges and walking through Core Creek Park. Hope for the Animals, a local rescue group, takes in homeless and unwanted animals, and readies them for adoptions to new homes. The fundraiser takes place one weekend day in late September 10 A.M.–3 P.M. 215/945-6204; www.hopeforanimals.petfinder.org.

Tails on the Trails Husky Hike and Picnic: It doesn't matter if your dog doesn't know mushing from flyball, all that matters is if you and your pup love to help other canines in need to participate in this annual fundraiser. Typically held the last Saturday in September, this event allows all participants to hike a mile or two with their pup (one dog per person). If someone you know would like to help but doesn't have a dog, foster dogs are available as walking companions. Pledges are encouraged in order to walk. At the event, helpful information will be provided on microchipping as well as sled dog demonstrations, canine good citizen tests, lunch, entertainment, pledge incentives, a silent auction, and more. Registration is at 9 A.M. and the hike starts at 10 A.M. The event is rain or shine and takes place at Core Creek Park. 267/566-5496.

Holiday Bazaar: Your pup is invited to view arts and crafts for sale at the Hope for the Animals' annual holiday bazaar held the first Sunday in December. Photos with Santa will also be available, for a $5 donation. The event is held at the Falls Township Senior Cititzens Center in Fairless Hills. 215/945-6204; www.hopeforanimals.petfinder.org.

Photos with Santa: Most weekends in December, you can take your pup to PetsMart in Fairless Hills to get his photo taken with everyone's favorite oversized elf, Santa. The cost is $10 for two photos, no appointment needed. All proceeds benefit Hope for the Animals. 215/945-6204; www.hopeforanimals.petfinder.org.

are available, as are restrooms, a playground, and benches along the lake to stop and take a breather with your leashed pup.

Take Route 1 North to the 213 exit (Maple Avenue). Make a right onto 213 to North Flowers Mill Road. Take a right onto North Flowers Mill Road. Go three traffic lights to Winchester Avenue and make a right. Take a left onto Bridgetown Pike. Hours are 8 A.M.–sunset. 901 E. Bridgetown Pk., Langhorne; 215/757-0571 or 215/348-6114.

16 Playwicki Park

🐾🐾 (See Bucks County map on page 146)

Located along the banks of Neshaminy Creek, Playwicki Park has been the subject of many artist renderings and photographs because of its lovely stone-arched railroad bridges. Within its 33 acres, Playwicki is a favorite spot among local dog walkers as there are hiking trails that follow the creek near the parking area and end at the railroad tracks. There are also picnic areas and a playground. All in all, it's a nice little park.

From Langhorne take 413 North to 213 East. The park is located on the right. Hours are sunrise–sunset. Route 213, Middletown (Middletown Township west of Langhorne); 215/757-0571 or 215/348-6114.

PLACES TO EAT

Charcoal Steaks N' Things: While not in Langhorne, it may be worth a drive to nearby Yardley to grab a bite here with poochie. Located right along the Delaware River, Charcoal offers everything from beef to veal to chicken and seafood. You two are welcome to sit at a picnic table alongside the river and enjoy the scenery while a-noshing. 11 S. Delaware Ave. (River Road/Route 32), Yardley; 215/493-6394.

PLACES TO STAY

Red Roof Inn Oxford Valley: If you're looking for an affordable place to stay with a poochie who is lighter than 80 pounds, and you don't mind a hotel with next to no amenities, this may be a good choice. A bare-bones motel, at least it doesn't charge extra for dogs and is only a half-mile to Sesame Place. Rates are $55–100. 3100 Cabot Blvd. W., Langhorne; 215/750-6200.

Sheraton Bucks County Hotel: If your doggy is less than 80 pounds and you're not looking for the most luxurious room around, this is a good option. The hotel itself is clean and inviting, and the service is extremely friendly, but the rooms aren't impeccable. However, the full-service health club with an indoor pool is a nice consolation prize. And there's no extra charge for your furry traveler, which is always good news. Rates are $89–182. 400 Oxford Valley Rd., Langhorne; 215/547-4100 or 888/625-5144.

Falls Township

Falls Township is one of the oldest townships in the state. It's believed that Dutch settlers came here decades before William Penn became proprietor of the state in 1681. His Pennsbury Manor home (a reconstruction of the original) is located in Morrisville in the township. Also part of the township are Oxford Valley Park and the town of Levittown, one of the state's first major suburban planned communities, dating back to 1952.

PARKS, BEACHES, AND RECREATION AREAS

17 Oxford Valley Park

☙ (See Bucks County map on page 146)

Lake Caroline is the centerpiece of this park which, sadly, doesn't have much in the way of beauty, mostly because it's next to the busy Oxford Valley Road and is relatively shadeless. You and puppers can hike around the lake and cross over a bridge or two to get to the other side of the lake, but there's no defined pathway outlining the lake. Also, you'll find some picnic tables under some trees, but sadly you're basically right alongside the busy road. Still, if you're in the area, it's not a bad place to stretch your collective legs or even get them wet in the lake. Hours are sunrise–sunset. Hood Boulevard and Oxford Valley Road, Oxford Valley (a half-mile southeast of Oxford Valley Mall); 215/757-0571 or 215/348-6114.

18 Queen Anne Park

🐾 (See Bucks County map on page 146)

Make sure your pup loves the great American pastime if you come here as there isn't much to do besides watch a game. This is really a baseball field more than anything else. Sure, it seems like if no one is here it'd be a great place to let your pooch off leash in the open outfield, but we don't take the chance as Nellie's recall isn't perfect, and the field is a bit too close to the street for our comfort. But there is a picnic table and a portable toilet if the need arises. Hours are sunrise–sunset. New Falls and Woodbourne Roads, Levittown (adjacent to government services building and Levittown Library); 215/757-0571 or 215/348-6114.

19 Frosty Hollow Tennis Center

🐾 (See Bucks County map on page 146)

As the name would indicate, this is not the first place that comes to mind to visit with your pup. In fact, Nellie didn't care much about walking here. But she sure had a heck of a time watching people playing tennis—her tail never stopped wagging. Although there are no official trails at this park, some makeshift ones meander through the wooded area. And while there were trash cans available, we didn't see any picnic areas here. Residents come here primarily to play tennis and to walk their dogs. We decided to check it out because it's one of the county's many parks where dogs are welcome.

From 413 South take a left onto New Falls Road and go about a quarter-mile and it's on your left. Hours are sunrise–sunset. New Falls Road, Levittown; 215/757-0571 or 215/348-6114.

PLACES TO EAT

Newportville Inn: A charming neighborhood favorite, the Newportville Inn serves some tasty German-American food with friendly service at a reasonable price. If you're really hungry, you might try the German appetizer that provides a sampling of the best 'wursts (brats and knockwursts) around. Otherwise, choose from menu items such as seafood, steaks, and weiner schnitzel. Overlooking Neshaminy Creek, the outdoor deck welcomes your pup to sit with you. 4120 Lower Rd., Newportville; 215/785-6090.

Bristol and Bensalem

Bristol is a city with a long, rich history. In fact, Bristol is the state's oldest borough and the first formal European settlement, founded in 1681. It's also home to the southernmost portion of the Delaware Canal, a National Heritage corridor, built in 1831 that helped carry coal, goods, and passengers 60 miles north to Easton.

Bensalem dates back to 1691 and was home to many Dutch, Swede, and English settlers. One of the most famous horses in recent history, Smarty Jones, also makes Bensalem his home.

Both Bensalem and Bristol are densley populated, busy suburban areas, but their collective parks make visiting here with your pup a little less hectic for both of you.

PARKS, BEACHES, AND RECREATION AREAS

🐾🐾 Silver Lake Park & Nature Center

🐾🐾 (See Bucks County map on page 146)

Considering it's located in a populous part of the county, Silver Lake Park is a pleasant spot to come relax and take in nature. Silver Lake is actually the terminus to Mill Creek, Queen Anne Creek, and the Black Ditch Creek Watershed. Containing the best-protected coastal plain woodland remaining in the state, it is highly cherished. You and your leashed pup will most likely run into many other nature lovers as this is also home to the Silver Lake Nature Center, which has a library and sponsors educational programs as well as nature walks. Speaking of walking, you and your pup can walk around Silver Lake as well as through the woods on the park's four miles of trails. You'll also find a pavilion, picnic areas, trash cans, and a playground.

Take the Route 13 Exit 358 from the PA Turnpike south towards Bristol for about two miles and take a right on Bath Road. The park is on your right. Hours are sunrise–sunset. 1306 Bath Rd., Bristol; 215/785-1177 or 215/757-0571.

21 Neshaminy State Park

😺😺 (See Bucks County map on page 146)

Upon entering the park, it doesn't appear too impressive even though it comprises 330 acres. But as Nellie got her nose to the ground she soon realized that this is more than just a big open space; it's where Neshaminy Creek meets the Delaware. And even though the river flows another 116 miles to where it meets the ocean, the tide water rises here making it a freshwater estuary. This phenomenon makes the area a home to many plants and animals originating from both the ocean and from upstream in Bucks County. Amazing!

You can check out some of the fascinating wildlife with your leashed doggy on the four-mile River Walk Hike through the park. Many interesting facts about the area are described in the River Walk Trail brochure provided by the park office.

Otherwise, you can see much of the beauty of the Delaware River and homes along it from the River Walk, and delight in the variety of boats that use this park as a launching area to the river. There's ample shade along the walk and many trash cans and picnic areas in the park, as well as a playground that is a bit of a throwback from a few decades ago, and a pool where dogs are not allowed.

Take 132 East to State Road. Take a left on State Road and see the park's entrance on your right. Hours are sunrise–sunset. 3401 State Rd., Bensalem; 215/639-4538; www.dcnr.state.pa.us/stateparks/parks/neshaminy.aspx.

22 Delaware River Access Area

😺 (See Bucks County map on page 146)

If you have a boat, this would be a great place to come with your pup because it's mainly a boat launching area, and only eight acres of this 100-acre park are developed. Also, it's a popular fishing spot for eager anglers. Picnic tables, benches, grills, and restrooms are available, too. But the best features of the park are the access to the water to cool your toes or paws, if needed, and to be able to see the New Jersey side of the river and all the boats that glide by.

Take Street Road (132 East) until it dead-ends at State Road. Take a right onto State Road and travel down about a mile. Take a left onto Station Avenue and follow the signs. Hours are sunrise–sunset. Station Avenue, Bensalem; 215/757-0571 or 215/348-6114.

PLACES TO EAT

Ted's Lakeside Deli: So you're working up an appetite while checking out nature at Silver Lake? Then drive down the road to always-tasty Ted's. Here, you'll find a variety of hoagies, steak sandwiches, onion rings, and Nellie's favorite: French fries. You two can eat at the picnic tables outside or take your food home. The cheesesteak hoagie, a traditional cheesesteak with lettuce, tomato, and onion, is one of the best items on the menu. 803 Bath Rd., Bristol; 215/788-5188.

PLACES TO STAY

Holiday Inn Bensalem: Recently renovated with an outdoor pool and a full-service restaurant, this is a comfy place for you to stay. But that's not all: Poochie is welcome with no extra charge and no weight restrictions. What could be better for an extra large pup? Rates are $89–119. 3499 Street Rd., Bensalem; 215/638-1500.

Radisson Hotel Philadelphia Northeast: An impressive option for your petite poochie (under 30 pounds), the Radisson makes a concerted effort to treat your pet like a guest. A special treat is provided at check-in and the hotel pet rooms are on the first floor with access to a handy courtyard for potty breaks. There's also an indoor and outdoor pool here for you to enjoy. Rates are $149. 2400 Old Lincoln Hwy., Trevose; 215/638-8300.

Red Roof Inn Philadelphia Trevose: Big pups need not apply. But if you have one dog weighing less than 50 pounds, he's welcome here for no additional fee. The hotel is in good condition and inexpensive, and about a 5- to 10-minute drive to Playwicki and Core Creek Parks. Rates are $55–65. 3100 Lincoln Hwy., Trevose; 215/244-9422.

Sleep Inn and Suites: Another solid bet for lodging with your hound in Bensalem is the Sleep Inn. The staff is friendly and the rooms are clean and comfortable. While there's no weight restriction for your dog to stay here, there is a $10 per day per pet fee. Rates are $95–130. 3427 Street Rd., Bensalem; 215/244-2300.

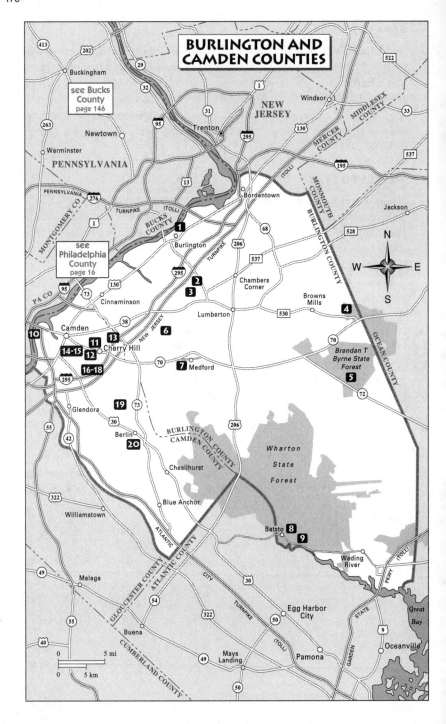

CHAPTER 6

BURLINGTON AND CAMDEN COUNTIES

Burlington and Camden Counties

Did you ever notice when you blow in a dog's face he gets mad at you? But when you take him in a car he sticks his head out the window.

Steve Bluestone

BURLINGTON COUNTY

New Jersey's largest county, Burlington extends from the Delaware River all the way to the Atlantic Ocean—in other words, it spans the state. That wide-open space is exactly why it's ideal to partake of with poochie. In fact, the county is loaded with doggy destinations. (Just be sure to put a tick collar on your dog as ticks carrying Lyme disease are relatively common in these parts.)

PICK OF THE LITTER—BURLINGTON AND CAMDEN COUNTIES

BEST DOG PARKS
Duke's Dog Run at Freedom Park, Medford, NJ (page 189)
Pooch Park at Cooper River Park, Cherry Hill, NJ (page 195)
Crows Woods, Haddonfield, NJ (page 199)

BEST PLACES TO EAT
Robin's Nest, Mount Holly, NJ (page 185)
Villa Barone, Collingswood, NJ (page 199)
Corner Bistro, Haddonfield, NJ (page 202)

BEST PLACE TO STAY
Haddonfield Inn, Haddonfield, NJ (page 202)

It's hard to believe that in New Jersey—the state that conjures up images of diners and exits off the Garden State Parkway—you could ever find yourself in the middle of the pristine, seemingly untouched lands of the Pine Barrens, chock full of streams and lakes, bird and animal life. Equally surprising is traveling the country roads where vineyards, blueberry fields, and cranberry bogs abound.

In fact, Burlington County is home to the largest blueberries in the world, and it's the second-largest cranberry-producing county in the country. Who'da thunk it?

Since the county is so vast, it encompasses not just the open areas, but also suburban towns with lots of history, charm, and, above all else, activities for your dog. From frolicking leash-free in a local dog park to strolling through historic towns, you and your four-legged friend will be happy you checked out the county of Burlington.

PINE BARRENS 101

For the pure nature of it, Burlington County is in a class by itself. In order to get a feel for the county, it's important to understand a major part of its natural landscape: the Pine Barrens, a.k.a. the Pinelands (more politically correct). New Jersey's Pine Barrens consist of about 1.4 million acres making it the largest tract of open space along the mid-Atlantic coast. It's believed that the term "pine barrens" was probably coined by early settlers who were not happy with the acidic, sandy soil—a less than stellar medium to grow crops. But this soil later was found to be ideal to grow blueberries and cranberries, produce the area is famous for today.

Also within the Pine Barrens live some rare and endangered plants and animals, like pygmy pine trees no taller than the average adult, and the endangered Pine Barrens treefrog. Plus, it has one of the continent's largest freshwater aquifers—accounting for 17 trillion gallons of water. Even more remarkable, this area is located in the most densely populated state in the country. With all of the parks and recreation areas available, Linus couldn't help but become sappy expressing his love for the Pine Barrens.

Burlington City

Dating back 325 years, Burlington City is a colonial village of understated charm. Home to New Jersey's first recorded European settlement and to a few Underground Railroad sites as well, this city boasts a wealth of history all within about one square mile. While the city is not a major destination for dog lovers, history buffs and ruffs will surely appreciate it.

PARKS, BEACHES, AND RECREATION AREAS

🚩 Riverfront Promenade

🐾 (See Burlington and Camden Counties map on page 178)

While visiting Burlington City, your pooch will no doubt want to check out the Riverfront Promenade that skirts the Delaware River. The promenade is essentially a paved walkway about a mile long that's also the center of the Delaware River Heritage Trail that stretches 115 miles through New Jersey and Pennsylvania. A few park benches are scattered along the area in case your pooch or you gets pooped and you want to gaze at the Delaware River. You can also see Burlington Island from this location, the first recorded European settlement in New Jersey, founded in 1624. (They were Walloons from Belgium who established a trading post to barter with the Native Americans.) Still, it's a good thing there's free parking in front of the promenade and summer concerts held here, because there's not much more to say about this spot. Don't forget to bring poop bags as the rules state to clean up after your dog.

From Burlington, follow High Street to its end and park on the right in the free parking lot. Hours are sunrise–sunset. 609/386-0200 or 609/386-4773; www.tourburlington.org.

PLACES TO EAT

Umm Ice Cream Parlor: After a hot day taking in Burlington history, you and your pup might want to chill out with some of the cold stuff and sit outside this authentic period ice cream parlor offering original ice cream flavors, coffees, and desserts. 236 High and Union Streets, Burlington, NJ; 609/387-9786.

DOG-EAR YOUR CALENDAR

Burlington Day: You and your doggy can join in on the fun in Burlington City by checking out the sidewalk sales and antique car show, street musicians, and food vendors at this annual community event in May. Most of the activity takes place around High Street. 609/386-0200; www.tourburlington.org.

Red, White and Blueberry Festival: Enjoy everything blueberry with your pup from the "blueberry capital of the world" in Hammonton. Berries of blue are featured on pies, bagels, Italian water ice, ice cream, and tarts. There are even pie-eating contests for humans. Sorry, pups! Also at the festival are live stage shows, arts and crafts, and car shows. The party surrounds Vine Street and takes place in late June or early July. 609/561-9080.

Festival of Lights Fireworks and Illuminated Boat Parade: An all-day fun-filled event usually held in August, this festival features live entertainment, kids' activities, as well as an evening concert, boat parade, and fireworks in Burlington City. Much of the fun takes place around High Street. Free parking and admission. 609/386-0200; www.tourburlington.org.

Batsto Village's Country Living Fair: Those into country will especially love this annual fair celebrating rural life. The fair, held the third Sunday in October, features crafts, food, antique cars, chainsaw art, quilting, and pony rides. 4110 Nesco Rd., Hammonton, NJ; 609/567-4559; www.batstovillage.org.

Mount Holly

A historic town that predates the American Revolution, Mount Holly is the county seat and parked along the banks of Rancocas Creek. It is worth a visit simply for the Robin's Nest Restaurant, which loves four-legged clientele. After a noshing, you and your pup might want to work off a few calories by strolling through the downtown section of Mill Race Village for some shopping or a little history lesson. Some of the old buildings in town are quite a sight, such as the Shinn Curtis Log Cabin (on Park Drive), built in 1712, and the Burlington County Historic Prison Museum (on High Street), built in 1810, the oldest prison in continuous use until 1965.

Whitesbog Dog Walk: Help preserve this historic cranberry and blueberry village in Brendan Byrne State Forest by participating in its annual fundraising dog walk in October. No doubt your leashed furry friend will be thrilled to get his four legs pumping with you for such a good cause. Cost is $5 per human/dog couple for the roughly three-mile walk. 609/893-4646; www.whitesbog.org.

Apple Festival: Held in October at Kirby's Mill, in Medford, you and your pup can sample a taste of the harvest in strudel, pies, muffins, ice cream, doughnuts, cider, and apple butter, while mingling with members of the community. 609/654-0563; www.medford-township.com.

Dickens Festival: Held the first week in December, you and puppers can join the fun on Medford's Main Street through its tree-lighting ceremony, then meet Santa and stroll and sing along with the festive carolers dressed as characters from *A Christmas Carol.* 609/714-8811; www.medfordvillage.org.

Holiday Parade: Another merry event in Burlington City is its holiday parade, usually held the first Saturday in December. Here you and your hound will be astounded by the high school bands, string bands, hometown heroes, beauty queens, antique cars, elves, and of course, our bearded buddy, Santa. 609/386-0200; www.tourburlington.org.

PARKS, BEACHES, AND RECREATION AREAS

☑ Smithville County Park

🐾🐾 🐾 (See Burlington and Camden Counties map on page 178)

While just a five-minute drive from Mount Holly, and not the ideal park for dogs, the 250-acre Smithville County Park is worth a visit. This former woodworking industrial complex surrounding Rancocas Creek dates back to the early 1800s. On the park grounds are the 25 surviving buildings, including the famous Smithville Mansion. Of course, you can't visit inside the mansion with your dog, but you can survey the lovely landscaped grounds with him, as long as he's on a short leash and is well behaved.

After viewing the flowery grounds, take a right onto Park Avenue. This is where picnic tables and park benches overlook the river. There you can sit, watch a waterfall, and just take in the quiet together. A launching pad for

THINK GLOBALLY, BARK LOCALLY

Doggie Easter Egg Hunt and Canine Blood Drive: And you thought the kids had all the fun at Easter? Your pup will be kidlike hunting for eggs at this annual event that benefits the Burlington County Animal Alliance. The Easter Bunny will also be on hand for photos with your pooch. (This funny bunny is apparently undeterred by dogs.) The cost is $5 registration per dog, and $5 extra for pictures with the Easter Bunny. In addition to the egg hunt, the American Red Cross will conduct a canine blood drive. So you and your pup can help other pets in two meaningful ways. Both events are usually held simultaneously two Saturdays before Easter, at the Burlington County Animal Shelter located in the County Complex off of Woodlane Road, in Westampton. 609/880-1235; www.bcaa.petfinder.org.

Dog Day Afternoon: Held in September, this Mount Holly event educates the public about adopting dogs from various shelters. Fun activities include pet contests, animal communicators, and various speakers. Bring poochie to enjoy a full day of free festivities. Mill Race Village on White and Church Streets. 609/267-9505.

Howl-O-Ween Contest and Photos: Help other pups by taking yours to the Petco in Willingboro for this howlin' fun event, usually held the Saturday before Halloween. Polaroid photos are $5 with proceeds benefiting the Burlington County Animal Alliance. Dogs (and cats) are available for adoption, too. 609/877-9711.

Adopt a Friend: Every Saturday 1–4 P.M., the Burlington County Animal Alliance introduces its rescued pups to the public at its Adoption Day at PetsMart in the East Gate Shopping Center, Nixon Drive, near Routes 295, 73, and 38, in Mount Laurel. 609/880-1235; www.bcaa.petfinder.org.

boats doubles as a watering hole for your thirsty pal. Park officials are currently planning on recreating the industrial village to include a footbridge extending a 595-foot span to connect one side of the park with the other.

Take Route 38 East through the intersection of Route 541, toward Pemberton. Follow for nearly three miles and make a left onto Smithville Road. Travel about three-quarters of a mile and turn left to enter the picnic area, onto Park Avenue. To enter the mansion grounds and visitor's parking lot, turn left onto Meade Lane. Hours are Monday–Friday 8 A.M.–4:30 P.M. 609/265-5068; www.burlco.lib.nj.us/county/smithville.

🔢 Rancocas State Park

🐾 🥾 (See Burlington and Camden Counties map on page 178)

Although it is called a state park, Rancocas is really not what most people would consider a "park." It's more of a territory. You'll find no picnic tables nor a visitor-friendly main entrance or an office with maps and information. However, there is an extremely interesting and inviting part of the park, which is the Rankokas Indian Reservation (note: different spelling). This 350-acre area is leased to the Powhatan Renape Nation by the state of New Jersey. Within the grounds, you'll find nature trails and animals like buffalo, deer, and horses, as well as a replica of a 1600s traditional woodland Indian village, and, of course, the Native Americans who live here and couldn't be friendlier.

Although the New Jersey Audubon Society also leases part of the Rancocas State Park property and has nature trails of its own, it does not allow dogs for fear of disturbing the birds and other wildlife. Hours are sunrise–sunset.

Take 676 West to 295 North; get off at the 45A Mount Holly exit. Proceed through two lights and after the second light, you'll see it on the right. 609/261-4747; www.powhatan.org.

PLACES TO EAT

Mount Holly Deli Station: Situated in a late-1800s train station, this eatery serves up the finest bagels and donuts this side of the Rancocas. Outdoor tables make eating with your pup a pleasure. 25 Madison Ave., Mount Holly, NJ; 609/261-2455.

Robin's Nest: Serving French-American cuisine and located in the middle of the Mill Race Village shopping district, the Robin's Nest is a definite must-do. First, the food is delicious. Try the pear salad and gazpacho. And not only are the people who work here friendly, but they love dogs. Plus, you can sit very peacefully right along the Rancocas Creek. Of course, dogs with good manners are the best customers because the tables are somewhat close together. Mine, luckily, had a good day, and was welcomed with a big bucket of water. Call ahead to let them know you'll be bringing your dog and they'll be happy to seat you on their deck. 2 Washington St., Mount Holly, NJ; 609/261-6149; www.mountholly.com/robinsnest.

PLACES TO STAY

Best Western Inn: About two miles from Mill Race Village and five to Smithville, this reasonably priced hotel is a good option, especially if you enjoy indoor pools and hot tubs. Although your dog may not be able to get into the swim of things with you, if he's 40 pounds or lighter he'll be welcome to sleep with you here. There is an additional $10 plus tax, per night pet fee. Rates are

$99–114. 2020 Rt. 541 Road 1, Mount Holly, NJ; 609/261-3800 or 800/633-8211; www.bestwestern.com.

Browns Mills

Located in the heart of the Pine Barrens, Browns Mills is a small community. But you may not think it's so small after you discover the plethora of recreation opportunities available for you and your pooch, such as the regular leashed dog walks held by Whitesbog Village.

PARKS, BEACHES, AND RECREATION AREAS

🐾 Whitesbog Village

🐾🐾🐾 🐾 (See Burlington and Camden Counties map on page 178)

With the word "bog" in the name, it's got to relate to cranberries in some way, right? Right, but ironically, Whitesbog Village, located in the northern part of Brendan Byrne State Forest, is actually the spot where blueberries were first cultivated. It happens to be where cranberry bogs were harvested—with a few still farmed today. This turn-of-the century agricultural settlement is a "berry" unique spot to take your dog because you'll probably see and hear things you don't every day. But be sure to bring insect repellent because, especially in summertime, this bog is quite muggy and buggy.

Upon entering Whitesbog, first be sure to get a map at the entrance sign in the front. You can choose to hike or drive the self-guided tour, which is about six miles long. This tour highlights the homes and buildings of what was the working family farm of the White family in the 1860s (hence, the name Whitesbog).

Once you get into the thick of the tour, be sure to stop, take a look around, and just listen. You will not believe you're in the bustling state of New Jersey. The area is pristine, almost prehistoric. The only thing you're likely to hear are buzzings of bugs, birds, and maybe a few frogs because you'll be surrounded by ponds, pines, and complete tranquility.

Take Route 70 East to 530, or Route 38 East, crossing over 206 onto Route 530. Follow to Mile Marker 13. Hours are sunrise–sunset daily; guided tours available by request. 120-13 Whitesbog Rd., Browns Mills, NJ; 609/893-4646; whitesbog@hotmail.com; www.whitesbog.org.

🐾 Brendan T. Byrne State Forest

🐾🐾🐾 (See Burlington and Camden Counties map on page 178)

A true gem of a state park, Brendan Byrne (formerly Lebanon State Forest) is the second-largest state forest in New Jersey. Those car air-fresheners can't hold a pine needle to the true pine smell you'll experience once you and your pup step outside of the car. In fact, this park prides itself on that very smell—its 32,012 acres of protected land include the predominant Atlantic white cedars that stand tall over its sandy trails and roads. Although dogs are not permitted to stay in the campsites or cabins in the park, they are allowed leashed in its recreation areas and along more than 25 miles of trails.

Pakim Pond, located within the forest, is the main picnic area and includes picnic tables, charcoal grills, restrooms, and a playground. (Interesting tidbit: This area was originally a reservoir for a cranberry bog. The name Pakim is derived from the Lenape Indian word for "cranberry.") A water fountain is also available for dogs if your pooch is a stickler for tap water and would rather not guzzle pond scum like my boy, Linus.

Don't forget to bring poop bags to the park as it has a carry-in/carry-out trash policy. Unfortunately, this is the worst aspect of the park when it comes to its dog-friendliness because driving around with a bag of poop in the car couldn't be more unpleasant. But because your dog is so furry and cute and will have a blast with you here, you'll withstand it with a smile, right?

The park entrance is located on Route 72. Follow east past the intersection of Route 70 to Milepost 1. Turn left into the forest at the entrance sign and make your first right. The park office is immediately on the left. Once you arrive, be sure to grab the free trail maps located at the office and at the entrance sign by Pakim Pond. Hours are sunrise–sunset. 609/726-1191; www .nj.gov/dep/parksandforests/parks/byrne.html.

Mount Laurel

While you're sure not to find a mountain here—more likely urban sprawl— Mount Laurel actually gets its name from a hill at the intersection of Hainesport–Mount Laurel and Moorestown–Mount Laurel Roads in the township. This town has many amenities in the way of parks and recreation, not the least of which is its off-leash dog park.

PARKS, BEACHES, AND RECREATION AREAS

6 Laurel Acres Park

🐾🐾🐾🐾 🐕 (See Burlington and Camden Counties map on page 178)

A lovely park on its own, Laurel Acres is an award-winner for its playgrounds, paved paths, baseball and soccer fields, and even its sledding hill. But this park's dog run could at least be nominated for a leash-free award if there was such a thing. The dog run is a fenced-in area that has two sections; one for dogs 40 pounds and heavier and a smaller section that's for dogs that are, uh, smaller. Late afternoon is one of the busiest times of the day at the run. No matter when you choose to go, you and your pup will meet friendly dogs and their people.

The run has poop bags available and a bench. The ground cover is mostly grass with a concrete walkway in the middle, which is key because it can get quite muddy. For your dog, though, it's another story. Unless you have no problem with a dirty, smelly dog trashing your car interior, it's advisable to stay away from the dog park the day after it rains because the mud can get extreme.

Dogs should stay on leash until entering the dog run. While the dog run is not immediately noticeable from the parking lot near Church Street, follow the walking path located near the middle of the park and you'll run right into the dog park. Laurel Acres Park can be accessed by both Church Street and Union Mill Roads.

From Route 38 take Church Street South. The park is on the left at the fifth traffic light. Another entrance is on Union Mill Road between Academy Boulevard and Elbo Lane. Hours are 7 A.M.–dusk. 856/234-2623; www.mountlaurel.com/dogrun.htm.

PLACES TO EAT

The Black Swan: After a good romp at Laurel Acres you might want to head over to this upscale restaurant. Of course, you can't eat inside with your dog, but the takeout option is well worth it. The menu includes everything from sandwiches to seafood and chicken, salads, and pasta. Larchmont Shopping Center, 127 Ark Rd. at Route 38, Mount Laurel, NJ; 856/866-0019; www.the-blackswanofnj.com.

PLACES TO STAY

Radisson Hotel: Moderately priced but not run-of-the-mill in appearance or quality, this hotel is one of the best in Mount Laurel that allows dogs to stay with their humans. Plus, it has an outdoor pool, fitness room, game room, tennis court, and basketball court. There is a $25 per day pet fee, but no size limit to your favorite furry friend. But it might be difficult to find a room at busier times of the year because pet-friendly rooms are fewer and are typically on the lower floors. So make sure to arrange your plans well in advance. Rates are $87–225. 915 Rt. 73, Mount Laurel, NJ; 856/234-7300.

Red Roof Inn: While Linus would not have made the cut here, if your dog is on the smaller side (no exact weight limit mentioned), then she might enjoy a stay with you at the Red Roof Inn at no extra charge. This hotel may not have all the bells and whistles that pricier hotels have, but it's got a friendly staff and clean, comfy rooms. Rates are $60–70. 603 Fellowship Rd., Mount Laurel, NJ; 856/234-5589.

Summerfield Suites: This is another solid alternative for hotel stay with your small dog (under 40 pounds), but has the suite feel. The only caveats are no more than two pets and antiflea treatments must be in use (I don't know how to prove a dog is using Advantage). A nonrefundable $150 cleaning fee is charged for a one-bedroom suite, a $200 fee for the two-bedroom suite.

There are lots of grassy areas to walk your pup. The most unique thing about this hotel? It's complimentary grocery delivery service, of course! Remember to call ahead because pet policies can change without notice, management advises. Rates are $129–200. 3000 Crawford Pl., Mount Laurel, NJ; 856/222-1313; www.summerfieldsuites.com.

TownePlace Suites: Homier than a hotel, these suites allow you to stay with your pup in a townhouse environment. The fee for dogs depends on how long you'll be staying, but if for five or fewer days, it's a one-time charge of $75. Plus, there is a nonrefundable sanitation fee of $150. Although there are no nearby parks within walking distance, there are designated walkways to take your dog for outings. Rates are $100–150 per night. 450 Century Pkwy., Mount Laurel, NJ; 856/778-8221.

Medford

Medford, a town "where everyone knows everyone," prides itself on its tight-knit community, especially evident during its festivals, which draw significant crowds throughout the year. Medford seems to have the same feeling about its dogs—and this could be why the town's dog park is one of the best.

PARKS, BEACHES, AND RECREATION AREAS

7 Duke's Dog Run at Freedom Park

🐾🐾🐾🐾 🦴 (See Burlington and Camden Counties map on page 178)

Now, this is what a dog park should be! Located within Freedom Park, Duke's Dog Run is actually a private, unfenced area that allows your runner the freedom to let loose, literally. Be sure he's got good recall, though, because he could dart off into the woods and make friends with some nearby horses.

Named after a German shepherd, Duke, a beloved park regular who died of megaesophagus (the same disease that Linus had), this dog park is definitely one of the best in South Jersey. Truly a dog's dog park, it includes a natural stream for fun-filled, four-legged romping. But be careful because if your playful pal is a water lover like Linus was, the minute you take that doggy off leash, he'll be likely to jump in the stream right away. It's only knee high, but if you just cleaned your car recently, prepare yourself for a new aroma dynamic.

A good number of regulars at the park will make your dog (and you) feel right at home. Some of the best times to come are on weekends at either the beginning or end of the day. The dog park is located within Freedom Park at Jones and Union Road off of Route 70. Park your car near the playground and start to walk across the fields following signs for the Dog Run; continue to walk with your leashed pup in the direction of the signs for about a quarter-mile. Eventually, you'll reach the gated area—and it's time for the leash release!

FETCHING NECESSITIES

You and Rover might be accused of putting on the dog by visiting **Scherzer Antiques,** a high-end antiques store in the heart of Historic Medford Village, but it's worth it. The antiques are gorgeous. Plus, both of you are more than welcome—the friendly, dog-loving owners of this charming shop often have at least one of their five pups roaming the store. 134 S. Main St.; 609/953-2950.

If you're in the market for high-end reproductions, then make a stop at **Heather Fine Furnishings,** where you and your pup are welcome to check out the furniture, paintings, wreaths, candles, and other accessories. The store owners have a Cavalier King Charles spaniel, and love to see all kinds of pups in the store. 62 S. Main St.; 609/654-9506.

Need to stock up on some doggy essentials after a romp at the park? Then look no further than the Willingboro **Petco.** You and puppers are welcome to shop together here. Plus, adoption events are held on Saturday afternoons where you could get your furry friend another furry friend. 4318 Rt. 130 N.; 609/877-9711.

Call the park or visit the website before your first visit to ensure that the dog park hasn't moved to another location. At press time, there were talks of moving it to another area, closer to the parking lot. Hours are sunrise–sunset. 609/654-2512; www.medfordtownship.com/recreation1.htm#PARKS.

PLACES TO EAT

Mom's Bake at Home Pizza: Linus (and I) never met a pizza that we didn't like, especially one that we could bake ourselves. If you're in the Medford area and have access to an oven, you must try Mom's Bake at Home Pizza. It's not only delicious but seriously fun. You tell the staff what you want on your pizza (more than 30 toppings to choose from), bring it home, and bake when you're ready for a hot and tasty pizza pie. Although it's a chain of restaurants, Mom's is one-of-a-kind when it comes to the pizza/fun factor. Ironstone Village, 560 Stokes Rd., Medford, NJ; 609/654-8885.

Hammonton

Known as "the Blueberry Capital of the World," this Pineland town hosts the popular Red, White and Blueberry festival every year in June. But even better is the gigantic state forest that surrounds the town, and Batsto Village, a preserved iron-ore-producing village.

DOG-EAR YOUR CALENDAR

Riverfront Summer Concert Series: For a paw-tapping good time, take your music-appreciating pooch to Burlington City for its weekly riverfront concerts at the Promenade Park Bandstand in July and August. Music includes pop, big band, jazz, and vintage rock and roll. Free parking and admission. Most concerts start at 7:30 P.M. 609/386-0200; www.tourburlington.org.

Valenzano Winery's Jazz and Blues Wine Harvest Festival: You and your leashed doggy are more than welcome to enjoy the September wine festival together. Some of the fun includes live blues and jazz bands, wine tasting, food vendors, discount wine sales, local crafters, as well as free pony rides, clowns, and children's activities. Tickets are $8 for adults, dogs and kids are free. 340 Forked Neck Rd., Shamong, NJ; 609/268-6731; www.valenzanowine.com.

PARKS, BEACHES, AND RECREATION AREAS

🐾 Wharton State Forest

🐾🐾🐾 (See Burlington and Camden Counties map on page 178)

A forest that encompasses three counties in New Jersey, Wharton State Forest is one massive state park. Named after Joseph Wharton, a successful Philadelphia financier who purchased 96,000 acres of the Batsto area in 1876, this forest was famed for the discovery of bog ore from nearby streams that was used to manufacture iron. In fact, the iron industry flourished in the Pine Barrens at the time of the Revolutionary War and the War of 1812. Then by the mid-19th century the iron industry declined and the disappearances of towns and villages that had evolved to support the industry soon followed.

What's left now is a beautiful park. Your dog and you will no doubt love that the majority of the forest has remained undeveloped in order to preserve the forest's natural habitat. And if puppers loves to hike with you, then you two will feel like you're in a hiker's dream. The forest provides a portion of the 50-mile Batona Trail, as well as 500 miles of unpaved roads. Although your doggy is welcome throughout the state forest on a leash, unfortunately, dogs are not allowed to camp or stay overnight here.

The Wharton State Forest has two main entrances: one at Atsion Recreation Area and the other at Batsto. Atsion has picnic facilities, a swimming area, and playgrounds, and is free throughout the year, except in summer months when there is a $5 entrance fee on weekdays, $10 on weekends. Atsion is on Route 206, eight miles north of Hammonton; 744 Rt. 206, Shamong, NJ; 609/268-0444. The other entrance, at Batsto, features the historic Batsto Village, as well as several trails with varying terrains and lengths. Batsto Village is located on Route 542, eight miles east of Hammonton; 4110 Nesco Rd., Hammonton, NJ; 609/561-0024. Both sites are open sunrise–sunset.

🖲 Batsto Village

🐾🐾🐾 🐕 (See Burlington and Camden Counties map on page 178)

If you're headed to Wharton State Forest, or even if you're not, you should seriously consider investigating Batsto Village, a former bog iron- and glass-making town. The uninhabited village, dating back to 1766, was founded at this location to produce bog iron, which was used to make everything from cannon balls to pots and pans. (Interesting tidbit: Water was mined for the bog iron ore that would settle at the top. This bog iron was derived from the surrounding decaying vegetation and iron-rich clays found in the slow-moving waters of the Pineland streams.)

Located on the same site as the state forest visitor's center at Batsto, you can pick up a map at the entrance and start your exploration. Then you and your dog can saunter along the sandy paths throughout the village and take a peek inside some of the homes of the workers who worked at Batsto. They're completely preserved with period furnishings and accoutrements. A little creepy for Linus, he was happy he wasn't allowed inside.

There's free admission to the village weekdays, $5 on weekends. As luring as it is to let your dog off leash here to run the wide-open spaces, park authorities say to keep poochie on leash and clean up after her. Hours are sunrise–sunset. (See directions under Wharton State Forest, above.) 4110 Nesco Rd., Hammonton, NJ; 609/561-3262; www.batstovillage.org.

PLACES TO STAY

Ramada Inn of Hammonton: A clean room at a good price and a friendly front desk is what you're likely to find here. Your stay includes a complimentary continental breakfast. If you plan to bring your dog with you, call first to confirm the pet policy, hotel management suggests. At the time of press, the pet fee was $15 per day per dog. Rates are $70–120. 308 S. White Horse Pk., Hammonton, NJ; 609/561-5700 or 888/298-2054.

CAMDEN COUNTY

Cross over the Ben Franklin Bridge from Philadelphia and you'll land in a New Jersey county that is in the midst of transformation, or shall we say renaissance? Once considered an eyesore and known for its go-go bars and strip clubs, Camden County has come a long way in enhancing its image in the past few years. In fact, the entrance into Camden County from the bridge has been completely renovated (partially incited by preparations for the 2000 Republican National Convention); the strip clubs and go-go bars are long gone-gone from this entranceway.

All sorts of improvement projects have been ongoing since then to bring visitors to the city of Camden, the county seat, and its waterfront. Within the past decade the following attractions have opened: the New Jersey State Aquarium, the Camden Children's Garden, a new stadium for the Camden Riversharks baseball team, Campbell's Field; USS New Jersey Battleship Museum; and next to it, an outdoor amphitheater, the Tweeter Center.

But Camden County isn't just Camden city, of course. It's a densely populated Philadelphia suburb with some of the region's most charming neighborhoods and proud residents. And the image makeover is not just helping the people who visit and live here but the pets, too. For such a small county, Camden boasts one of the leading Philadelphia area dog parks (and one of the oldest): Pooch Park at Cooper River Park. It also hosts one of the newest, Connolly Park in Voorhees, as well as one of the most controversial, the unfenced Crows Woods in Haddonfield. Plus, cities like Collingswood are finding ways to make their downtowns enticing not just for people but for their dogs, too.

Just keep in mind when visiting New Jersey parks, there is a high incidence of Lyme disease, so check your dog thoroughly for small deer ticks about the size of a pin head.

Camden City

The city of Camden has improved its waterfront, attracting 2.5 million people every year, and is in the midst of an aggressive citywide revitalization plan. But the city still doesn't have a lot in the way of restaurants or other attractions outside of the waterfront. And at this point, you may not want to venture too far from there as the surrounding area is not the most traveler-friendly. Maybe city renovation will be the answer. Until then, there's a park on the waterfront you can visit with your pooch as well as a dining option.

PARKS, BEACHES, AND RECREATION AREAS

10 Camden Ulysses Wiggins Waterfront Park and Marina

🐾 (See Burlington and Camden Counties map on page 178)

The name makes it sound amazing, but this isn't much of a park, per se. It's more of a passive-use park or a landing. In fact, it's directly across the Delaware River from Penn's Landing, so maybe that's why? The park encompasses a 50-slip marina, the Tweeter Center, the USS *New Jersey*, the New Jersey State Aquarium, the Children's Garden, Campbell's Field, and the River Stage. Of course, you can't take your dog inside any of these facilities, which makes the park not that desirable. But you might enjoy a free, outdoor concert with poochie at the River Stage, or walk along the promenade or simply sit and gaze at the Delaware River.

From Philadelphia, take 695 over the Ben Franklin Bridge, follow 695 to Mickle Boulevard all the way to the end and you'll be in front of the park. Hours are sunset to sunrise. 856/541-7222 or 856/795-PARK.

PLACES TO EAT

Crossroads Café: As long as your pooch is well behaved, you're welcome to sit outside together at this café and enjoy coffee or sandwiches and salads together. 2 Riverside Dr., Camden, NJ; 856/365-1770.

Cherry Hill

Probably best known for its mall (one of the first), Cherry Hill is actually a former agrarian community called Delaware Township. But because of the beautiful cherry trees that grew at a nearby farm and a notorious hotel called the Cherry Hill Inn that existed at this site, the citizens of Delaware Township elected to change the name of the community to Cherry Hill, right about the time the mall opened in 1961. Every springtime, bountiful cherry trees with fluffy pink blossoms line Chapel Avenue in the township. Cherry Hill might be most famous among dog owners for its incredible off-leash dog park, one of the first.

DIVERSIONS

Barclay Farmstead: If you and your pup are looking to soak in a bit of history while you enjoy the outdoors, you might want to take advantage of the 32 acres available to explore at this carefully preserved farm and farmhouse. Hours are Tuesday–Friday noon–4 P.M., 1–4 P.M. the first Sunday of each month; closed Mondays and national holidays. Admission is $2 for nonresidents and $1 for senior citizens and children. Dogs must be on a leash at all times. 209 Barclay Ln., Cherry Hill, NJ; 856/795-6225; www.barclayfarmstead.org.

Yappy Hour: Looking for frolicking fun indoors? Look no further than the Moorestown PetsMart. You and your pup are invited for puppy playtime Thursday nights. If your dog is less than 30 pounds, he can attend the session 7–7:30 P.M.; if he's heavier than 30 pounds, he can attend 7:45–8:15 P.M. 1331 Nixon Dr., Moorestown, NJ; 856/439-9899.

PARKS, BEACHES, AND RECREATION AREAS

🔟 Pooch Park at Cooper River Park

🐾🐾🐾🐾🐕 (See Burlington and Camden Counties map on page 178)

Paws down, this is definitely one of the area's best dog parks. Pooch Park, located in the eastern section of Cooper River Park, has all the amenities a great dog park should have, not the least of which are fun and friendly dogs and people. There are two separate fenced areas: one for dogs 30 pounds and under and a larger one for bigger dogs. As a whole, the park offers a good amount of shade, park benches, poop bags, water bowls, a water fountain, and lighting. A cement walkway in the middle of each fenced area is especially useful for people on damp, muddy days.

The only thing missing that would make this the perfect park is a swim area. But who needs perfection when you're outdoors with your pup?

Regardless, on our last visit Linus could not control his enthusiasm as the minute we entered, he grabbed a Kong toy and ran like a fool with it in his mouth (trying to bark), all the while frolicking with a friendly standard poodle.

Because of its popularity, Pooch Park is definitely one of the busiest dog parks around. Depending on your availability, it may be best to come during weekdays, as weekends can be jam-packed with pooches. Also, make sure to keep your small dog in the small dog area, even if he's alone. It's better to be safe than sorry: There was one incident in which a small dog was attacked and killed by a much larger dog.

Kids younger than 12 are not allowed here. However, the good news for people with disabilities is that this park has been altered recently to make it wheelchair accessible.

Before heading to the park, make sure your dog has proof of vaccinations and a municipal dog license as Camden County Police are known to come and check for such things.

Take Route 70 to Cuthbert Boulevard South and turn left onto North Park Drive. Follow North Park Drive all the way to the end. Pooch Park will be on the right and there's a parking lot on the left. Hours are 6 A.M.–10 P.M. 856/795-PARK; www.co.camden.nj.us/government/offices/parks/pk_pooch.html.

12 Challenge Grove

 (See Burlington and Camden Counties map on page 178)

While this park has won awards for its facilities' complete accessibility to people, it's no accessibility-winner for dogs. Although it has two playgrounds and a .25-mile track where it would be great to rollerblade with your pup, these areas don't allow dogs—even on leashes. But because the park skirts the Cooper River, it has some aesthetic value to doggies and their owners.

It's located at Brace and Borton Mill Roads in Cherry Hill. Take 295 to Exit 32 (Route 561) toward Haddonfield. Proceed on Route 561 about 1.2 miles to Route 154 North (Brace Road). Turn right onto Route 154 north and proceed to the second traffic light. Turn left at the light onto Borton Mill Road. Challenge Grove is on the right. Hours are sunrise–sunset. 856/795-PARK.

13 Maria Barnaby Greenwald Park

(See Burlington and Camden Counties map on page 178)

Linus had no idea what we were in for when we came here. But we were pleasantly surprised to discover that at Greenwald Park, you and your pooch can walk the mile-long bike path that runs along the outer edge of the park, or hike the Watchable Wildlife Trail, which is about two miles total and hugs the Cooper River. Brochures about this trail are available at the Parks Administration Building on North Park Drive as well as at spots along the trail. Go to the parks building for a guaranteed brochure.

Along the wildlife walk, the brochure will direct you to awesome finds like a freshwater marsh and the wildlife that rely upon it, as well as point out a wooded hillside, a willow island, a black gum tree, and lots of other fascinating sites. You may even see some rare birds, turtles, or even a muskrat (looks like a groundhog with a tail). Linus was once startled by a sweet little squirrel, but that's as close to animals as we were able to get. The park is bounded by Park Boulevard (just south of Route 70), Grove Street, and Kings Highway. Hours are sunrise–sunset. 856/795-PARK.

PLACES TO EAT

Big John's: If you're looking for a cheesesteak as good as one from South Philly without crossing the Delaware River, then call Big John's and they'll deliver right to your door. If cheesesteaks aren't your thing, you might try the Italian hoagie or any of the pizzas, sandwiches, and salads. 1800 E. Rt. 70, Cherry Hill, NJ; 856/424-1186.

PLACES TO STAY

Holiday Inn: When you're a big guy like Linus was, finding a place to stay can be ruff. Luckily the Holiday Inn in Cherry Hill welcomes gentle canine giants with open arms. The only requirements are a $75 deposit and a signed pet waiver. The good news for humans is an indoor and outdoor pool, as well as a fitness center on site. The good news for both of you? The hotel is only a mile from the super Cooper River Park's Pooch Park. Rates are $97–129. Route 70 and Sayer Avenue, Cherry Hill, NJ; 856/663-5300; www.holidaycherryhill.com.

   Residence Inn: If you need a place to stay for more than a night or two in Camden County, you might want to check out this extended-stay hotel. Linus was relieved to hear that there was no size limit on dogs here. However, there is a $50 per day pet fee/cleaning fee for the first four days, then after that time, the fee decreases and varies, according to management. Still, one of the biggest selling points to the furry one was the fireplace to lie in front of, and the doggy bags from the daily complimentary breakfast buffet. Rates are $109–189. 1821 Old Cuthbert Rd., Cherry Hill, NJ; 856/429-6111.

Collingswood

As part of Camden County's revitalization, Collingswood is definitely making a name for itself. Once a run-down, struggling borough, this South Jersey town is now one of the top places to live in the Philadelphia area. Within the past five years, a record number of businesses have popped up all over town, and a vibrant community has ensued. This community spirit has been extended to dogs by many of the borough's businesses and events organizers.

PARKS, BEACHES, AND RECREATION AREAS

14 Knight Park

😺😺 (See Burlington and Camden Counties map on page 178)

More of a suburban park rather than an outdoor escape, 64-acre Knight Park has bike paths, playgrounds, a gazebo for outdoor concerts, picnic facilities, ice skating in the winter, and baseball fields. Pups are welcome as long as they're on leash. The last time we were there together, Linus discovered a duck pond with lots of feathered friends. Of course, this sent him running on the retractable leash and jumping into the muckiest part of the pond to say

FETCHING NECESSITIES

Vintage Rose: This friendly, eclectic gift shop offers a bit of everything, including jewelry, baby gifts, hand-painted furniture, picture frames, and even miniatures. The workers here will happily give your pooch a treat while visiting. 720 Haddon Ave., Collingswood, NJ; 856/833-0900.

Serenity Home: Serenity Home offers modern home accents and gifts from around the world, including garden sculptures, feng shui items, and Asian-inspired goods. Your dog may especially love the metal dog sculptures available. Needless to say, the staff here welcomes you and your pooch. 689 Haddon Ave., Collingswood, NJ; 856/833-1414; www.Serenityhome.biz.

Velvet Paws: With a name like this, is it any wonder that only the best will do for shoppers at this upscale pet store? With everything from beds and leashes to toys and high-end gifts, you and your doggy can have fun shopping here together, and the staff will even provide treats for puppers. 107 Kings Hwy. E., Haddonfield, NJ; 856/428-8889.

hello to a few ducks. Of course, he wouldn't have known how to hurt them. Too bad the ducks didn't know that about my friendly boy. But he never was dirtier or smellier than after that experience.

There is word of the park having an informal dog-walking group, but according to city officials, it's not welcome. Apparently, the one-bad-apple scenario happened here and officials claim that not enough people are cleaning up after their dogs. So there could be an end to dogs being welcome at the park even by the time this book is in print.

Take Route 70 to Cuthbert Boulevard south to Haddon Avenue. Take a right on Haddon Avenue, follow through Collingswood and take a left at Collings Avenue. The park is on the right. Hours are sunrise–sunset. 856/858-0533.

15 Newton Lake

🐾🐾 (See Burlington and Camden Counties map on page 178)

If you and your pup are looking for a peaceful walk lakeside, then this is the spot for you. A 2.25-mile newly paved bike path surrounds the lake, which is shaded on one side and sunny on the other. On your excursion you'll run into lots of runners, bikers, and dogs and their humans. There's also a playground here and picnic tables. In all, the park consists of about 103 acres for your leashed pup to enjoy with you.

Take Route 70 to Cuthbert Boulevard south through Collingswood. The park will be on the right. Take a right on Lakeshore Avenue and park anywhere along that street. Hours are sunrise–sunset. 856/858-0533.

PLACES TO EAT

Grooveground: This groovy coffee shop allows your pup inside with you to order your favorite beverage and browse the CDs for sale, and outside to eat. Coffee is the specialty here, but delicious juice drinks and sparkling coolers are available, as well as breakfast and lunch sandwiches, and desserts. 647 Haddon Ave., Collingswood, NJ; 856-869-9800; www.grooveground.com.

Villa Barone: Authentic, fresh Italian food at moderate prices is served at this BYOB eatery that's an absolute local favorite for people and their pups. Definitely try any of the paninis at lunchtime or the Ravioli Rosa for dinner. You and your doggy can dine alfresco when the weather's warm, and when it's not, there's always takeout available. Even though it's located on busy Haddon Avenue, free parking is available. 753 Haddon Ave., Collingswood, NJ; 856/858-2999.

Haddonfield

Charming and quaint, yet bustling with activity, Haddonfield is a historical place with tree-lined streets and many striking Victorian and Federal-style homes and buildings. The sense of community fostered in the town is what makes Haddonfield so special, so say its residents. Never mind the high taxes, ask anyone about their home town, and they'll tell you they love it here because of the friendliness of Haddonfielders. Dogs are not left out; a few of the businesses on Haddonfield's main street, Kings Highway, welcome dogs to eat or shop with you. And its Crows Woods park is a doggy nirvana.

One especially interesting tidbit about Haddonfield is that it has not been enjoyed just by dogs, but probably by dinosaurs at one time, too. In fact, the first complete dinosaur skeleton ever unearthed was found here. You can see the discover site in Pennypacker Park.

PARKS, BEACHES, AND RECREATION AREAS

16 Crows Woods

🐾🐾🐾🐾 🐕 🐾 (See Burlington and Camden Counties map on page 178)
What better way to enjoy a fall (or even a spring, summer, or winter) day than to walk in the woods with your canine companion off leash? That's exactly what you'll get at this unique wooded area. Plus, the company you'll meet here couldn't be friendlier—the pooches as well as their people. This spot consists of dense woods with sandy walking trails and a swimming hole for dogs. The trails are outlined with tree trunks and marked on nearby trees

DOG-EAR YOUR CALENDAR

May Fair: An annual Collingswood event, the May Fair has arts, crafts, and music and a kids' zone with rides and games. More than a hundred artists and crafters display and sell their unique creations in a juried show. Tens of thousands of people show up for the event, so keep your pup on a short lead. 866/BE-IN-COLLS.

Summer Evening Concerts: If Spot likes to relax to music, then by all means bring him with you to the summer concert series. Sponsored by Haddonfield's Rotary Club and held each Friday in the summer months, these concerts offer something for everyone. Be sure to bring a lawn chair and come early to secure a spot for you and your furry friend. Concerts start at 7 P.M. 856/216-7253.

Crafts and Fine Art Festival: If you and poochie are looking for something fun to do as well as get a little shopping in, you might check out this Haddonfield festival offering one-of-a-kind works of art and crafts for sale and lots of yummy food, along Kings Highway one July weekend. Hours are usually Saturday 11 A.M.–6 P.M., and Sunday noon–5 P.M. Admission is free and there is plenty of free parking. 856/216-7253.

Blessing of the Pets: Holy Trinity Episcopal Church in Collingswood celebrates the Feast of St. Francis in October with an outdoor service and blessing of the animals. 856/858-0491.

Pets on Parade: Dress up Fido and head over to the Garden State Discovery Museum in Cherry Hill to join other four-legged friends in a parade to celebrate Halloween. Dressed-up doggies parade through the museum and outside it. Prizes are awarded for all sorts of categories. Entrance fees for the museum are $7.95 for adults and children older than 1; seniors are $6.95. Garden State Discovery Museum, 2040 Springdale Rd., Cherry Hill, NJ; 856/424-1233.

Halloween Party: The PetsMart Howl-o-Ween Yappy Hour costume party takes place every year around the haunting holiday. All pets can participate in the costumed party. Other activities include games, costumes contests, treats for tricks, photos, and costume parade. 1331 Nixon Dr., Moorestown, NJ; 856/439-9899.

Christmas Tree Lighting Parade: An annual event the whole town of Haddonfield looks forward to, the Tree Lighting Ceremony and Santa's Arrival is held the Saturday after Thanksgiving. White lights and luminarias line the streets with strolling carolers and other free events and entertainment. 856/216-7253.

to prevent you from getting lost. But Linus felt that if he had to get lost, this would be the place to do it. (Be sure to bring poop bags as signs dictate cleaning up after your pup.)

Haddonfield residents don't know how lucky they are to have such a prime dog spot. Or do they? At press time, dog lovers were in the midst of fighting local officials and off-leash opponents about whether the area should allow dogs off leash all the time as was previously done, at certain hours and days of the week, or not at all. While various people and dogs had used the area up to this point, opponents contested that off-leash dogs were ruining the area and were posing a danger to people. At press time the park was leash-free seven days a week, except for the hours of noon–5 P.M., when dogs must be leashed. In 2005 the borough of Haddonfield should be finished with its field study to determine the feasibility of allowing dogs off leash at all. Hopefully, our friends will win their fight to make the area off leash as much as possible.

Follow Kings Highway west (towards the train overpass bridge). At the next traffic light, make a left onto Warwick Road and follow for approximately one mile. Make a left onto Upland Way and follow to the train bridge. Immediately after you pass under the bridge, make a right at the sign for Crows Woods. Continue to the parking lot on the left. Once you see the covered picnic area, you've found the dog park. Hours are sunrise–sunset. 856/429-4700.

17 Pennypacker Park

(See Burlington and Camden Counties map on page 178)

Listed on the New Jersey Register of Historic Places, this park is famous for one major event, the discovery of the *Hadrosaurus foulkii*, the world's first nearly complete skeleton of a dinosaur. Visiting the site, you'll see a stone and bronze plaque explaining what happened the eve of the Civil War in 1858, when William Parker Foulke unearthed the skeleton. And behind the plaque, you'll see a steep ravine where bones of *Hadrosaurus foulkii* were originally excavated. Also, you might see a ledge where kids bring and leave all sorts of toy dinosaurs.

Aside from its prehistoric significance, the park isn't all that impressive. Although the park encompasses Driscoll Pond, Hopkins Pond, and a section of the Cooper River, the park itself is not well marked and it's hard to determine how to get to the footpath, especially from the dinosaur site. So find your way to Hopkins Pond and you'll see a path on the other side of Hopkins Lane across from the lake where the parking lot is and you can hook up with the Watchable Wildlife Trail there.

To get to the dinosaur site from downtown Haddonfield, take Kings Highway to Grove Street. Take a left on Grove Street and follow it to Maple Avenue and make a right. The dinosaur site is at the end of this dead-end street. You can park along the street. Hours are sunrise–sunset. 856/795-PARK.

To get to the Pennypacker Park trails, take Kings Highway to Grove Street and take a right on Hopkins Lane. Follow it until you reach the parking lot on the right and park there.

PLACES TO EAT

Corner Bistro: A true Haddonfield hometown favorite, the Corner Bistro appeals to vegetarians and non-vegetarians, even your favorite furry carnivore. The dog-friendly bistro will welcome you and your pooch to sit outside and enjoy any of its bistro fare like overstuffed sandwiches, wraps, salads, pastas, and fish. The only thing this great eatery doesn't have is a liquor license, so you and your pup can always BYO. 59 Kings Hwy. E., Haddonfield, NJ; 856/354-8006.

Starbucks: Want a nice, hot cup of java and a cool, bowl of water for your best pal, too? Not a problem. The Haddonfield Starbucks welcomes its furry customers and their owners at its streetside seating. But do use caution as the staffers explained that the New Jersey Department of Health insists that dogs are not allowed in serving areas in or outside restaurants. You might get a hairy eyeball from customers who aren't of the hairy variety, but staffers will look the other way. If there's a problem sitting here, there's always takeout for the two of you. 216 Kings Hwy. E., Haddonfield, NJ; 856/429-8110.

PLACES TO STAY

Haddonfield Inn: If Fifi likes to go frou-frou and she isn't a barker, then by all means stay here. The owners of this beautiful inn, who have their own German Shorthaired Pointer, welcome all dogs who are well behaved and can stay in a crate when you're not in the room with them. Because it's a small inn, there is only one suite available for dogs to stay in. Called the Monaco, this French-country room has a fireplace and even its own entrance that makes it great for late-night potty breaks. But because it's the only dog-friendly room at the inn, it is coveted. So you might want to reserve it early on. There is an additional $15 charge for dogs. Rates $139–229. 44 West End St., Haddonfield, NJ; 856/428-2195; www.haddonfieldinn.com.

Haddon Heights

Another charming community in Camden County with busy shops and restaurants on its main street, Station Avenue, Haddon Heights is also a prime spot to visit with Spot. This area has its share of interesting architecture, too, in its homes and downtown buildings.

PARKS, BEACHES, AND RECREATION AREAS

18 Haddon Lake

🐾🐾🐾 (See Burlington and Camden Counties map on page 178)

Spanning nearly 80 acres through Haddon Heights, Audubon, and Mount Ephraim, this county park is worth a visit. Maybe you and your pup like to take it easy, or maybe you have a high-energy dog who needs his exercise? Regardless, this is the spot for you as long as Fido is on a leash.

With a cross-country trail and miles of bike paths, some that encircle the lake, as well as picnic areas, pavilions, volleyball courts, an inline hockey court, a softball field, and an outdoor amphitheater, this park has it all. You can spend a good chunk of an afternoon here enjoying nature or attending an outdoor concert or community sporting event. There are even indoor restrooms. And if you and your pooch like to take in quiet time together, small boats without motors are permitted in the lake.

While there are several different entrances to the park, the most direct one is to take a right on East Lake Drive off of Kings Highway and follow it all around the lake and park on the opposite side (the west side) along the lake. Hours are 6 A.M.–10 P.M. 856/795-PARK.

PLACES TO EAT

Anthony's Restaurant: Excellent service and good, moderately priced Italian food are offered at this eatery. Pups are welcome with you outside if one of the few tables is open (you may want to call first). If you have time and space for dessert, definitely try the crème brulee. It's doggone delectable. 512 Station Ave., Haddon Heights, NJ; 856/310-7766.

Voorhees

The town of Voorhees has a thriving community. Because it's experienced rapid growth in the past few decades, if you take a look around, it seems as though everything is new—the buildings, the businesses, the homes—and now even its dog park. But the township's master plan that is enacted for the next decade emphasizes preserving open space and limiting development.

PARKS, BEACHES, AND RECREATION AREAS

19 John Connolly Park

🐾🐾🐾🐕 (See Burlington and Camden Counties map on page 178)

This is one fancy-shmancy park. A former industrial site, this 43-acre tract of land was made into a park with the help from the state-funded Green Acres Program. The beautifully landscaped park features picnic tables, a gazebo, walking trails, and a dog run. However, now the not-so-good news: Dogs are

THINK GLOBALLY, BARK LOCALLY

Fun Run Dog Walk: Benefiting the Animal Welfare Association in Voorhees, the annual Paws & Feet Run and Fun Walk is a 5K run and one-mile run-walk that draws hundreds of human and canine walkers to Cooper River Park in Cherry Hill every May. The event fee is $15 and helps homeless animals. 856/424-2288; www.awanj.org.

Woofstock Festival: Benefiting the Animal Orphanage of Voorhees, this annual event takes place at Voorhees' Lions Lake Park 11 A.M.–4 P.M. one Saturday in September. Admission is $3 donation (seniors and kids under 12 are free). Here, your pup can visit a pet astrologer, watch agility demonstrations, dress up for pet costume contests, and win prizes. 856/753-4169; www.theanimalorphanage.org.

Annual Dog Walk: More than just a 1K–3K walk, this full-fledged doggy event that takes place the first Sunday in October at Haddon Heights county park gives you the opportunity to talk to vets, speak with a dog psychic, shop for crafts and treats, listen to music, eat, and enter your dog (and you) in a costume contest including but not limited to: strangest song (pet or owner), biggest feet, littlest dog, longest tail, and dog/human look-alikes. The fee is $15 and sponsor donations are encouraged. Dogs must be on leash at all times and should have current rabies vaccination. Water and bowls will be provided. The event benefits the no-kill Animal Adoption Center in Lindenwold, NJ. 856/435-9116; www.animaladoption.com.

allowed only in the dog run, not on the walking trails or anywhere else in the park. But if your dog's like mine was, she won't care. It's better to be off-leash and frolicking free, right?

The park's dog run has two sections: one for dogs more than 35 pounds and the other for smaller dogs. Within both sections, there are poop bags available, trash cans, bowls for water, benches, trees, and shade. The word on the street is that a water line will be installed for a fountain and that the large dog section of the area might be expanded. Aggressive dogs are not allowed here, nor are children younger than 12. Also, a valid municipal license is required for all dogs in the run.

Take 295 North to Exit 32. Take a right onto Route 561 toward Berlin-Voorhees. Follow Route 561 (Haddonfield Berlin Road) for approximately three miles. Make a left onto Clementon Road and follow for about 1.5 miles. Take a left into the entrance for Connolly Park. Hours are dawn–dusk. 856/428-7480.

PLACES TO EAT

Diane's Italian Water Ice: Another great option of eating a Philadelphia specialty without crossing the river, is Diane's Italian Water Ice. If it's a warm-weather month, you know that Diane's is open because the lines can wrap around the block. But there's a reason it's so popular: The water ice is yummy. The tried and true area lemon is always a safe bet, but some wacky flavors like chocolate-chocolate chip or Reese's Peanut Butter Cup might be worth a try. You and your pup are welcome to eat your cold treat outside together on the benches. Located in the Avian Center on Evesham Road. 2999 E. Evesham Rd., Voorhees, NJ; 856/751-9704.

Laceno Italian Grill: A Voorhees favorite, this moderately priced, Italio-contemporary eatery serves up delectable seafood, pastas, and wood-fired pizza. While the restaurant doesn't have outdoor seating, you and poochie can still enjoy its takeout menu. You'll love it. If you like seafood, try the fried calamari and sole. White Horse Road, Eschelon Village Plaza, Voorhees, NJ; 856/627-3700.

Berlin

A small South Jersey town located near the junction of Routes 73 and 30, Berlin isn't necessarily the hot spot to visit, but if you're near the area and need a place to stretch your collective legs, your pup won't mind that it's not breathtakingly beautiful.

PARKS, BEACHES, AND RECREATION AREAS

20 Berlin Park

☙ (See Burlington and Camden Counties map on page 178)

While this park is huge (more than 151 acres) and includes about five miles of nature trails, two miles of bike paths, and fishing facilities along the Great Egg Harbor River, it's not very pretty, nor did we find the visitors there very friendly. Dogs are not allowed on pathways and in the playground. Linus was not amused. But if your goal is to get some exercise with your furry friend on a leash and traverse some nature trails, then this is definitely an option.

And while you can't visit this part with your dog, this park is known for being home to the Camden County Environmental Studies Center, a reference library and learning facility for teachers in the area.

Take the White Horse Pike (Route 30) west. Take a left on Park Drive and follow the arrow for Route 561. Follow 561 after the basketball courts and park in the lot to the right. Hours are sunrise–sunset. 856/795-PARK.

PLACES TO EAT

Los Amigos: If you're a fan of authentic Mexican food, you must try this little eatery that's a smidge on the pricey side. Although it doesn't have any dog-friendly outdoor seating, it does have takeout as an option. And if you can't decide on something off the incredible menu, the tequila shrimp is always a hit. 461 N. Rte. 73, West Berlin, NJ; 856/767-5216.

CHAPTER 7

Beyond the Delaware Valley

The average dog is a nicer person than the average person.

Andrew A. Rooney

Sometimes you just need to get away, no matter how much you love where you are—it's human nature to branch out, and apparently canine nature, too. Linus loved every minute of every car ride no matter how long or how far we'd go. As long as he could shed every hair in his top coat and slobber on the majority of the back three windows on the way, we were golden as far as he was concerned—no pun intended.

One of the greatest things about living in Philadelphia or the surrounding area known as the Delaware Valley is that you're only one to two hours away from other excellent yet dramatically different destinations, such as the Jersey Shore, the Pocono Mountains, and Pennsylvania Dutch Country (a.k.a. Lancaster County—pronounced in these parts "LANK-uh-ster"). Lucky for my furry friend, all three destinations are happy to accommodate pups in their own unique ways.

PICK OF THE LITTER— BEYOND THE DELAWARE VALLEY

BEST PARK
Delaware Water Gap National Recreation Area, Pocono Mountains (page 218)

BEST DOG PARK
Buchanan Park Dog Park, Lancaster, PA (page 221)

BEST BEACH
Sunset Beach, Cape May, NJ (page 214)

BEST PLACES TO EAT
The 4th Street Café, Ocean City, NJ (page 211)
The Lobster House, Cape May, NJ (page 215)

BEST PLACES TO STAY
The Sealark Bed & Breakfast, Avalon, NJ (page 212)
Billmae Cottage, Cape May, NJ (page 216)
Hollinger House Bed & Breakfast, Lancaster, PA (page 223)

BEST EVENT
Basset Hound BoardWaddle, Ocean City, NJ (page 210)

NEW JERSEY SHORE

If you're from Philly, the outskirts, or New Jersey, you refer to the coastline as the "shore," not the "beach." If you are not from these parts, do everything in your power not to refer to it as the "beach," or you'll be immediately pegged as an outsider and probably laughed about. Say instead, "I'm goin' down da' shore." Once you arrive, you can say you're headed to the beach. That's the place where the sand and water meet.

Of course, the Jersey Shore is as long as the state. For the purposes of this book, we'll focus on the section where many Philadelphians vacation for a day trip or more: Cape May County.

Linus's first experience with the Jersey Shore was something that will stay with me forever. It was the first time my husband and I let him off leash without a fence to corral him. He ran as far as he could on the beach, but then suddenly it occurred to him that he was far from us. He would look back and then wait for us to catch up. Then he ran directly into the water, got scared from a ripple in the water (some water dog!), and ran back to shore. Later, he was found lying in a sand pool of water soaking in the early spring sun and enjoying the salt air. This, of course, was in the off-season of late March, before the no-dogs-allowed ban goes into effect at many Jersey beaches.

Actually, it's most fun to go to the Shore before the beginning of spring and after mid-fall as your pup can have off-leash fun frolicking on the beaches and walking along the boardwalks. However, if you do go in prime season, there are still some free (read: no beach tags necessary) shore-y spots to take your pup even if she has to be on a leash.

Ocean City

Ocean City is definitely one of the area's most popular shore towns, with eight miles of pristine beaches, a two-mile boardwalk lined with eateries offering everything from pizza to popcorn, and touristy stores galore, as well as terrific rides and fun for the kiddies. But for dogs, Ocean City beaches and boardwalks are open only October 15–May 15, not too bad compared to other shore towns. The most exciting news is that a year-round, off-leash dog park is scheduled to open in OC in 2005.

PARKS, BEACHES, AND RECREATION AREAS

Ocean City Dog Park

Ocean City, known for its family-friendly environment, is getting even more inclusive with plans to open an off-leash dog park because, after all, "dogs are family, too," according to the Ocean City Dog Park Association's tag line. Slated to open in 2005, the spectacular planned park is to be the first of its kind on the South Jersey Shore. The 45,000-square-feet fenced park will encompass three areas: a small dog park, a large dog park, and a separate dog run. Each section will be double-gated with an unleash entryway. The park itself is to be nicely landscaped and equipped with dog and people fountains, bag dispensers, memorial benches, and a four-inch layer of pea gravel as ground cover.

Trained "pet ambassadors" will be on hand to guide newbie park visitors. In addition, the park will be physically accessible and parking will be available for all visitors.

However, an application process is required to ensure that only immunized and licensed dogs have access to the park. The Pooch Paw application form will be posted to the website (www.oceancitydogpark.org).

The completed park will be located on 45th Street off of West Avenue in Ocean City, adjacent to the public works building. Hours will be sunrise–sunset.

THINK GLOBALLY, BARK LOCALLY

Ocean City Pet Fashion Show: Get out those bonnets and black ties and head down to Ocean City on Easter Saturday. It's the day of the ever-so-popular annual Woofin' Paws Pet Fashion Show that takes place at Ocean City High School's Carey Stadium. Dogs as well as other pets compete in such categories as Best Dressed, Best Bonnet, Swimsuit Division, Pet/Owner Look-a-Like, Intelligent Pet Tricks, Cutest Tail Wagger, and Best Face Licker as well as Best in Show. No prior registration is necessary; just come with $3 per dog to enter the fashion show. All proceeds benefit the Humane Society of Ocean City. 609/525-9300; www.njoceancity.com.

Basset Hound BoardWaddle: Can you imagine as many as 500 basset hounds strutting down the Ocean City boardwalk to help raise money and awareness for homeless basset hounds? An annual fundraiser for Tri-State Basset Hound Rescue, Inc., the BoardWaddle is usually held the first Saturday after April 15 and is part of the larger Ocean City Doo Dah Parade. If you share your life with a basset, you both are welcome to join the parading pack. If you don't, you and your pup will have a hoot watching from the sidelines. All that's requested are pledges to participate. Prizes are awarded for the top 20 pledges, and a picnic follows the event for all participants. www.tristatebassets.org.

Dog Walk Ocean City: Dogs are welcome on the Ocean City boardwalk Memorial Day weekend as part of the newly annual "Barks on the Boards" fundraiser for the Humane Society of Ocean City. Dozens of happy pooches walk the boardwalk in order to help their fellow animals, and vendors and rescue groups provide information. Elvis made a special appearance at the event in 2004. 609/399-2018 or 609/525-9300; http://hsoc.petfinder.org.

To donate to the effort, contact the Ocean City Dog Park Association, P.O. Box 145, Ocean City, NJ 08226; 609/545-0778; www.oceancitydogpark.org.

PLACES TO EAT

Blue Planet Diner: Anything and everything you could want to eat, you can find at the Blue Planet, and inexpensively, to boot. Serving up a mostly American diner menu, the Blue Planet has your favorite sweet and savory breakfast foods, sandwiches and burgers, seafood and steaks, and even vegetarian items, too. Plus, your pup is welcome to sit outside with you. 841 Asbury Ave., Ocean City, NJ; 609/525-9999.

The 4th Street Café: Whether you stop by for coffee and an outstanding scone or for a creative, home-cooked meal for dinner, you will be glad you did. Serving American cuisine with a fusion twist, the dinner menu isn't cheap, but the meal will be well worth it. 400 Atlantic Ave., Ocean City, NJ; 609/399-0764.

PLACES TO STAY

Residence Inn Somer's Point Hotel: If you want to be near Ocean City and are looking for amenities like a TV with cable and a VCR, an outdoor pool and tennis court, and a nice, clean room, you and your pooch are welcome to stay here for a nonrefundable deposit of $75. All rooms have kitchenettes; some come with a fireplace. A daily complimentary breakfast is available. Rates are $149–209. 900 Mays Landing Rd., Somers Point, NJ; 609/927-6400 or 800/331-3131.

Sea Cottage Inn Bed & Breakfast: This lovely Victorian B&B with an inviting front porch is located a half-block from the beach. If it's summertime and your pup is under 25 pounds, you're welcome to bring her for an extra $10 per night. But puppies under one year old are not allowed, nor are dogs with bad manners—any time of year. During the off-season, there are no weight restrictions on canine guests, but you must get prior approval from the B&B owner. It's also requested that families with small children *and* dogs find other lodging as the rowdy combo could disturb other guests. Rates are $115–175. 1136 Ocean Ave., Ocean City, NJ; 609/399-3356 or 888/208-1927; www.seacottageinn.info.

Avalon and Sea Isle City

Located one mile further east than its neighboring shore towns, Avalon boasts it's "Cooler By a Mile." You and your pup will be equally cool if you visit this Jersey Shore favorite prized for its restaurants and family environment. Sea Isle is the family-friendly neighbor north of Avalon, also a hot spot for dining and beach recreation. Speaking of family members, your furry one is welcome on Avalon and Sea Isle beaches October–March.

PLACES TO STAY

Sea Isle City Townhouse: This comfy pet-friendly townhouse allows your dog(s) to stay with you for one $150 refundable deposit. One block to the bay and two-and-a-half blocks to the beach, this townhouse is equipped with three bedrooms and 1.5 baths, two double beds, and two queen-size beds. It also has a front deck with gate and full-size fenced back yard, as well an outside shower. Rates are $300–1,250. 238A 39th Street, Sea Isle City, NJ; 215/725-4863.

The Sealark Bed & Breakfast: Our first introduction to B&Bs with Linus happened to be at the Sealark. It's comforting to know the same owners still run the lovely B&B and provide the same great service we enjoyed years ago. This nicely decorated Victorian guest house has one pet-friendly room (open all year) with a private porch and entrance, and even a fenced area in back. Pet-friendly apartments (open May–October) located across the street are now part of the Sealark. There is no extra charge or size limit for your pup, and you can leave him in the room when you go out provided he's quiet and polite. Rates are $50–240. 3018 First Ave., Avalon, NJ; 609/967-5647.

Cape May

No Jersey Shore town is quite as distinctive as Cape May. Boasting more than 600 vintage Victorian structures, the entire town has been designated a National Historic Landmark District. You can't help but smile while walking around town gazing at the amazing architecture and gardens of the bright, colorful homes. Your pup is sure to smile, too, at the plethora of lodging options and year-round dog-friendly beaches, some in Cape May and others in nearby North Wildwood. Although the city of Cape May bars dogs from its promenade and shops, dogs are allowed on the public beaches November–March and in North Wildwood September 16–May 14. There are also a couple of bayside beach spots that are doggone wonderful and open to pups.

PARKS, BEACHES, AND RECREATION AREAS

Cape May Point State Park

Home of the still-functioning Cape May Lighthouse, a magnificent 157-foot lighthouse dating back to 1859, this state park is one of the few areas along the South Jersey Shore to take your leashed dog for a walk in the grass.

The site of the park was used as a coastal defense base during World War II. Bunkers were built in 1942, and while they were originally located about 900 feet from the sea, coastal erosion has washed away the land in front of and under the bunker in the park. Locals say that at low tides you can still see remains of gun mounts in front of the bunker.

FETCHING NECESSITIES

Sunset Beach Gift Shops: So you are away with your pooch having a wonderful time, don't you want something to remember it by? Of course! Good news for the two of you: you are welcome at any of the Sunset Beach Gift Shops where you can find nature items, visit a garden center, buy seasonal clothing and Cape May t-shirts and sweatshirts, and jewelry made with the quartz crystals from Sunset Beach. They'll even provide your pup with a dog treat just for visiting. 123 Sunset Beach Rd., Cape May Point, NJ; 609/884-7079.

The park itself consists of 153 acres of ponds, marshes, and wooded areas, but for some reason dogs are not allowed to access them via the four miles of hiking trails. Linus, who didn't believe it, pulled me onto the trail until a hiker warned us that it was, indeed, against the rules.

It's too bad because there's so much to explore in the park's nature area. A resting and feeding area for thousands of migrating birds and monarch butterflies, Cape May Point is also one of the premier spots in North America to view the fall migration, from the wildlife observation platform.

This park also has picnic tables at three different locations. The trash policy is carry in/carry out, so don't forget the poop bags.

While dogs are not allowed on the beach during the warm-weather months, they are permitted September 15–April 15, a small but worthy consolation for their exile from the park's nature areas.

The park is located on Sunset Boulevard. From Cape May take Lafayette Street to West Perry, which becomes Route 606 (Sunset Boulevard) at Broadway. Make a left into the park when you see the lighthouse. Hours are sunrise–sunset. 609/884-2159.

Higbee Beach Wildlife Management Area

Hideaway Higbee Beach is truly a doggy oasis in Cape May. Okay, so there's no shade here, but it's the beach and your dog is welcome! How glorious for your hot, sticky pup to plunge into the water with off-leash abandon. (Although dogs are supposed to be on leash here, if your pup will come when you call her, there shouldn't be a problem.) This half-mile stretch of beach contains the last remnant of coastal dune forest on the bay shore, and it's managed as a migration stop-over for southern bound birds.

It is a beautiful, rustic beach, but it's also rocky, so you'll need some rugged shoes. The area is also quite buggy, so remember your insect repellent. Don't forget the poop bags, as there are trash cans here for cleanup, and portable toilets for you should the need arise.

DOG-EAR YOUR CALENDAR

Cape May Pet Parade: One Saturday in September, bring your hairy best friend to the shore and enjoy or take part in the annual Cape May Kiwanis Pet Parade. Here, your pup can parade and be judged on her costume. Lots of animals, including birds and cats, participate so it's best that Fido remains on a leash. Registration is at 10 A.M., judging is at 10:30 A.M., and the parade starts at 11 A.M. The free event is held at Cape May Elementary field on Lafayette Street near Madison. 609/884-9565.

Sunset Beach Flag Ceremony: Every night mid-May–September at about 20 minutes before dusk, a 40-year tradition of lowering the flag to the sound of *Taps*, Kate Smith's version of *God Bless America*, and the *Star Spangled Banner* continues in Sunset Beach. All the flags flown here are the casket flags of deceased veterans. Children usually help in the ceremony and learn how to properly fold an American flag. You and your patriotic pup are always welcome to see this very special ceremony every night of the season. 609/884-7079.

If the beach isn't enough for you two, explore the two miles of hiking trails within the wildlife management area.

Take Route 9 south from the village of Cape May. Turn left onto Route 626. Cross the bridge and turn right onto New England Road. The road dead-ends at Higbee Beach. Once in the general area, veer right and follow the sandy road to the parking area. Walk down to the beach and enjoy. Hours are sunrise–sunset. 609/628-2103; estiles@dep.state.nj.us.

Sunset Beach
😺😺😺😺 🐾

Aptly named, this beach is famous for its incredible open-water sunsets as it is located in the southernmost point of New Jersey on the Delaware Bay. Your pup may come here leashed or not as long as she is in control of herself. Use extreme caution when swimming as the currents here, where the bay meets the ocean, are highly unpredictable currents—you can walk about four feet in the water and the floor can suddenly drop to 15 feet deep. Be careful! Swimming is not advised for either humans or canines, but it is done here regularly anyway.

One of the most fascinating things about this beach, in addition to it being dog-friendly, is the "Cape May Diamonds" that wash ashore here. Actually, they're pure quartz crystals that you or your four-footed digger can discover and take home for free. Native Americans believed that these crystals held special powers of bringing success and good fortune. So you can bet they're

made into all types of jewelry that you can find in the nearby Sunset Beach Gift Shops.

Sunset Beach is also known as having a daily flag-lowering ceremony at sunset during the summer months that is a must-see. Plus, if you're visiting the Cape May Point State Park, you're just a few steps away to Sunset Beach down Sunset Boulevard.

Take Lafayette Avenue south and bear to the right to West Perry Street, which turns into Sunset Boulevard; continue for about three miles. Sunset Boulevard ends at Sunset Beach. Parking is free. Hours are sunrise–sunset. 609/886-2005.

PLACES TO EAT

The Lobster House: Very few restaurants exude that authentic Jersey Shore ambiance, but this one takes the claw...or is it paw? In fact, all four of your pup's paws are welcome here in the Raw Bar open-air area of the restaurant. You can grab a nice cold mug of beer and some moderately priced oysters or mussels, and your salty dog can enjoy the smells and sounds of Fisherman's Wharf. This restaurant actually has its own fleet of fishing boats. You will no doubt have a memorable experience visiting here with your pup. Don't forget your camera. Fisherman's Wharf, Cape May, NJ; 609/884-8296; www.thelobsterhouse.com.

Sunset Grill: You and your pup are welcome to grab a sandwich, a wrap, a hamburger or hotdog, ice cream or water ice and enjoy it at this little water's-edge eatery located in the Sunset Beach Gift Shop area on Sunset Beach. 123 Sunset Beach Rd., Cape May Point, NJ; 609/884-7079 or 609/884-7095.

PLACES TO STAY

Billmae Cottage: Maybe poochie is a little bit "rock and roll," as many dogs are, but if you're a little bit "country" you might enjoy staying at this super-dog-friendly establishment that's open all year-round. Decorated in a rustic country motif, each suite at the cottage has a kitchen and a private bathroom. A large screened-in porch makes it easy for you and your any-size pup to relax. There's a fenced-in yard area for your doggy, too, as well as handheld outdoor shower facilities for easy rinse-off. This cottage loves dogs so much they'll likely ask you for your pooch's picture for their guest book. The fee for staying with your dog ranges $50–100, depending on length of stay, and proof of shots is requested. Rates are $150–240. 1015 Washington St., Cape May, NJ; 609/898-8558; www.billmae.com.

The Highland House: Only four blocks to the beach, the Highland House is a great location, but even better is that your doggy can stay here with you at no extra charge. One of the pet-friendly rooms has a private entrance, great for potty breaks. This lovely inn, dating back to 1850, has a large front porch and gazebo where you can relax and reflect together. And it's just a few minutes' drive to Sunset and Higbee Beaches. Rates are $105–135. 131 N. Broadway, Cape May, NJ; 609/898-1198.

Marquis De Lafayette: Located in the heart of Victorian Cape May, the oceanfront Marquis De Lafayette welcomes your pooch with no weight restrictions. Although the location is great, don't expect stellar service or immaculately clean rooms. Plus, this section of Cape May doesn't encourage dogs during the warm-weather months. Off-season might be the time to come here as the rates are half of those in summer. Plus, you'll be able to take your dog on the beach with you. The pet fee is $20 per night. Rates are $99–309. 501 Beach Ave., Cape May, NJ; 609/884-3500.

New England Motel: About 15 minutes from Cape May, this family- and dog-friendly motel has been newly renovated. Two outdoor pools are available for humans only (sorry, pups). There is no weight restriction for dogs, but he must be crated when you're out of the room. And you must let the staff know if your dog likes to bark before staying here. The pet fee is $35–175 (for carpet cleaning), depending on length of stay. Rates are $75–200. 11th and New Jersey Avenues, North Wildwood, NJ; 609/522-7250 or 800/9-UTMAID; www.gwcoc.com/newengland.

Surf 16 Motel: Open May–October, this motel is located in nearby North Wildwood. The motel owners are dog lovers themselves and welcome your pup with no weight restrictions, just a $10 per day fee. The motel is only two blocks to the beach, but dogs are not allowed on it May 15–September 15. Still, there's a fenced-in dog run available for your pooch. Rates are $75–220. 1600 Surf Ave., North Wildwood, NJ; 609/522-1010.

POCONO MOUNTAINS

Okay, so Pennsylvania can't lay claim to the seashore, but it certainly can boast the stunning Pocono Mountains. The Native American word Pocono actually means "stream between two mountains," referring to the striking Delaware Water Gap area, where the Delaware River cuts between two mountain regions of Pennsylvania and New Jersey. Other natural springs and brooks are scattered throughout the Poconos, too.

Encompassing 2,400 square miles, 150 lakes, and seven state parks as well as one national park, the Poconos are the place to go when you want to really enjoy the great outdoors for an extended time with your furry friend. Dogs are welcome in all national and state parks and forests as long as they're on a leash. And they're allowed at most campsites throughout the region.

The hiking trails in the Poconos are some of the best on the East Coast, especially the Appalachian Trail, accessible at various points throughout the Delaware Water Gap National Park.

While summer is an opportune time to hit the Poconos because it's cooler up there and there are tons of things to do, fall is probably the best for hiking and witnessing the beauty of nature. From early September through October you can watch the dramatic, reds, golds, and yellows pop from the mountain trees. Since the timing of fall foliage varies, call the fall foliage hotline (570/421-5565) for weekly updates on where the leaves are at their most spectacular.

PARKS, BEACHES, AND RECREATION AREAS

Beltzville Park

More of a recreation spot than a natural, quiet escape, Beltzville has much to offer you and your leashed doggy. Its centerpiece is the 949-acre Beltzville Lake, with 19.8 miles of shoreline. If your interest is hiking, 15 miles of trails can take you through wooded pathways, old roads and creek valleys, as well as more historical sights like a slate quarry from the 1700s and a mill race from a former gristmill. A covered bridge, once used by horse-and-buggy traffic, was relocated from the Pohopoco Creek to the area between the picnic areas and the beach, so pedestrians with or without pups can investigate it. Although there is a beach for human swimming at the park, dogs are not allowed in this area or the nearby picnic areas. However, at the far end of the parking lot where the water meets the land, in the "No Mooring Zone," dogs do swim there. While it's not encouraged (in fact, it's against the rules), it happens. Use discretion if your poochie wants to do some doggy paddling.

From the Northeast Extension of the Pennsylvania Turnpike, take Exit 74 and follow the signs to the park. It's right off the exit. Hours are sunrise–sunset. 2950 Pohopoco Dr., Lehighton, PA; 610/377-0045.

Bushkill Falls

If you're in the Poconos, you must see the "Niagara of Pennsylvania," also known as Bushkill Falls. Sure, it's a bit of a tourist trap and admission is charged to see the eight different falls, unlike at its more famous northern counterpart. But it's the quintessential Poconos experience, attracting tourists for more than 100 years.

Your leashed pup is welcome with you on your hike, which can span 15 minutes to two hours or more, depending on your interest. The area is downright beautiful—hilly, too. You'll encounter lots of steps, so take that into consideration. On your travels, you'll venture through the woods, across quiet paths along rushing streams, and stop at towering lookouts to view each of the eight waterfalls. When you're finished with your hike, you can refresh with a picnic in the picnic area or visit the shops near the entrance that can provide you and your doggy with whatever sustenance you need.

Bushkill Falls is open April–October and, weather permitting, in November. Entrance fees are $8 for adults, $7 for seniors and groups, $4 for children aged 4 to 10, and free for kids 3 and under.

Take I-80 East to Exit 309, Route 209 north. Turn left onto Bushkill Falls Road at the blinking light in Bushkill. Parking is free. Hours are 9 A.M.–5 P.M. 570/588-6682; www.visitbushkillfalls.com.

Delaware Water Gap National Recreation Area

When thinking about Pennsylvania and New Jersey together, exquisite scenery probably wouldn't enter your mind…at least not at first. But if you visit the Delaware Water Gap, that will all change. This natural gorge between the two states is carved by the Delaware River right at the Appalachian Mountains in Pennsylvania. It creates cliffs of nearly 1,200 feet on each side of the gap, and although the actual gorge is only about two miles long, the entire Delaware Water Gap National Recreation Area is 40 miles long encompassing 70,000 acres of ridges, forests, lakes, and rivers on both sides of the Delaware.

Lucky for you and your four-footed traveling companion, it's part of the National Park Service park system, so it's well marked and well traveled. As long as puppers is leashed, she is welcome throughout the park, with the exception of the beaches. You two could easily spend an entire day in the car just checking out all of the sights along Route 209 (River Road). You'll likely come across rural areas, hilly sections, beaches (dogs not allowed, though), and even some waterfalls.

Another great opportunity is being able to hike a 25-mile portion of the 2,000-mile Appalachian Trail (which travels from Georgia to Maine) in the park.

If you want to see only the actual Gap, it's located in the town of Delaware Water Gap, Pennsylvania, located off of Route 80 at the southern tip of the park.

You can also catch scenic views of the Gap from the Kittatinny Point Visitor Center, right over the river in New Jersey. You can pick up maps and literature there, too. It is open Memorial Day weekend–Labor Day 9 A.M.–5 P.M.; after Labor Day it's open weekends 9 A.M.–5 P.M. Don't try the Bushkill visitor center because it's closed.

Although there are no fees to use the Delaware Water Gap park, if you choose to use the access areas at Bushkill and Dingman's Falls, there is a $5 fee for weekdays; $7 weekends.

To get to Kittatiny Point Visitor Center from Pennsylvania, take I-80 at the Water Gap. Go eastbound, take the first ramp after the toll plaza, and continue straight at the end of the ramp. Park hours are sunrise–sunset. 570/828-2451; www.nps.gov/dewa/index.htm.

Lehigh Gorge State Park—Glen Onoko

Another seriously gorgeous gorge is located in this southern section of the Poconos. The 4,548 acres of Lehigh Gorge State Park run along the Lehigh River. But the best part of this area, at least according to Nellie, is the Lehigh Gorge Trail, the surface of which is ballast/crushed stone. The trail's 26 miles of abandoned railroad grade follows the river throughout the park. Shaded and peaceful, it takes you past stunning scenery, including white-water rapids. In some sections, all you can see are the cliffs and the river; in other sections, only waterfalls and trees. But be careful here as some people have gotten seriously hurt or even died along this trail because of the steep terrain, poorly marked trails, and fast-moving water.

Take the Northeast Extension of the Pennsylvania Turnpike to Exit 74. Follow US 209 south to Jim Thorpe. Then take PA 903 north across the river to Coalport Road. Turn off of Coalport to Glen Onoko and follow to the parking area on right. Hours are sunrise–sunset. RR 1 Box 81, White Haven, PA 18661; 570/443-0400.

PLACES TO EAT

Vinny D's Deli & Catering: An award-winning deli that uses only the best cheeses and meats, and makes its own breads and focaccia, Vinny's is the place for takeout breakfast or lunch. The number of choices on the menu makes it tough to decide. If you're in the mood for a cheesesteak but aren't satisfied with the selection, you can design your own. But don't forget your carnivorous and hairy friend. 730 Milford Rd., Strawberry Fields Plaza, East Stroudsburg, PA; 570/421-6868; www.vinnyds.com.

Werry's Pub: Although there's outdoor seating here and the restaurant owner's dog, Chelsea, inspired the names of some menu items, dogs are not allowed here. But takeout is an option, and you're sure to be satisfied as the huge menu offers traditional pub fare as well as tasty entrées. The pub is located about a mile from the Delaware Water Gap recreation area. P.O. Box 270—Jay Park, Marshalls Creek, PA 18335; 570/223-9234.

PLACES TO STAY

Blueberry Mountain Inn: Although the inn itself isn't what you'd picture in the Poconos, the warm hospitality and cozy environs inside make the Blueberry Mountain Inn an excellent retreat. Even better is that up to two large size pooches (no Saint Bernards, apparently) can stay with you for $10 per day. A full hot breakfast is served daily. The B&B is situated on hundreds of acres among the mountains, streams, lakes, and ponds. Plus, it's only a 15-minute drive to the Lehigh Gorge. Thomas Road, HC 1 Box 1102, Blakeslee, PA 18610; 570/646-7144; www.blueberrymountaininn.com.

Delaware Water Gap KOA Campground: Open April–October, your pooch is welcome to stay with you in the campsites here at no additional fee— that is, unless he's a rottweiler, doberman pinscher, German shepherd, or pit bull. (Apparently, insurance companies now exclude certain breeds from liability coverage. Sorry!) There is a pet walk available, and the campsite is only two miles to the Delaware Water Gap. Your dog must be on a leash at all times, and crated if you leave the campground without her. Rates are $31–35 for two adults, plus $5 for each additional adult or child. 233 Hollow Rd., East Stroudsburg, PA; 570/223-8000; www.koa.com/where/PA/38101.htm.

Ramada Inn Pocono: Fun for the whole family is available here, including your pooch, of course awaits at this Ramada Inn. There's no extra fee for your pet, just a $50 deposit if paying with cash, but none with a credit card. There are no weight restrictions on dogs here, either. For you and/or the kids, there's a snowman-shaped indoor pool open year-round, as well as a recreation room featuring a mini-golf course. Close to outdoor activities at Lake Harmony, and about five miles to Lehigh Gorge. Rates are $75–115. Route 940, Lake Harmony, PA; 570/443-8471.

LANCASTER, PENNSYLVANIA

Best known for its large population of Old Order Amish (Pennsylvania Dutch) people, Lancaster County is a fascinating place to learn about the history of these private, separatist people who live a simple life without electricity or use of cars. They dress simply, much like people did in the 19th century, and drive horse-and-buggies. The Amish live life on their terms, successfully, by relying heavily on family and religion (strict interpretation of the Bible) and farming. It might surprise you to know that the Pennsylvania Dutch aren't Dutch at all; of German descent, they speak a German dialect, as well as English.

Although most of Lancaster's attractions, the many Amish museums and homes open to the public, are not conducive to bringing your pup, there are a few spots that you two can visit together on the off hours.

While 25,000 Amish reside in Lancaster County, this once old-fashioned area has become quite progressive in recent years. Walking through the charming, bricked sidewalks in Lancaster City, you'll see some swanky new restaurants serving cutting-edge cuisine. One even lets you bring your pooch. Plus, the city has one of the best dog parks that Linus ever visited.

PARKS, BEACHES, AND RECREATION AREAS

Buchanan Park Dog Park

Named after Philadelphia's favorite son, Benjamin Franklin, Franklin and Marshall College has lots to brag about. First of all, it's a respected liberal arts school with a charming campus, and now has a pawsome dog park. Your pup will think he's in college and not want to come home when visiting here, and neither will you because of the friendly feel of the park. In fact, everyone, including the people, has fun here. In fact, one regular admitted that park users think the park is for the dogs, but it's really for the people.

This dog run has a double-gated entrance, a separate area for smaller dogs, a good amount of shade, picnic tables, donated poop bags and dispenser, water bowls, and a large area for dogs to run that's on an incline, giving Fido the extra exercise. Linus made instant friends here with some greyhounds and a Labrador. Some regulars drive to this popular park from 25 miles away just to provide their dog with some fun and socialization. But if you're visiting Lancaster County, all you need to do is get yourself and your dog to the campus of Franklin and Marshall, located in Lancaster City. The park is located behind the North Museum on campus.

Take Route 30 East towards Lancaster and exit at Harrisburg Pike. Turn right toward Franklin and Marshall College and continue approximately two miles. Pass under the elevated walkway. Turn right at the second light onto College Avenue. Then turn right at the first light onto Buchanan Avenue. Try

DIVERSION

Drive-In Movies: Just outside of Lancaster, the Columbia Drive-In offers you and your pup a night of flicks under the stars, seven days a week, rain or shine Memorial Day–Labor Day. Adults are $7, children 2–12 and seniors $3. The only requirement is a car radio or portable FM radio. The staff loves hairy movie buffs (dogs), especially. 4061 Columbia Ave., Columbia, PA; 717/684-7759 or 717/684-7708.

to find a parking spot on Buchanan or on College Avenue. Hours are sunrise–sunset. 120 N. Duke St., Lancaster, PA; 717/291-4841.

Central Park

Right outside the Lancaster City limits, sprawling 544-acre Central Park borders the Conestoga River. This park has just about every recreational activity available including multiple playgrounds, hiking trails, playing fields, a swimming pool, and even garden plots. Dogs are welcome all over the park on a leash.

Upon entering on Duke Street, if you take a right on Rockford Road and follow it you'll see parking, picnic areas, and then a playground, and the river behind the area. People and dogs have been known to swim in this section, although signs warn to do so only "at your own risk." There's no easy edge to get in and out of the water, which definitely poses a problem if your dog can't get back on land. Hiking trails, both short and long, meander through the park.

The most interesting feature of the park is the Garden of the Five Senses. It consists of paved pathways with raised herb and flower gardens, scent boxes, reflecting pools and water courses, and interpretive signs leading you and your pup through a natural explanation of the five senses. Plus, there's a nearby gazebo and picnic area with numerous seasonal flower displays for you and your pup to enjoy.

From Lancaster City, take Duke Street south through the city until Chesapeake Street. Take a right onto Chesapeake Street; go .2 mile and turn left into the park. Hours are sunrise–sunset. 1050 Rockford Rd., Lancaster, PA; 717/299-8215.

Chickies Rock Park

Derived from the Native American word Chiquesalunga, meaning "place of the crayfish," Chickies Rock Park was named when it was first developed in

1977. Here, you'll find hiking trails including a portion of the Susquehanna Heritage Trail, as well as creeks and portions of the Susquehanna River. While there are some nice overlooks at the sections of Breezy View and Chickies Overlook, towering 200 feet above the Susquehanna River, the park as a whole is not user-friendly. It's difficult to find the various sections of the park as they're poorly marked on both sides of Chickies Mill Road, which northbound turns into River Road, making it even more confusing.

Take Route 30 West 10 miles from Lancaster City to the Columbia/Route 441 exit. From the exit turn right onto Route 441 North and go one mile to the parking area on the left to the Breezy View Overlook. Hours are sunrise–sunset. 1050 Rockford Rd., Lancaster, PA; 717/299-8215.

PLACES TO EAT

El Serrano: Exceptional and affordable Mexican/Peruvian food is what this place is known for. Sadly, they don't have dog-friendly outdoor seating, so only takeout will do. The good news is it's only two miles from the Buchanan Dog Park. 2151 Columbia Ave., Lancaster, PA; 717/397-6191.

Molly's Pub: Although it looks like a 19th-century brick row home, you'll know it isn't when you see the cute black Labrador's profile on the sign. So it's no surprise they love dogs here. In fact, the owners of this darling pub encourage you to come with your pooch where you two can sit at the sidewalk seating. They'll greet your pup with a bowl of water and at the end of your meal, provide him with a treat. Molly's Pub is a warm and friendly place serving burgers, soups, stews, and salads. 253 E. Chestnut St., Lancaster, PA; 717/396-0225; www.mollys-pub.com.

PLACES TO STAY

Holiday Inn Lancaster: There's nothing fancy about this hotel, but it's convenient to Lancaster City and the Amish countryside. The Holiday Inn welcomes your dog if she's under 25 pounds for a $25 one-time fee. Only one dog is allowed, but the pet-friendly rooms have exterior entrances, helpful for potty breaks. Rates are $99. Route 30, 521 Greenfield Rd., Lancaster, PA; 717/299-2551.

Hollinger House Bed & Breakfast: Situated about three miles south of downtown Lancaster, the 1870 Adams-period brick home is a friendly and peaceful respite in the country. They love dogs here as there are several who live here from time to time, as part of a rescue mission. It's clean and the service is warm and friendly. The grounds surrounding the home are available for off-leash frolicking. An extra $25 is charged per night for your furry friend to stay with you, and proof of rabies and bordatella shots is required. If needed, dog-walking service can be arranged for $8. Rates are $120–145. 2336 Hollinger Rd., Lancaster, PA; 717/464-3050 or 866/873-7370; www.hollingerhousebnb.com.

The Old Square Inn: A gorgeous, old brick home located in nearby Mount Joy, the Old Square Inn invites your pup for an extra $10 per day. Fido will be provided with treats and bowls. You will enjoy a full country breakfast every morning and an outdoor pool, as well as a comfy room with private bathroom and a fireplace. Rates are $109–239. 127 E. Main St., Mount Joy, PA; 757/653-4525 or 800/742-3533.

Sickman's Mill Campground: Located in the tree-covered hillside surrounding the Pequea Creek, this campground is quiet and peaceful. All of the campsites are wooded and next to a freshwater stream that's great for swimming and white-water rafting. Dogs are welcome everywhere as long as leashed and picked up after. Some amenities include a snack bar, toilets, and hot showers. A five-story brick-and-stone 1790s gristmill on site is also available for touring. Rates are $16–30. 671 Sand Hill Rd., Conestoga, PA; 717/872-5951; www.sickmansmillcampground.com.

RESOURCES

Community Groups

Want to meet like-minded individuals both human and canine? Try visiting these sites and you'll meet some great people who love their dogs just like you, and you can get involved with fundraisers and social events.

Chester County Canine Hiking Club: 610/933-1506 or misspoop@comcast.net.

Developing Horsham Dog Park: www.horshamdogpark.com.

Developing Main Line Dog Park: www.Mainlinecanine.com.

Eastern State Dog Pen: www.Fairmountdog.org.

MonDaug Bark Park: www.Mondaugbarkpark.com.

Orianna Hill Dog Park: www.oriannahill.org.

Schuylkill River Dog Run: www.Phillyfido.net.

24-Hour Emergency Animal Hospitals/ Veterinarians

Hopefully, you'll never need any of these emergency services, but just in case you do most are open on weekends and at night, some even 24 hours.

PHILADELPHIA COUNTY

Ryan Veterinary Hospital at the University of Pennsylvania (VHUP):
3900 Delancey St., West Philadelphia; 215/898-4685 (emergencies); 215/898-4680 (appointments); www.vet.upenn.edu.

DELAWARE COUNTY

Animal Emergency Hospital: 4009 Market St., Aston; 610/494-6686.

CHESTER COUNTY

West Chester Animal Emergency Clinic: 1141 West Chester Pk., West Chester; 610/696-4110.

MONTGOMERY COUNTY

Gwynedd Veterinary Hospital: 1615 West Point Pk., Lansdale; 215/699-9294; www.gwyneddvethospital.com.

Hickory Veterinary Hospital: 2303 Hickory Rd., Plymouth Meeting; 610/828-3054.

Mainline Emergency Animal Hospital: 24 E. Athens Ave., Ardmore; 610/642-1160.

Metropolitan Veterinary Emergency Services: 915 Trooper Rd., Norristown; 610/666-0995.

BUCKS COUNTY

Veterinary Specialty and Emergency Center: 1900 Old Lincoln Hwy., Langhorne; 215/750-7884; www.vsecvet.com.

BURLINGTON COUNTY, NJ

Columbus Veterinary Hospital: 3075 Rt. 206, Columbus, NJ; 609/298-4600.

Mt. Laurel Animal Hospital: Mt. Laurel Rd., Mt. Laurel, NJ; 856/234-7626.

CAMDEN COUNTY, NJ

Clementon Animal Hospital: 210 White Horse Pk., Clementon, NJ; 856/784-2610 (nights/weekends) or 856/784-2304.

TRAVELING VETERINARIANS

Can't lift your 150-pound Saint Bernard out the door? Then have the health care come to you.

American Association of Housecall Veterinarians: www.homevet.org.

Karen Collins, VMD, The Home Pet Doctor (serving Bucks County): 215/504-9097.

Mark Johnson, VMD, Vetcare (serving Bucks and Montgomery Counties): 215/914-0966.

Shannon Stanek, DVM (serving Montgomery and Chester Counties): 610/207-6390.

Dog Physical Therapy and Acupuncture

Sometimes your pooch needs more rehab after illness or injury than a traditional vet can provide. If that happens, you might want to get in touch with these specialists.

Anwell Veterinary Rehab Center: Quakertown; 610/346-7854; www.pvah.com.

Physical Therapy for Your Pet: 203 Kresson Gibbsboro Road, Voorhees, NJ; 856/346-3200; www.petpt.com.

Veterinary Acupuncture: Berwyn Veterinary Center, 1058 Lancaster Ave., Berwyn; 610/640-9188.

Natural and Nutritional Supplements

Great Pumpkin Health Foods: 607 E. Market St., West Chester; 610/696-0741.

Lionville Natural Pharmacy: 309 Gordon Dr., Lionville; 610/363-7474.

Pet Sitting/Dog Walking Services/Day Care

Whether you need someone to walk your dog once or you're looking for a week's worth of care, try these dog-sitting experts.

Doggie World Day Care Inc: 858 N. 3rd St., Philadelphia; 215/238-7200.

Doggone Dependable Pet Sitting: 856/985-6461 (NJ); www.doggonedependable.com.

Karen's K-9 Care: 457 Lancaster Ave., Frazer; 610/725-8973; http://karensk9care.com.

La Dolce Vita Pet Care: P.O. Box 63765, Philadelphia, PA 19147; 267/242-5190 or 215/551-9859; www.home.earthlink.net/~philadelphiapets.

Pacey's Pampered Pets: 7236 Kindred St., Philadelphia; 215/728-0665.

Paws and Purrs: 610/574-0078; fran@pawsandpurrssitters.com; www.pawsandpurrssitters.com.

PhiladelphiaPawsandClaws.com: 215/482-6799; philadelphiapaws@aol.com.

Philapets.com: 1710A Bainbridge St., Philadelphia; 215/893-0894; www.philapets.com.

Pet Transportation

Best Friends Express: Landsdowne; 610/284-9969.

Pet Taxi c/o La Dolce Vita: 267/242-5190 or 215/551-9859; PhiladelphiaPets @earthlink.net.

Waste Removal Services

Somebody's gotta do it. If poop is not your thing, it is for these folks.

Clean Scoop: 23 Bridge St., Oreland; 215/887-7698.

Miss Poop: 115 Forge Hill Ln., Phoenixville; misspoop@comcast.net; www.misspoop.com.

Poopie Scoopers R-Us: Cheltenham; 215/379-0183.

Dog Training and Behavior

It's never too late or too soon to teach Fido some manners. Here are some local training services. Dog training is also available at all PetsMart stores.

Amazing Tails: 651 Scroggy Rd., Oxford; 717/529-6875.

Dog Training Club of Chester County: Whiteland Business Center, Exton; 610/687-4808.

K-9 Training & Behavioral Therapy: Center City (Queen Village); 215/551-5254; www.k-9training.org.

Paws on the Run, Inc.: 319D Norristown Rd., Horsham; 215/675-1160.

Philadelphia Dog Training Club: Haverford; 610/853-9601.

Ruth Cionca: Philadelphia; 215/248-PLAY.

What a Good Dog: 811 Newtown Rd., Villanova; 610/688-0516.

Y2K9s: 1000 E. Mermaid Ln., Wyndmoor; normanland@comcast.net; www.y2k9s.net.

Grooming

Every dog has his day, and it's usually in the mud or poop. If you're tired of cleaning and grooming your pooch, you have to try letting someone else do it—it's doggone liberating.

Betty's Snip & Dip Grooming: 2908 Mount Carmel Ave., Glenside; 215/884-8215.

Bow-Wow Boutique: King of Prussia; 610/265-3646.

Bow-Wow Mobile Dog & Cat Grooming: Philadelphia; 215/464-5159.

Clippen Dales: 6208 Ridge Ave., Philadelphia; 215/482-4840.

Doggie Wash N' Go: 461 Bethlehem Pk., Fort Washington; 215/283-9525; www.doggiewashngo.com.

Groomingdales: 1012 E. Willow Grove Ave., Wyndmoor; 215/233-5233; www.groomingdales.biz.

Heights Pet Styles: 151A Haddon Ave., West Berlin, NJ; 856/767-1875.

K-9 Kingdom: 588 Glassboro Rd., Woodbury, NJ; 856/848-4737.

Kool Clips (traveling groomer): 610/405-8675.

Oh So Pretty: 614 S. 3rd St., Philadelphia; 267/767-7532.

Personal Touch Pet Care: Route 30, Frazer; 877/594-6998.

Pooch Caboose Mobile Dog Grooming: Southampton; 215/682-9000.

Scissors N Suds: 811 Haddon Ave., Collingswood, NJ; 856/858-6262.

Portraits

Couldn't you just stare at that sweet, furry face for hours? Well, now you can. Get a professional photo or drawing done of your fur-covered loved one.

Petdrawings.com: 877/364-8697.

Pet Poses: 856/596-5944.

Scott Ellis Photography: 302/239-3632.

Dog Bakeries/Boutiques

The latest trend is dog bakeries and boutiques under one ruff...uh, roof. Here are some of the area's finest.

The Bone Appetite K9 Bakery & Boutique: 122 E. Lancaster Ave., Wayne; 610/995-2663; www.theboneappetite.com.

Bone Jour: 14 N. 3rd St., Philadelphia; 215/574-1225; www.bonejourpetsupply.com.

Braxton's Animal Works: 620 W. Lancaster Ave., Wayne; 610/688-0769; www.braxtons.com.

Chic Petique: 616 S. 3rd St., Philadelphia; 215/629-1733, www.chicpetique.com.

Henley's: 113 E. King St., Malvern; 610/296-0100.

Jake & Elwood's House of Chews: 122 S. Main St., New Hope; 215/862-2533 or 866/285-1800.

Lick Your Chops: 700 2nd St. Pk., Richboro; 215/322-5266.

Pooch: 2020 Locust Street, Philadelphia; 215/735-0793.

Reigning Dogs & Cats: 30 West Rd., Newtown; 215/497-7477.

Reigning Dogs & Cats: 950 State Hwy. 33, Hamilton, NJ; 609/588-9300.

Velvet Paws: 107 Kings Hwy. E., Haddonfield, NJ; 856/428-8889.

Whiskazz and Pawzz: Chadds Ford Shops—Bldg. #1, Routes 1 and 100, Chadds Ford; 610/388-7010; www.whiskazzandpawzz.com.

Area Animal Shelters and Rescues

Make a promise to yourself that the next dog you get will be an adopted one. There are simply too many great dogs out there who don't have homes—both mixed breeds and purebreds, from puppies to adults. Rescues take dogs and provide homes for them, while shelters have dogs on site. Whatever your choice, most people who work or volunteer in this area are well informed about dog behavior, and try not to place a dog with you unless it's a good match.

Animal Orphanage, Inc.: 1 Cooper Rd., Voorhees, NJ; 856/627-9111; www.theanimalorphanage.org.

Animal Welfare Association in Voorhees: 856/424-2288; www.awanj.org.

Bucks County SPCA: 1665 Street Rd., Lahaska; 215/794-7425; www.bcspca.org.

Burlington County Animal Shelter: 15 Pioneer Blvd., Mount Holly, NJ; 609/265-5073.

Chester County SPCA: 1212 Phoenixville Pk., West Chester; 610/692-6113; www.ccspca.org.

Delaware County SPCA: 555 Sandy Bank Rd., Media; 610/566-1370; www.delcospca.org.

Delaware Valley Golden Retriever Rescue: 60 Vera Cruz Rd., Reinholds; 610/678-4981; info@dvgrr.org; www.dvgrr.org.

Delaware Valley Siberian Husky Rescue, Inc.: P.O. Box 773, Horsham, PA 19044; 215/412-0270 or 610/666-1816.

Furry Friends Network: A great organization that serves the Philadelphia area. 290 Fairview St., Carlisle; www.furryfriendsnetwork.com.

Hope for the Animals: P.O. Box 877, Morrisville, PA 19067; 215/945-6204.

Main Line Rescue: 303 W. Lancaster Ave., PMB #191, Wayne; 610/337-9225; http://mainlinerescue.com.

Make Peace with Animals: P.O. Box 488, New Hope, PA 18938; 215/862-0605.

Montgomery County SPCA: 19 E. Ridge Pk., Conshohocken; 610/825-0111; www.montgomerycountyspca.org.

Morris Animal Refuge: 1242 Lombard St., Philadelphia; 215/735-3256; http://morrisanimalrefuge.org.

Mutts N More: This great group serves New Jersey, Pennsylvania, Delaware, and Maryland. Toms River, NJ; www.muttsnmore.com.

Pennsylvania SPCA: 350 E. Erie Ave., Philadelphia; 215/426-6300; www.pspca.org.

People-Pet Partnership: P.O. Box 63575, Philadelphia; 215/218-9212; www.peoplepetpartnership.com.

Petfinder.org: The best website and resource for looking for your next pet. You can search by breed, size, age, location, and gender to find the perfect furry friend.

Spay and Save, Inc.: P.O. Box 122, Lafayette Hill, PA 19444; 610/279-9714.

Pet-Friendly Real Estate

With all the fun things to do with your pup and the great dog communities within the city, why not live here? Here are some apartment options that are dog-friendly.

Bank Street Court: 23 N. 3rd St.; 215/351-9193.

The Barclay: 237 S. 18th St.; 215/545-1500.

Brandywine Construction & Management: Dogs under 25 pounds. 47 N. 3rd St.; 215/351-9193.

Chocolate Works Apartments: Dogs under 25 pounds. 231 N. 3rd St.; 215/351-1535.

Delancey Place: Small dogs only. 321 S. 19th St.; 215/735-5757.

Independence Place: 233-241 S. 6th St.; 215/545-1500.

Juniper East: 1329 Lombard St.; 215/732-5700.

Locust Point: 2429 Locust St.; 215/564-3322.

The Metropolitan: 117 N. 15th St.; 877/563-6753.

One Rittenhouse Square: Small dogs only. 135 S. 18th St.; 215/735-5757.

Parkway Apartments: Dogs under 25 pounds. 2601 Pennsylvania Ave.; 215/232-2601.

The Parkway House: 2201 Pennsylvania Ave.; 215/564-4750.

The Pennsylvania House: 1500 Chestnut St.; 215/569-8174.

Phoenix: 1600 Arch St.; 267/514-0444.

Pier 5: 7 N. Christopher Columbus Blvd.; 215/545-1500.

Riverloft: 2300 Walnut St.; 215/568-1002.

Riverside Presbyterian Tower Independent Living: Dogs under 30 pounds. 158 N. 23rd St.; 215/563-6200.

Summit Park Communities: 8201 Henry Ave.; 215/482-0788.

The Touraine: 1520 Spruce St.; 215/735-3850.

Missing Dog Websites

Every dog lover's worst nightmare. I hope you don't ever need this list. But if you do, first contact your animal shelter if your dog is lost. After you do that, here are some websites just in case.

www.1888pets911.org

www.Lostapet.org

www.missingpet.net

www.Sherlockbones.com

Pet Bereavement/Grief

They're never "just" a dog. If you need help dealing with the death of your hairy best friend, don't deny yourself. Call these folks—they are pros.

PetFriends, Inc.: Staffed by volunteers, each of whom has completed a 15-hour training course on grief, crisis intervention, active listening, and veterinary issues. Moorestown, NJ; 609/667-1717 or 800/404-PETS (long-distance calls will be returned collect within 24 hours).

The University of Pennsylvania School of Veterinary Medicine: Philadelphia; 215/898-4529.

INDEXES

Accommodations Index

Restaurant Index

General Index

M

Malvern: general information 99; parks 99; places to eat 100–101; places to stay 101

Malvern Movies: 90

Manayunk: general information 29–30; parks 30–31; places to eat 31–32

Manayunk Arts Festival: 22

Manayunk Canal Towpath: 31

Maria Barnaby Greenwald Park: 196

Mario Lanza Park: 62

markets: 65

Marsh Creek State Park: 95–96

May Fair: 200

McKaig Nature Education Center: 139

Medford (NJ): general information 189; parks 189–190; places to eat 190

Media: general information 73; parks 73–75

missing dog information: 233

MonDaug Bark Park: 135–136

MonDaug Bark Park's Dog Walk: 122

MonDaug Bark Park's Flea Market/ Dog Costume Party: 123

Montgomery County: Ambler 121–126; Cheltenham Township 142–143; Conshohocken and Lower Merion Township 143–145; festivals/ events 122–123, 131, 134; general information 113–115; Green Lane 115–116; highlights 114; Horsham Township 126–128; King of Prussia and Upper Merion Township 137–140; map 112; Montgomery Township 120–121; Norristown 130–133; Schwenksville 117–118; shopping 123; Skippack Township 118–120; Springfield Township 140–141; Upper Dublin Township 133–136; Upper Moreland Township 136–137; Upper Providence Township 129–130; veterinarians 227; see also specific destination

Montgomery Township: general information 120; parks 120–121; places to eat 121; places to stay 121

Montgomery Township Bark Park: 120–121

Mount Airy: see Chestnut Hill, Mount Airy, and Blue Bell Hill

Mount Holly (NJ): general information 182; parks 183–185; places to eat 185; places to stay 185–186

Mount Laurel (NJ): general information 187; parks 187–188; places to eat 188; places to stay 188–189

movies: 25, 90, 131, 222

Mummer's Parade: 36

murals: 20

music: see festivals/events; outdoor concerts

Myrick Conservation Center: 105–106

N

Neshaminy State Park: 176

New Hope: general information 156–157; parks 157–159; places to eat 159–160; places to stay 160–162

New Hope Canal Boat Company: 155

New Hope Winery: 157

New Jersey Shore: Avalon and Sea Isle City (NJ) 211–212; Cape May 212–216; festivals/events 214; general information 208–209; Ocean City (NJ) 209–211; shopping 213

Newlin Grist Mill: 81–82

Newlin Grist Mill Fall Festival: 83

Newton Lake: 198–199

Newtown: general information 169; parks 169–170; places to eat 170–171

Nockamixon State Park: 164

Norristown: general information 130–131; parks 132; places to eat 132–133; places to stay 133

Norristown Farm Park: 131, 132

Northbrook Canoe Company: 107

Northeast Philly: general information 27; parks 27–29; places to eat 29; places to stay 29

Northern Liberties: general information 38; parks 39–40; places to eat 40–41; places to stay 41

Acknowledgments

Writing this book has been an exhilarating and hilariously fun experience at times, to dreadfully sad after Linus died. Because of all the kind words and assistance I received along the way, the very least I can do is be grateful in print.

Linus, I realize you can't read but I know you'd at least try to lick the page. Maybe someone in Doggy Heaven can translate for you. I want to thank you for not just inspiring me to write this book and helping me do it, but for making me a better person and parent. There's not a day we don't think about you. We miss your silliness and unbelievable sweetness. We miss your hugs…your physical presence…even those tufts of golden hair and dried slobber all over the house and car. We love and miss you dearly. Take good care of your bunny brother, Hopkins.

Wags and kisses to the love of my life: my extremely supportive and tolerant husband. I can't express how much I appreciate all the extra work and sacrifice you endured so I could get this accomplished. Thank you for listening and coaching, being flexible, and most of all, believing in me even when I didn't. It wouldn't have been at all possible if it wasn't for you. Thank you. I love you.

Gushie: Thank you for your commitment in helping me get all the work done I needed to for as long as you did. I know it wasn't easy with the monkeys.

Susie: I seriously couldn't have done it without your undying support and always positive words of wisdom. Thank you.

Mom and Dad: I can't thank you enough for making special trips to spend with the boys so I could work. And for understanding the profound loss of my beloved dog and that he wasn't just a dog.

McLaughlin Parents: Thanks so much for watching the boys at a moment's notice so I could track down a new park, and for being Linus's favorite visitors.

Wooden and Fee: Thanks for taking Monkey Muchacho off my hands to Auntie Annie's Fun House.

To the rest of my pack in the field and behind the scenes: Billy, Joey, Tommy, Nellie, Kathryn, Mia, Rebecca, and all the other good people at Avalon, Nancy Ashton, Rob Raymond, Sharon Breske, Karin and John Murphy, Linda McLaughlin, Melissa and Rob Halfpenny, Karen Lindenbaum, Stephanie Donofry, Bill Zardus, and Amy Yellin.

As well as the scores of park, restaurant, hotel and event people and anyone else that I've been in touch with who's nicely pointed me and my hairy companion in the right direction. Thank you!

Wags,
Chris

Keeping Current

Note to All Dog Lovers:
While our information is as current as possible, changes to fees, regulations, parks, roads, and trails sometimes are made after we go to press. Businesses can close, change their ownership, or change their rules. Earthquakes, fires, rainstorms, and other natural phenomena can radically change the condition of parks, hiking trails, and wilderness areas. Before you and your dog begin your travels, please be certain to call the phone numbers for each listing for updated information.

Attention Dogs of Philadelphia:
Our readers mean everything to us. We explore Philadelphia and the surrounding areas so that you and your people can spend true quality time together. Your input to this book is very important. In the last few years, we've heard from many wonderful dogs and their humans about new dog-friendly places, or old dog-friendly places we didn't know about. If we've missed your favorite park, beach, outdoor restaurant, hotel, or dog-friendly activity, please let us know. We'll check out the tip and if it turns out to be a good one, include it in the next edition, giving a thank-you to the dog and/or person who sent in the suggestion. Please write us—we always welcome comments and suggestions.

The Dog Lover's Companion to Philadelphia
Avalon Travel Publishing
1400 65th Street, Suite 250
Emeryville, CA 94608, USA
email: atpfeedback@avalonpub.com